Mozambique: the Revolution and its Origins

D1261729

Mozambique: the Revolution and its Origins

Barry Munslow

London   New York   Lagos

Longman Group Limited,
Longman House,
Burnt Mill, Harlow,
Essex CM20 2JE,
England
and Associated Companies
throughout the World

Published in the United States of America
by Longman Inc., New York

First published 1983

British Library Cataloguing in Publication Data

Munslow, Barry
   Mozambique: the revolution and its origins.
   1. Mozambique – Politics and government
   I. Title
   967'.903   DT463

   ISBN 0-582-64391-0
   ISBN 0-582-64392-9 Pbk

Library of Congress Cataloguing in Publication Data

Munslow, Barry
   Mozambique: the revolution and its origins.
   Bibliography: p.
   Includes index.
   1. Mozambique – Politics and government – To 1975.
   2. National liberation movements – Mozambique.
   3. Mozambique – Politics and government – 1975–.
   I. Title.
   DT463.M863   1983   320.967'9   82-16204
   ISBN 0-582-64391-0
   ISBN 0-582-64392-9 Pbk

Set in 10/11 Times Roman
Printed in Great Britain by
Butler & Tanner Ltd, Frome and London

To the people of Mozambique;
to my parents, Tom and Joyce Munslow;
to Pauline and Karl

The photograph on the cover depicts FRELIMO leader Samora Machel addressing village people in Tete province.
We are grateful to Dr Basil Davidson for permission to reproduce this photograph.

Contents

List of abbreviations

ANM	Association of Natives of Mozambique
APIE	State Housing Corporation
ARA	Armed Revolutionary Action
CANM	Central Association of Mozambican Negroes
CONCP	Conference of Nationalist Organisations of the Portuguese Colonies
COREMO	Mozambique Revolutionary Committee
DGS	General Directorate of Security
DOI	Department of Interior Organisation
EEC	European Economic Community
FNLA	National Front for the Liberation of Angola
FPLM	Popular Forces for the Liberation of Mozambique
Frelimo	Front for the Liberation of Mozambique
g.d.s	Dynamising groups
GEs	Special Groups (in the colonial army)
GEPs	Special Paratrooper Groups (in the colonial army)
GUMO	United Group of Mozambique
ILO	International Labour Organisation
Iscor	South African Iron and Steel Industrial Corporation
KANU	Kenya African National Union
KIEC	Kurasini International Education Centre
MANU	Mozambique African National Union
MPLA	Popular Movement for the Liberation of Angola
MRN	National Resistance Movement
NESAM	Nucleus of Mozambican Secondary Students
OJM	Mozambican Youth Organisation
OMM	Organisation of Mozambican Women
PAIGC	African Party for the Independence of Guinea and Cape Verde
PCP	Portuguese Communist Party
PIDE	International Police for the Defence of the State
PSP	Public Security Police
SADCC	Southern African Development Co-ordination Conference
TANU	Tanganyika African National Union
UDENAMO	National Democratic Union of Mozambique
UN	United Nations
UNAMI	National Union for Mozambican Independence
UNEMO	National Union of Mozambican Students
UNITA	National Union for the Total Independence of Angola
UPA	Union of Angolan Peoples
WNLA	Witwatersrand Native Labour Association
Zamco	Zambezi Consortium

Preface

My thanks extend to many people over a long period of time for all the help and support they have given in producing this book. Above all, thanks must go to the people of Mozambique and members of Frelimo, who extended their fullest co-operation throughout the field research and without whose patience and understanding this project would not have been possible. Great intellectual and theoretical stimulus was provided by the members and associates of the Centro de Estudos Africanos at the Eduardo Mondlane University in Maputo, in the period that I was working there. Certain individuals have provided special inspiration – in particular, Basil Davidson, whose personal example, pioneering work on Portuguese Africa and constant encouragement have been of inestimable benefit. The many talks with Iain Christie and Aquino da Bragança, two very knowledgeable people on the history of Frelimo, also deserve mention. A special word of thanks must go to Professor William Tordoff for his help and supervision of my doctoral thesis, on which part of this book is based. Amongst the many other individuals who have played a part, I will mention only Ong Bie Nio, Phil O'Keefe, Diane Jelley, Bo Westman, John Ellis, Maria Brown, Neil Murtough and Ralph Young. To those not mentioned by name, my gratitude is no less great. My parents, Joyce and Tom Munslow, enabled me to be in a position to write the book, and their support has been unbounded. The Social Science Research Council generously provided me with a grant to do the early research work. Many people have helped type the manuscript in the universities of Liverpool and Manchester, and my thanks go also to them. Finally, I would like to thank all those who have read and commented on parts of the manuscript, but none of course bears any responsibility for the views, errors and interpretations contained herein, which are entirely my own. The book is offered in all humility with the hope that it will make some small contribution to the understanding of Mozambique and the revolution that Frelimo initiated.

Barry Munslow
Department of Political Theory and Institutions
University of Liverpool

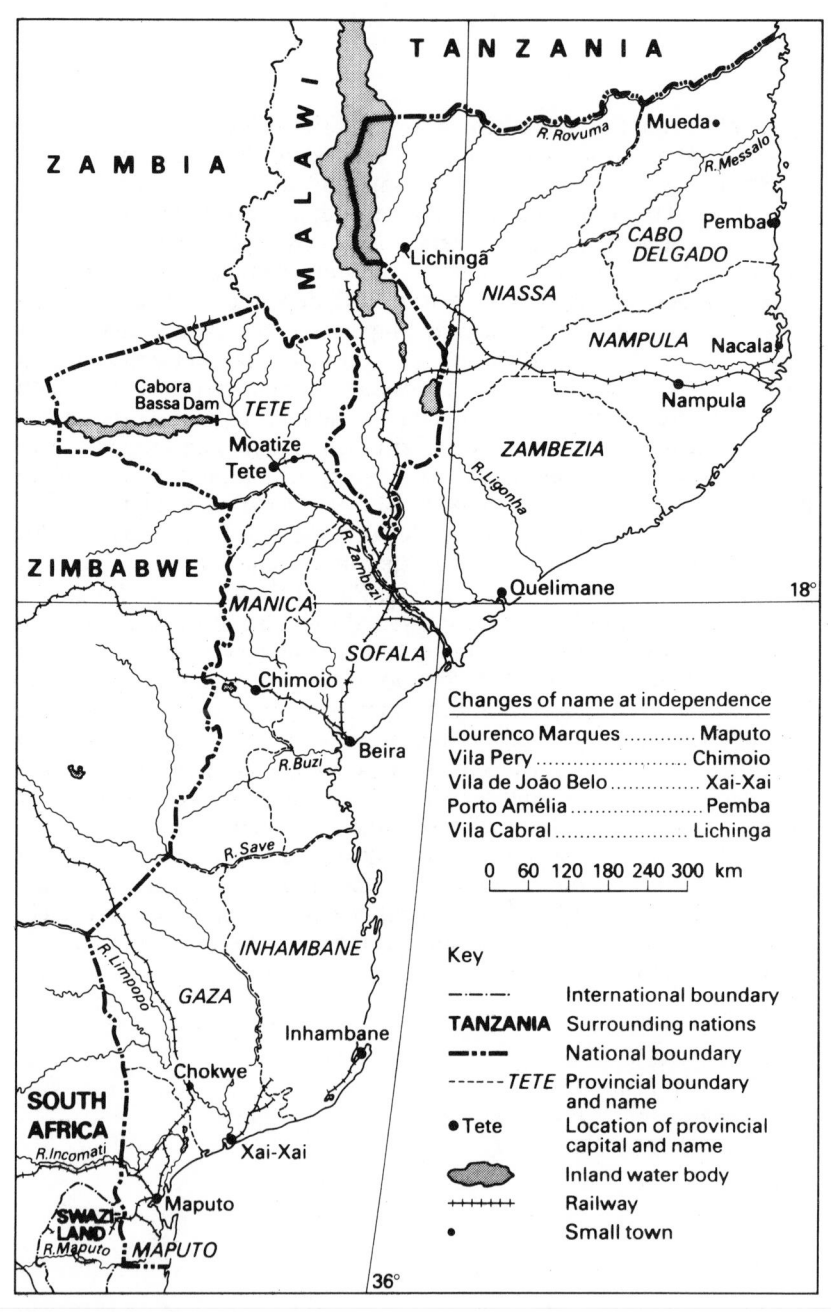

Changes of name at independence

Lourenco Marques .... Maputo
Vila Pery .... Chimoio
Vila de João Belo .... Xai-Xai
Porto Amélia .... Pemba
Vila Cabral .... Lichinga

0   60 120 180 240 300 km

Key

—·—·—   International boundary
TANZANIA   Surrounding nations
—■—■—   National boundary
------*TETE*   Provincial boundary
and name
●Tete   Location of provincial
capital and name
   Inland water body
+++++++   Railway
●   Small town

Map of Mozambique

xii

PART ONE

The political economy of Mozambique

1 An introduction

> We often say that our great victory in the course of our struggle has been the fact that we were able to transform the armed struggle for national liberation into a revolution.
>
> (Samora Machel)[1]

Mozambique achieved its independence ten to fifteen years after most other African countries. Some clue as to why this should be lay, perhaps, in the army uniforms worn by President Samora Machel and other leaders of Frelimo (the Front for the Liberation of Mozambique) at the Independence Day celebrations in June 1975. These marked the end of a decade of guerrilla warfare against the Portuguese colonial authorities. But why had it been necessary to fight such a war before this particular colonial power would relinquish its grip on the African continent? More puzzling still, why should Portugal, the poorest of the colonial powers in Africa, hang on for the longest period of time? These are just some of the questions that we will try to answer in what must surely be one of the most fascinating chapters in Africa's history.

The continent has seen numerous armed struggles, many of them associated with an independence movement, but rarely has a nationalist party transformed an armed struggle into a revolution. This above all else marks the importance of the Mozambican experience for the study of Africa. An analysis of how and why this occurred must inevitably be one of our central themes. It was not an overnight metamorphosis; there was no single visionary messiah leading the people from the colonial wilderness to the promised land of socialism. Only after an extended period of crisis did Frelimo make a decisive break with the mainstream of traditional African nationalism and take a revolutionary path. The necessary but not the sufficient condition for this option stemmed from the sub-metropolitan nature of the colonising power, as we explain in Part One of the book. Mozambique found itself increasingly under the sway of its South African neighbour rather than that of Portugal, and this proved a far more troublesome legacy for the newly independent country.

Although an analysis of the political economy of Mozambique provides the essential foundation for a detailed study of Frelimo and the Mozambican revolution, the political economy of Mozambique cannot be understood in isolation from its colonial, regional and international linkages, for it was these which were to shape the country's development. As Wallerstein has written:

> At a certain point in time, both Europe and Africa (or at least large zones of each) came to be incorporated into a single social system, a capitalist world-economy, whose fundamental dynamic largely controlled the actors located in both sectors of one united arena. It is in the reciprocal linkages of the various regions of the capitalist world economy that we find the underlying determinants of social actions at a more local level.[2]

As with other parts of Africa, contact with the West over many centuries contributed to Mozambique's underdevelopment and dependency. It began with the era of piracy and plunder by merchant capital and was consolidated by a century of direct colonial rule. Pre-capitalist African societies were penetrated, and the existing social, economic and political systems were disrupted and refashioned to serve the interests of the dominating powers. Much has already been written about the theory of underdevelopment, and little more of a general nature need be said here. Various mechanisms were established to exploit the colonised peripheries for the benefit of the colonial metropoles. Initial investments of capital produced returns which far exceeded the sum invested, and forms of unequal exchange were established to the detriment of the African countries.[3]

When speaking of dependency, it is clear that the nature of the countries on which a peripheral society is dependent will determine the form which that dependency takes. The uniqueness of the colonial experience that we are examining is that *the economies of both the colonised and the coloniser were in relationships of dependency.*

Portugal, the colonising power, was itself on the periphery of Europe, exhibiting many of the features of a typical third world economy, importing manufactured products and exporting raw materials and labour. As a result of the weakness of the Portuguese economy, Mozambique's dependency was to take a very particular form. It was not to be dominated by the colonising power's capital; quite simply, that capital was not available. Instead, Mozambique became an integral part of a regional sub-system dominated by the peripheral centre, South Africa. Portugal was a sub-metropolitan power, whose principal feature was the non-articulation of political and economic power over its colony. Political control was exercised by one sub-metropolitan power, Portugal, whilst another sub-metropolitan power, South Africa, exerted the main economic control. As we shall see, the sub-metropolitan nature of the colonising power was to have vital implications in the unfolding of subsequent events.

In Part Two of the book we trace the changing patterns of resistance to colonial rule, relating these to the previously charted transformations in the political economy. Over time, various disparate threads were gradually woven into the nationalist tapestry when Frelimo was finally formed in 1962. The third part of the book explores the ensuing confrontation between Frelimo and a seemingly immovable colonial power. Portugal's intransigence was to compel the taking up of arms. This in its turn was to set in train a whole range of internal conflicts and changes within the movement. As Frelimo's long-standing representative at the United Nations was to remark: 'There was no other way open to us but that of identifying in theory and practice the beginning of the Revolution with the beginning of the armed struggle, because there can be no partial or peaceful struggle against Portuguese colonialism.'[4]

Over the next decade the post-independence policies of Frelimo were to be shaped, as it wrestled with the problem of building a new society in its steadily expanding liberated areas. The policies and principles then devised were to provide a guide for the future. In place of the Africanisation of existing political and economic structures after independence, Frelimo was to try to create a new form of state, make the transformation into a Marxist–Leninist vanguard party and attempt to build entirely new social relations of production. The new government was also to begin the difficult task of disengagement from the South African-dominated regional sub-system. However, the problems it had then to face were enormous – in particular, those associated with controlling and transforming the inherited state apparatus. We turn our attention in the final part of the book to these post-independence developments and try to assess the successes and the failures to date.

Notes

1 S. Machel, *Estabelecer Poder Popular para Servir as Massas*, Maputo, 1979.

2 I. Wallerstein, 'The Three Stages of African Involvement in the World Economy', in P. C. W. Gutkind and I. Wallerstein (eds.), *The Political Economy of Contemporary Africa*, London, 1976, p. 30.

3 See, for example, A. Emmanuel, *Unequal Exchange: a Study of the Imperialism of Trade*, New York, 1972.

4 Frelimo, *Petition Submitted to the United Nations Fourth Committee*, 14 Oct. 1969.

2 Portugal and the economics of colonialism

The scramble for Africa

In the final quarter of the nineteenth century the industrial powers of Europe began systematically dividing up the African continent. Britain, France, Germany and Belgium needed raw materials for their factories and later markets for the goods they produced by transforming those raw materials into finished products. Portugal was the odd man out amongst the colonial powers with its predominantly pre-industrial economy. Since the Methuen Treaty of 1703, the Portuguese economy had been beholden to British manufacturers. Under this agreement, British textiles could freely enter the Portuguese market, thus effectively hampering the growth of Portugal's own domestic industry, and in return Portuguese wine had preferential entry into Britain. Portugal paid for this uneven trade balance with Brazilian gold, and this helped to consolidate London as the financial centre of Europe. As Portugal's most famous historian, Oliveira Martins, so eloquently described the situation, 'The gold of Brazil merely passed through Portugal and cast anchor in England, to pay for the flour and textiles with which [England] fed and clothed us. Our industry consisted of operas and devotions.'[1] Martins neatly encapsulated the later relationship when he posed the following question: 'People think that England is bound to look after us; but what [will happen] when there are no more Africas with which to pay her?'[2]

The economic dependency on Britain transformed Portugal into a virtual neo-colony. That Portugal gained as much territory as it did in Africa was largely due to the support that Britain gave to its claims. However, at the time of the 'scramble' many fears were voiced in Lisbon that Britain would take away Portugal's colonies, and there were certainly clashes on a number of issues.[3] Britain's main concern, though, was thwarting its real competitors in West Africa, who were threatening to control the whole of the Congo basin. At its crudest, as one author astutely observed: 'The bigger powers were jealous of one another, and would rather lose a trick to Portugal than to each other.'[4] Defending Portugal's claims to Angola was a way for Britain to get a back-door entry into the region. However, when Portugal attempted to lay claim to all of the land between Angola and Mozambique, thus interfering with the Cape-to-Cairo dreams of British imperialists, the final result was never in doubt. At the Berlin Congress, the frontiers of the proposed colony of Mozambique were considerably reduced in size to favour the British. Then in 1890 a British ultimatum threatened the use of naval force, obliging Portugal to withdraw from more territory in the Zambezia region. Between 1898 and 1912 there were even negotiations between the British and the Germans concerning the possible partition of the Portuguese African colonies.

The extent of Portugal's dependency internationally has been the subject of some debate, but it is undeniable that British capital exerted an enormous sway over the sub-metropolitan and colonial economies. This influence was not solely restricted to the sphere of finance capital. From 1865 to 1879, between a half and two-thirds of Portugal's exports went to Britain.[5] Nine-tenths of all exports were agricultural products (wine was 40 per cent of the total), and the existence of a single stable market for exports (in England) reinforced Portugal's position as a dependent, predominantly agricultural economy. Over this same period England provided between 37 and 59 per cent of Portugal's imports.

The origins of empire

Portugal's African colonies of Angola, Cape Verde, Guinea Bissau, São Tomé and Príncipe, and Mozambique were the remnants of its merchant trading empire of three centuries earlier. The new empires of Britain, France and Germany were based on the Industrial Revolution, which had bypassed Portugal. Wealth accumulated by pillage and unequal exchange had not been converted into productive investment. Hence Portugal was completely unable to compete on an equal footing with its northern European neighbours. Portugal imported raw materials from its colonies and supplied finished products in return, but in relation to its other main trading partners the pattern was the reverse of an imperial economy. In the twentieth century Portugal exported cork, fish products, wine, timber, olive oil and wolfram as well as its two main commodities – textiles and labour. Heavy industrial goods, consumer durables, foodstuffs and fuels provided Portugal's major import items. In other words, Portugal was in the same position in relation to the major industrial powers that the African colonies were to Portugal. As late as 1950, the primary sector (agriculture, fishing, foodstuffs and forestry) employed half of Portugal's manpower. This was a virtually unique pattern of under-development in Europe for a colonising power; Belgium, with a similar population, had only one in ten of its workforce in the primary sector.

It has been argued that the case of Portugal demonstrates the thesis that colonialism was not overridingly concerned with economic self-interest. Hammond goes as far as entitling his book *Portugal and Africa 1815–1910: a Study in Uneconomic Imperialism.*[6] Although it is certainly true that other factors were present – in the case of Portugal, the political myths of grandeur of empire and the 'civilising' mission which served to buttress rule at home – the bulk of the evidence appears to contradict this thesis of uneconomic colonialism, as will become apparent with the unfolding of our analysis. Hammond correctly points to Portugal's weak economic capacity, yet the *dependent* nature of Portuguese capitalism cannot substantiate the theory of *uneconomic* imperialism. In spite of the relatively underdeveloped nature of the

Portuguese economy, the sub-metropole benefited from the colonies by having a cheap and protected source of raw materials, a guaranteed market and the opportunity of earning hard currency for an ailing balance of payments.[7]

The puzzle of why the poorest country in Europe should have a huge empire in Africa can only be resolved by going back in history. There was an enormous expansion of Portuguese merchant capital in the fifteenth and sixteenth centuries which had two essential aims. The first of these was the acquisition of gold from West Africa, and the other was the control of the Indian spice trade. By the middle of the sixteenth century, the Portuguese occupied and controlled much of the Indian Ocean in a vast arc of naval bases stretching from Macão in China, through Indonesia, the Malay Straits, Ceylon, Goa in India, the Persian Gulf, down through Mombasa in Kenya to Sofala in Mozambique. Wealth flowed into Lisbon, making it the richest city in Europe, and the foundation of this wealth was based on the barter of one type of primary commodity for another. This differed from the imperialism of the nineteenth century, which relied on taking raw materials from the colonies for manufacture in the metropoles with the colonies also serving as a market for these self-same goods.

Portugal's East African bases, then, originally served as a transit and depot zone for Indian shipping; indeed, Mozambique was even governed from Goa in India until 1752. However, with the collapse of the spice trade the *raison d'être* for the Portuguese occupation disappeared, and the Portuguese presence in Mozambique dwindled markedly, to be revived only later with the ivory and slave trade.

In the second half of the nineteenth century a different phase of imperialism began, and the thrust behind this new expansion was industrial. Yet, unlike the empire building of Britain, France and Germany, it was not the internal logic of Portugal's economy which led to the consolidation of its colonies. Although Portugal's presence in Africa predated that of the other European powers, its entry into the scramble for Africa was almost the last. The colonisation of Africa by these industrial powers set in motion Portugal's own colonial diplomacy, and its military campaigns of occupation followed its humiliation at the Congress of Berlin. The chartered companies provide the most persuasive evidence for this argument, being the 'exact institutional notations of the new imperialism. The impetus behind the "scramble for Africa" came from the driving economies of Western Europe: its spearheads were logically the great marauding companies.'[8] The European states politically consummated the process of colonisation after the economic *fait accompli* by the companies. Portugal, however, had no equivalent of the chartered companies, and herein lies the difference. Its proportion of international trade remained infinitesimal in comparison with those of other colonial powers. For Portugal

> was utterly unable to effect or even begin the conversion from an extractive to a transformer imperialism. This fact is the root determinant of the structure of the Portuguese colonies today. It provides the master-explanation both of the individual sectors of the

Portuguese colonial system, and of integration into the ensemble.[9]

However weak the sub-metropolitan economy, and thus limited in its ability to utilise the colonial labour force, there is no denying that profit was still the major incentive. If one reads the work of the great colonial architect, Dr Oliveira Salazar, undisputed ruler of Portugal for four decades, one is left in no doubt as to the colonial power's economic intentions towards the colonies:

> we must revise and put into execution plans for public works that are indispensable within the moderate financial resources available and have *a guarantee of an effective return*; and, before everything, as the highest and noblest work of all, we must organise on the best possible lines measures for safeguarding the interests of those *inferior races* whose inclusion under the influence of Christianity is one of the greatest achievements of Portuguese colonisation.[10]

Not only does this passage indicate the financial motivation underlying colonisation; it also highlights the racism within the colonial ideology of the 'civilising mission', and gives the lie to the official multiracial mystique. In fact the racism in the ideology was necessary to guarantee an effective return, as 'civilised' wages and working conditions could then be considered unnecessary for Africans.

Multiracial theory and practice

Officially Portugal boasted of its multiracial policy, but the reality was very different.[11] Of the major historians and social scientists writing on the Portuguese colonies this century, almost all are sceptical if not completely cynical about the official Portuguese claim to colour blindness. Even the most sympathetic to the Portuguese regime, such as Hammond, admit that multiracialism extended to only a few thousand people on the coastal settlement and 'was not something that commended universal approval among the Portuguese governing class'.[12] Professor Boxer, in his extensive survey of the Portuguese empire covering four centuries, noted the presence of a consistent racism throughout.[13] Ronald Chilcote offers an insight into the origins of the multiracial ideal when he writes, 'The myth of racial harmony in the African territories has its basis in the fact that the Portuguese male freely mated with coloured women.'[14] Yet miscegenation was perfectly compatible with racism – the large coloured population of South Africa attests to this – and in fact what was originally merely erotic expediency became colonial policy only in retrospect.

 Enshrined in Article 133 of the Portuguese Constitution is the philosophy of the 'civilising mission' which reads: 'It is of the organic essence of the Portuguese Nation to carry out the historic function of colonising the land of the Discoveries under its sovereignty, and to communicate and spread among the populations existing there the benefits of its civilisation.' This undoubtedly formed an important part of the ideology of the *Estado Novo* and was a reason, although not a principal one, for the reluctance to decolonise. To lose the colonies was to lose an important prop for the dictatorship associated with the mystique of empire and Portugal's historic mission.

The ramifications of the 'civilising mission' will be examined in greater detail, but one may note, in passing, that according to official government statistics, the illiteracy rate in 1959 was 97.8 per cent in Mozambique, 96.97 per cent in Angola, 98.85 per cent in Guinea and 78.5 per cent in Cape Verde. Apart from economic gain, the other goals of colonial policy appear to have been remarkably unsuccessful, at least if we measure the 'civilising mission' in terms of educational criteria. And if the Portuguese multiracial theory is confronted with the actual racism existing in colonial societies, then very little of substance appears to remain of the exaggerated claims. They even managed to depict the slave trade as a part of their civilising mission. One final point to make, however, is decisive before passing judgement upon the debate on the economic or uneconomic theory of Portuguese colonialism. The main means adopted for 'civilising' the 'natives' was enforced wage labour. Although slavery was officially abolished in 1869, it continued for a much longer period of time, and in 1899 a decree was issued facilitating the smooth transition from slavery to forced labour. Colonial administrators, such as Vieira Machado and Marcelo Caetano, continually stressed the importance of teaching the 'lazy native' how to work. Antonio Enes, the man who established early colonial policy in Mozambique, put the issue in a remarkably frank manner: 'If we do not learn how . . . to make the negro work and cannot take advantage of his work, within a short while we will be obliged to abandon Africa to someone less sentimental and more utilitarian than we . . . .'[15] One is obliged to draw the conclusion that whatever the rationales of empire, economic considerations underpinned them.

This becomes strikingly apparent when we examine the three distinct phases in the development of the Portuguese economy which can be identified up to the time of the April coup of 1974. Each was to have a major impact on Mozambique and we will examine them in turn.

The pre-Salazar period

Until 1910 Portugal was ruled by a monarchy; then followed a brief sixteen-year period of the Republic, followed by a military *coup d'état* in 1926 heralding the Salazar takeover. In the period leading up to the coup, the Portuguese treasury was bankrupt, inflation was rampant, foreign interests were controlling more and more of the economy at home and in the African territories, and accompanying all of this was a major political crisis. The Republic began with a severe handicap. It inherited a floating debt of £16 million and a consolidated debt of £120 million, and only twice did the Republic achieve a budget surplus. From 1914 onwards the government ran a permanent and growing deficit and the cost of living increased twenty-five-fold.

In 1916, after Portugal complied with Britain's request to enter World War I, the economic and political situation worsened. The country had four governments in 1919, nine in 1920, five in 1921, and five governments and three attempted military coups in 1925. Over the entire Republican period the country had eight Presidents, forty-four cabinets, twenty-four uprisings and revolts, and one hundred and fifty-eight general strikes. Between 1920 and 1925 police reports indicated three hundred and twenty-five bombs exploding on the streets of Lisbon. Small wonder, therefore, that the colonies were neglected and left to foreign capital to exploit.

By the end of the 1920s Portugal was no longer entirely a feudal economy, but the newly emergent classes were not sufficiently developed to enable the birth of a stable bourgeois liberal democracy. Eduardo de Sousa Ferreira has analysed the metropolitan social formation at that time as follows:

> There existed on the one hand agrarian capital, conservative, not sufficiently developed for concentration and unable to maintain a stand against the other factions of capital and take over power; on the other hand [there] existed financial and commercial capital. Still without developed industries or infrastructures as fields of investment, living on commercial and financial speculation, it was unable to exercise a hegemony; the monopolies for their part were far from ruling over the economy and prepared themselves in an attitude of reserve for the consequences of competition, against which the middle and petty bourgeoisie, at that time – very dynamically – still in possession of the political power, offered resistance.[16]

No single class or fraction of a class was able to gain ascendancy, and the danger of self-destruction in the face of a rising militancy amongst the Portuguese workers led to a compromise – a supra-factional political leadership was established under Salazar in the form of a corporate state.

Salazar's closed-door economy, 1926–1960

With the Salazar takeover there was a substantial change of direction as attempts were made to bring the economy, sub-metropolitan and colonial, more closely under national control. Effectively, however, all that happened was a slowing down in the level of foreign investment as political will alone could not transform the backward and dependent Portuguese economy. Yet it would be wrong to deny that there were changes, and these were wrought by one man in particular, Antonio de Oliveira Salazar. He set up the *Estado Novo* (New State), modelled on the Italian fascist system; he abolished all parties but one, and created *sindicato* state unions for workers and *gremio* organisations for employers. His political policies were anti-democratic at home and doubly so in the colonies. In 1958 he was reported as saying: 'I do not believe in universal suffrage, because the individual vote does not take into account human differentiation. I do not believe in equality but in hierarchy. Men, in my opinion, should be equal before the law, but I believe it dangerous to attribute to all the same political rights.'[17] His economic policy was fairly straightforward: cuts in wages and government expenditure and an increase in taxation. Between 1939 and 1955, real wages in Portugal dropped by a third.[18] Budgets had to balance, and the notion of debt became a blasphemy. One notorious criminal, Arthur Virgilio Reis, printed millions of escudo notes in a celebrated attempt 'to steal the country' in 1925, and this undoubtedly had a reinforcing effect on Salazar's anti-inflationary policies.[19]

Salazar completely eschewed the new Keynesian economic theory, pursuing instead ultra-conservative fiscal policies. The vulnerability of the sub-metropolitan economy was highlighted in the Great Depression as the Portuguese bourgeoisie was essentially commercial and its fortunes, therefore, were intrinsically linked to levels of trade. The downturn in world trade severely affected them. This vulnerability elicited an isolationist response from Salazar, and the country was progressively closed off from the world economy.

Internally there was a slow development of agriculture, but in industry there was a consolidation rather than an expansion. Government permission was required to open new factories or install any machinery that would increase production.[20] Permission was also required if the ownership or working of an industry was to be transferred to foreigners or to concerns in which Portuguese citizens did not have a controlling majority. More stringent controls were later introduced when it became compulsory for a fixed proportion of the shares in every foreign enterprise to be held by Portuguese nationals or Portuguese-based companies, and fixed rates of profit repatriation for foreign investors were set. This strong nationalist policy was a reaction to Portugal's dependent status, but the extent to which these measures truly wrested control from foreign capital is open to question. A foreign company may be content to have minority shares in a company, leaving indigenous capital in the majority, because it knows that the enterprise is only viable on the basis of foreign patents, foreign materials and supplies and foreign technical capital. In this way local capital becomes the prisoner of its foreign partner.

Economic and political power was extremely concentrated inside Portugal, with the government and industry being run by a closed shop of rich and influential people with interrelating interests based on the maintenance of the status quo. Portuguese industry was inefficient and therefore uncompetitive on the world market. The colonies provided one of the few possibilities for external investment. Even so, only a limited amount was invested there, as the sub-metropole remained predominantly a backward agrarian peasant society. Salazar did, however, try to make the exploitation of the colonies more efficient. He introduced legislation obliging every colony to draw up a balanced budget according to a unified plan, so that each one's expenses had to be met by its own revenues. These conservative fiscal policies enabled the colonies to become more effective sources of raw materials, foreign exchange and markets for the sub-metropole.

This can be most clearly demonstrated in the case of the textile industry. Until Salazar came to power, most cotton imports for this textile industry came from countries with little reciprocal trade with Portugal. For example, in 1926 the colonies provided only 1 167 tons of cotton in comparison with total cotton imports of 16 471 tons.[21] Forced cotton cultivation in the colonies and preferential measures taken in the sub-metropole meant that by 1946 the colonies were providing 96 per cent of cotton imports.[22] This rapidly produced a significant saving in foreign currency, as Portugal radically reduced the imports of finished cotton goods which it was now producing itself. In addition, Portuguese textile exports to the colonies had a good market because there were high tariffs against foreign products.

This period marks the beginning of a more systematic exploitation of the colonies, utilising intense 'labour-repressive' policies. Forced cash-crop cultivation, especially of cotton, and forced labour increased significantly. Nevertheless, this new phase could not alter the basic facts concerning the political economy of Portugal: it remained a backward country dependent on foreign capital, Salazar's 'nationalist' economic policies notwithstanding.

Opening up to foreign capital, 1960–1974

The third and final period stretches from 1960 to 1974, and is mainly characterised by the impact of the nationalist struggle in the colonies causing an opening up to foreign investment. The domestic economy began to throw off its archaic inheritance, and the working population involved in agriculture, forestry and fishing fell by nearly 10 per cent between 1960 and 1967, as compared with a fall of 5.5 per cent between 1950 and 1960.[23] In 1950, less than a quarter of the working population was involved in industry, but by 1967 it was well over a third. These changes were closely related to massive increases in foreign investment, and this is a clear symptom of a dependent economy. The percentage of foreign capital in total annual investments increased from 0.8 per cent in 1959 to 26.7 per cent in 1966.[24] Between 1947 and 1960 a mere 1.9 million contos were invested in Portugal. Then from 1961 to 1971 an astonishing 40.2 million contos of foreign investment poured into the country.[25] Of the one hundred largest industrial enterprises in 1970, foreign capital participated in forty-one.

The three colonial wars in Angola, Guinea Bissau and Mozambique were decisive in forcing changes in Salazar's policy. In spite of some post-Second World War development, Portugal still remained an underdeveloped capitalist power unable to finance the colonial wars without opening the doors to foreign investment. The foreign investment in the sub-metropole was more than matched by that in the colonies, with, for example, 60 per cent of the total sum invested in the escudo zone by foreign firms in 1969 going to the colonies.[26] Of these investments in the colonies, 98.5 per cent came from five countries: the United States, South

Africa, Britain, the Federal Republic of Germany and Belgium. After the Second World War Portugal gradually changed from being under the dominant metropolitan influence of the British, with the role of the United States and West Germany becoming more important.

The continuing underdevelopment of the Portuguese economy is an important factor in understanding why the potential was created for the emergence of a revolutionary movement in the colonies. Portugal did not wish to *decolonise* at the end of the 1950s or in the 1960s because it could not *neocolonise*. The reformist option, a controlled decolonisation with the nationalists inheriting the existing political and economic structures, did not exist; they had to engage in armed struggle, and thereby a revolutionary dynamic was set in motion within the nationalist movement itself. The benefits accruing to Lisbon from the colonies were entirely dependent on the exercise of *direct* political control. In this way Portugal avoided 'open' competition with the advanced industrial nations and could import cotton from its colonies, for example, at half the world price. Dr Francisco Nogueira, Foreign Minister for many years in the Portuguese government, sketched out the implications of the sub-metropole's economic weakness in relation to its colonies: 'Portugal was neither France nor England. It was very clear that once the political links were severed or weakened all the other links would disappear.'[27]

Major changes were taking place in the Portuguese countryside in the 1960s, and these too were to have a big impact on the colonies. There was increased mechanisation of agriculture, increasing rural proletarianisation and a dramatic reduction in the numbers employed in agriculture – falling by 355 000 from 1960 to 1970. Over this same period the total working population in Portugal fell by 150 000 as a result of emigration to the colonies and to Western Europe. The colonies acted as an important overspill for mass unemployment in the sub-metropole. By the early 1970s over one and a half million had found employment abroad.[28] A majority of the emigrants came from the newly unemployed of the rural areas, hence many of the white settlers in the colonies were illiterate former peasants. Unlike the British and French colonists, the Portuguese settlers occupied not only the senior and middle positions in the social–technical hierarchy of each colony but provided a fair proportion of the semi-skilled workers also. This clearly had important implications for emerging African class formation in Mozambique and Angola (in Guinea Bissau there were very few settlers), and it also gave the lie to the philosophy of the civilising mission.

The colonies were a major source of foreign exchange for the sub-metropole. Although each country had its own currency, issuing bank, annual budget and individual foreign exchange fund (holding its reserves of gold and foreign exchange), there was one common unit of exchange within the empire, the escudo. The Bank of Portugal operated the over-all system of interterritorial payments, producing a monthly balance of debits or credits for each territory. Settlement had then to be made in escudos. Each country had a reserve account with the Bank in which its escudo holdings were kept. If these were insufficient to pay the debts incurred by each colony, then they would be obliged to buy metropolitan escudos with their own reserves of gold or foreign exchange. There was a permanent trade deficit between the colonies and the sub-metropole, and this system simply acted as a channel through which, say, the gold earned in Mozambique by the migrant labour to the South African mines would flow directly back to Lisbon.

Turning to trade, we see some new patterns beginning to emerge. Although exports and imports between the sub-metropole and the colonies increased absolutely, the relative importance of the colonies declined. Throughout the 1960s the colonies had provided a quarter of all Portugal's exports, but by 1973 they represented less than 15 per cent. The declining share of Portugal's colonial imports was less severe – 14 per cent to 10 per cent over the same period – but was none the less significant. The main reduction in the colonies' share of trade with the sub-metropole stems from 1970, with Portugal's trade in Europe becoming increasingly important. On 22 July 1972, Portugal's Minister of Foreign Affairs put his signature to an agreement with the European Economic Community, and press reports linked the granting of nominal 'self-government' to the colonies at this time with the desire to obtain closer co-operation with the EEC.[29] There was clearly a shift in trade patterns towards Europe and away from Africa.

The effects of the unfavourable pattern of trade enforced by the sub-metropole on the colonies also began to emerge in this period. The outstanding debt of Mozambique and Angola with Portugal increased from 2 900 million escudos in 1968 to over 9 000 million escudos in 1971.[30] As a result of these debts, imports from Portugal had to be subjected to the same restrictions as those from other foreign countries, and this contributed to the reduction in the sub-metropole's trade with its colonies.

Although the relative importance of the colonies may have diminished, effectively they remained a crucial prop to the sub-metropole. In the face of an uncompetitive industrial base in comparison with the metropolitan powers, Portugal relied heavily on the super-cheap raw materials imported from the colonies to provide a counterweight. Textiles provided a fifth of export earnings and employed a third of the manufacturing workforce. This textile industry was built upon a price for raw cotton well below the world price, and this was guaranteed by colonial occupation and control. In 1969, 99 per cent of Mozambique's exports of raw cotton, sugar and groundnut oil went to countries of the escudo zone.[31] In 1973, the final year before the coup, Mozambique exported 51 000 tons of cotton which was converted into 50 million tons of fibre, and almost all went to the sub-metropole.[32] The colonies therefore remained important sources of raw materials right up to the end.

The colonies also remained an important market for the sub-metropole. More than a third of Portugal's cotton manufactures were exported back to the colonies. In 1969, for example, 81.5 per cent of Mozambique's undyed cotton fabrics were imported from the escudo area and 92.9 per cent of the dyed cotton fabrics.[33] Wine, as well as textiles, provided an important export. Indeed, the colonies spent more on wine imports than on imports of industrial and agricultural machinery. In order to enlarge the colonial market for manufactured alcoholic drinks attempts were made to eliminate local brews, frequently under the guise of combating alcoholism.[34]

Portugal was the poor man of Europe, dependent upon Britain and later the other major industrial powers. It did not have the capital to exploit the colonies extensively itself, and in the pre-Salazar period this was done almost entirely by proxy. With the accession to power of Salazar, there was the increasing use of the colonies to produce raw materials for the sub-metropole, and an attempt was made to reduce foreign dominance over the economy. Then in the 1960s, with three wars in Africa, it was only by opening the doors wide to foreign investment that Portugal was able to finance the massive military presence in the colonies for as long as it did.

By the time that big capital inside Portugal, supported by foreign investors, was in a position to arrange some form of neo-colonial solution it was already too late. As we shall show, the nationalist movements in the colonies had been transformed into organisations with revolutionary goals and were not prepared to discuss 'federal' solutions. If the absence of a neo-colonial solution was one of the main reasons for a revolutionary potential in the colonies, the other, extreme 'labour-repressive' policies, also stemmed from the backward nature of the Portuguese economy. The weakness of the colonial power increased the extent to which Mozambique was drawn into servicing the needs of the South African economy which dominated the Southern African region as a whole, and it is to this topic that we now turn our attention.

Notes

1 J. P. Oliveira Martins, *História de Portugal*, Vol. II, 7th ed., Lisbon, 1908, p. 149.

2 *Ibid.*, p. 429.

3 J. D'Arriaga, *A Inglaterra, Portugal e Suas Colónias*, Lisbon, 1882, p. xx.

4 V. Kiernan, 'The Old Alliance', a paper delivered at the National Conference on Revolutions in the Portuguese Colonies, Manchester, June 1973.

5 R. da Costa, *O Desenvolvimento do Capitalismo em Portugal*, Lisbon, 1976, p 18.

6 R. J. Hammond, *Portugal and Africa 1815–1910: a Study in Uneconomic Imperialism*, Stanford, Ca., 1966.

7 See A. Castro, *A revolução industrial em Portugal no século XIX*, Porto, 1976, p. 72, for a table showing how even in the early stage of colonial rule commercial benefits ensued.

8 P. Anderson, 'Portugal and the End of Ultra-colonialism', *New Left Review*, 15, 1961.

9 *Ibid.*, 102.

10 O. Salazar, *Doctrine and Action*, London, 1939, p. 177 (italics added).

11 See G. J. Bender, *Angola under the Portuguese: the Myth and the Reality*,

London, 1978; with A. Isaacman, 'The changing Historiography of Angola and Mozambique', in C. Fyfe (ed.), *African Studies since 1945*, London, 1976, pp. 228–31.

12 R. J. Hammond, 'Race Attitudes and Policies in Portuguese Africa in the Nineteenth and Twentieth Centuries', *Race*, ix, 2, Oct. 1967, 207.

13 C. R. Boxer, *The Portuguese Seaborne Empire 1415–1825*, London, 1969. See ch. 11.

14 R. H. Chilcote, *Portuguese Africa*, Englewood Cliffs, N.J., 1967, p. 11.

15 Quoted in E. Mondlane, 'Nationalism and Development', in *Portuguese Colonies: Victory or Death*, Havana, 1971, p. 171.

16 E. de Sousa Ferreira, *Portuguese Colonialism from South Africa to Europe*, Frieburg, 1972, p. 144.

17 *Le Figaro*, 3 Sept. 1958.

18 A. de Figueiredo, *Portugal and Its Empire: the Truth*, London, 1961, p. 55.

19 M. T. Bloom, *The Man Who Stole Portugal*, New York, 1966.

20 F. Cotta, *Economic Planning in Corporative Portugal*, London, 1937, p. 130.

21 *Ibid.*, p. 137.

22 N. S. Bravo, *A Cultura Algodoeira na Economia do Norte de Moçambique*, Lisbon, Junta de Investigações do Ultramar, Estudo De Ciências Políticas e Sociais, 66, 1963, p. 70.

23 See A. Castro *et al.*, *Sobre o Capitalismo Português*, Coimbra, 1971, p. 71.

24 De Sousa Ferreira, *Portuguese Colonialism*, p. 55.

25 The figures are compiled from R. da Costa, *Desenvolvimento*, p. 141, and *Portugal, an Informative Review*, 28, 1972.

26 See De Sousa Ferreira, *Portuguese Colonialism*, W. Minter, *Portuguese Africa and the West*, Harmondsworth, Mdx., 1972, for further details.

27 *Expresso*, Portugal, 23 March 1978.

28 *The Economist*, 26 Feb. 1972.

29 *Daily Telegraph*, 5 Dec. 1970.

30 *Financial Times*, 2 Feb. 1972.

31 *Anuário Estatístico 1969*, Vol II, Instituto Nacional de Estatística, Lisbon.

32 *Economia de Moçambique*, xi, 6, June 1974.

33 *Anuário Estatístico 1969*, *op. cit.*

34 See J. Capela, *O Vinho Para o Preto*, Porto, 1973.

3 South Africa: the spinning of the spider's web

The last hundred years have seen a remarkable growth in South Africa's economic power within the region. From being originally just another exporter of raw materials from the third world, the country has now become an important industrial nation in its own right. In the process, other states became entangled in a web of dependency, with the South African spider at the centre sucking out the labour and services of its surrounding victims. The weakness of the colonial power, Mozambique's juxtaposition to South Africa and its lack of rich export commodities (such as the diamonds, iron ore, coffee and oil that Angola possessed) contributed to making this country especially dependent on South Africa, and this was to present the post-independence government in Mozambique with particularly complex problems. The relative ease with which ties with Portugal were broken stands in marked contrast to Mozambique's continuing dependency on South Africa.

The origins of the migrant labour system

The mining revolution in the final quarter of the nineteenth century provided the foundation for South Africa's growth as the centre of a regional sub-system. By the turn of the century 54 000 Africans were working on the mines, and three out of four of these came from outside South Africa's borders.[1] The initial reluctance of the peasantry living closest to the mines to be incorporated into a cheap wage-labour system led to a far-reaching regional search for labour, stretching as far north as Tanganyika and Angola. Foreign migrants have consistently accounted for the majority of the mine labour force. Their labour, in other words, has been employed to build up South Africa's economy and not that of their own countries. The persistent absence of a large percentage of the fittest section of the workforce (40 per cent of Lesotho's male labour, for example)[2] could only contribute to the underdevelopment and peripheralisation of the remainder of the region. Although the need for a huge labour force to exploit the mineral deposits meant that pressure had to be put on the peasantry to create a migrant proletariat, this was a slow and uneven process. The first migrant labourers came in the 1860s, to work on the sugar plantations of Natal. It was the inability to 'free' the local peasantry from the soil which precipitated the migration of Indian and Mozambican labour even at this early stage.

South Africa's internal labour shortages have been portrayed as being the result of 'deficiencies' in the 'traditional' societies, meaning the

Africans' inability either to adapt their pre-capitalist economy or to forsake it for participation in the market economy. Colin Bundy has presented an altogether more convincing explanation for the shortage of labour willing to work on the mines.[3] He has shown that there was a substantially more positive response by African agriculturalists to market opportunities than is usually indicated. An adapted form of the traditional subsistence methods initially provided hundreds of thousands of Africans with a preferable alternative to wage labour. However, discriminatory and coercive means were used to disadvantage the South African peasantry, and 'market forces' were structured in such a way as to give preference to the white capitalist sector. An alliance was formed between mining and agriculture. Both mine owners and large white farmers required cheap labour, and to get this they had to destroy the basis of African peasant agriculture. For the farmers it was essential to transform their black competitors into their labourers, and it was the state's role to ensure the curtailment of African farmers' competition with the whites. The 1913 Land Act virtually guaranteed this by restricting blacks to only 13 per cent of the land area of South Africa, and labour-repressive laws guaranteed the continuation for generations of a cheap labour system.

Over time, then, there was a tranformation of the South African peasantry into a permanent migrant proletariat, which when not directly engaged in wage labour was returned to the Bantustan labour reserves. This pattern of incorporation of the peasantry was repeated outside South Africa's territorial boundaries, as every country, without exception, in the southern African region came to furnish migrant labour to a greater or lesser extent to serve the needs of the South African economy. Migrant workers came from Basutoland (now Lesotho), Bechuanaland (Botswana), Swaziland, Northern Rhodesia (Zambia), Southern Rhodesia (Zimbabwe), Mozambique, Nyasaland (Malawi), other African countries further to the north, and for a brief period in 1904, when other supply lines were disrupted, 60 000 workers were imported from southern China.[4]

To explain the reason for the use of migrant labour in more detail we refer to Marx's theory of value. The wage paid for the sale of labour is not the full value created by the labourer's work. The difference appropriated by the owners of the means of production is called surplus value, which is unpaid labour. Labour power under capitalism becomes a commodity to be exchanged in the same way as other commodities, based on the socially necessary labour time expended on its production and reproduction. This means, in other words, that the value of labour power is the value of the means of subsistence necessary for the maintenance of the labourer over time. However, labour may be purchased at a cost below its value, and so the level of surplus value expropriated by the capitalist may be increased. By preventing a permanent proletarianisation and instituting a migrant system, a wage *below* the immediate cost of reproduction of the labour force can be paid. With full proletarianisation, a man's wage has to pay for the housing, food, clothing, education and so on of the whole family – that is, the present and the future generation of workers. With a migrant labour system the cost of rearing the next generation of workers is carried by the woman who remains working on the peasant plot. This plot also has to provide sustenance for the male labourer between contracts and after he is no longer fit to work.

Although many countries furnished labour, Mozambique consistently provided the highest proportion of migrants for the gold mines. The development of mining in South Africa totally transformed the Mozambican formation. Between one-quarter and one-third of the total Mozambican workforce was annually exported outside the country, not only to South Africa but also to other adjacent countries.[5] A class of worker-peasants was formed in the south of the country. A transport infrastructure was built to serve as an outlet for South Africa's raw material exports, and it also facilitated the easy flow of men to and from the mines. That flow of men was necessarily a constant and highly regulated one, as we shall see.

The influence of the South African economy on Mozambique was, and remains still, so great that the phases in its development help us to understand the changes which took place in Mozambique itself. Broadly speaking, there are two periods. The period 1875 to 1924 was that of mining capital hegemony: diamonds were discovered in the 1860s and gold in the 1880s, and mining rapidly came to dominate the entire economy. A second period, from 1925 to the present, was marked by the dominance of manufacturing and the emergence of South Africa as an industrial power.[6]

The mining era

Diamond mining opened up the new era and created conditions favourable for the rapid growth of gold mining, which was to assume a far more important role in South Africa and to have a devastating impact on the political economy of Mozambique. Kimberley's diamond mines created a group of entrepreneurs having connections with international capital markets and in possession of a ready supply of capital.[7] The high profits made from diamonds were soon invested in the gold mines, and the ownership of both was highly centralised. Just prior to the First World War, only two of the nine leading gold-mining companies were outside the control of the De Beers and the (closely associated) Werner Beit group of financiers. Major inputs of foreign capital were necessary to permit the development of these mines as the capital available locally was insufficient. It soon became available in Britain and Europe, however, because of an existing capital surplus and the urgent need of the international economy for gold currency. Between 1887 and 1913, £125 million was invested from abroad in gold mining, and by the latter part of the period less than 15 per cent of the shares were South African-owned.[8]

In a book published to commemorate the fiftieth anniversary of the proclamation of the Witwatersrand and the jubilee of the city of Johannesburg (in 1936) there is a remarkably frank appraisal of the role which black labour had to play in the gold-mining industry: 'The principal factor of limitation to the expansion of the Rand is the availability of native labour in sufficient quantities.'[9] Later in this same work we read:

> The scale of operations of the mines expands or contracts more or less in direct ratio to the number of natives employed, and therefore the numbers of white employees, the amount of money expended by the mines in working costs, the profits earned, the taxation paid and the dividends disbursed, are in the main determined by the numbers of natives employed.[10]

As Johnstone has argued in his meticulous and detailed study of the gold-mining industry, the accumulation of profit was circumscribed by the unique cost structure of the industry.[11] These were the low average grade of gold (half that found in Western Australia); an internationally fixed gold price, which meant that increases in the costs of production could not be passed on to the consumer in higher prices, and output could be maximised indefinitely without jeopardising profit (unlike the diamond-mining industry); there was also a high level of development and overhead costs dependent upon deep-level gold mining. The main cost components were labour and materials. Since companies had a limited ability to control the input of the latter, labour was the crucial area of cost minimisation. In other words, there had to be a *maximisation of ultra-cheap labour*.

The mining companies faced three problems in attaining these aims. There was a continuing measure of economic independence amongst Africans, as we have already seen; there was competition among employers in different sectors for labour inside South Africa; and finally, as a consequence, there was an internal shortage of non-white labour. Companies confronted these problems in three ways. Compulsion upon Africans to work was increased. There were transformations in the structure of the ownership of means of production; tribal tenure in the reserves was undermined with the splitting up of the land into family holdings, and systems of loan advancement and debt inducement were introduced. Traders created indebtedness and were paid a capitation fee for every African they secured to labour in the mines.[12] Secondly, there was the monopsonisation of labour recruiting with the founding of the Witwatersrand Native Labour Association (WNLA) in 1896. This eliminated wasteful competition and duplication amongst the mining companies, reduced capital overheads and improved the general organisation of the labour supply. The WNLA came fully into operation after the Boer war, and between 1913 and 1924 it enabled the cost of recruiting to fall by 20 per cent.[13] The third measure taken by the companies was the importation of non-white labour from outside South Africa. Given the finite nature of South Africa's supply and the unpopularity of mine work along with the high political and economic costs of employing unskilled white labour, this appeared to be a logical step. The employment of foreign migrants brought an additional bonus by exerting a down-pressure on African wage rates within South Africa and exported many of the problems that intensive labour exploitation would cause. The nature of capital accumulation on the Transvaal required vast quantities of cheap labour and Mozambique was to become the principal supplier, which influenced the entire development of the country's political economy and class formation, as succeeding chapters will show.

The industrial era

The mineral revolution alone was not sufficient to account for South Africa's domination of the region. Settler power exerted through the state ensured that the economy would not remain a mining enclave but would develop its own industrial base. In the second period from 1925 to the present, manufacturing became dominant. The rapid growth of this sector was predicated upon an apartheid state which guaranteed a continuing supply of cheap labour producing high profits. Revenues from gold mining provided the state with the means to establish the infrastructure of the manufacturing industry. The 1920s saw the formation of the South African Iron and Steel Industrial Corporation (Iscor), and between 1933 and 1945 the number of private manufacturing establishments rose by almost 50 per cent.[14]

Several factors stimulated the development of the secondary sector. After the depression, South Africa followed Britain in going off the gold standard, and gold export earnings increased considerably as a result. Then in the Second World War military manufacture and the import substitution of goods no longer available in wartime conditions provided a second stimulus, as they had with Portugal. Exchange controls introduced in 1948 produced an enforced isolation from foreign markets, and this was followed in the early 1950s by the Korean war boom which inflated raw material prices and thereby encouraged South African agriculture. Then a fifth stimulus was provided by the opening of the Orange Free State gold mines and the discovery of uranium. From the 1960s onwards there was a policy to build up a self-sufficient military machine in response to sanctions. Finally, with the depression of the 1970s and 1980s coupled with the oil crisis, the price of gold increased considerably.

Throughout this century, with minor exceptions, foreign migrants have accounted for between a half and three-quarters of the total mine labour force.[15] The employment of black South Africans in their place would have considerably reduced the internal reserve army of labour for secondary manufacturing, thereby increasing costs and reducing the high investible surplus which was an important factor in maintaining the high rate of growth in this sector.[16] Foreign migrant labour was used to create an 'artificial' reserve army of labour exerting a downward pressure not only on wages in the secondary sector but specifically in mining. Average wages per shift stayed more or less constant between 1910 and the Second World War and were below those in manufacturing. As one spokesman of the mining companies put it: 'Actually we prefer to hire these country chaps . . . . Otherwise we would have to compete with local industry in wages, and the urban African gets more money than we are willing to pay.'[17]

Migrant labour was far from being the only thread in the South

African web of regional dominance. South African investment in Mozambique increased when Portugal lifted controls on investment in order to help finance the colonial wars in 1965. South African capital moved into mining ventures, fishing industries, manufacturing projects and citrus and agricultural development.[18] Where the investment was not directly South African in origin, most transnationals expanded their operations into Mozambique by way of their South African subsidiary. Frequently investment was carried out on a joint basis. In the 1960s, South African investment in Mozambique amounted to £10 million and non-South African investment to £30 million.[19] In addition to investments, Mozambique also acted as an export market for South African manufactured goods. The transit rail and port facilities that Mozambique provided were of vital importance to its economy, as we will show in succeeding chapters. Tourism for white South Africans was a relatively new feature of the situation, with Mozambique becoming a holiday playground for the Europeans who had benefited from the economic privileges accruing to their race under apartheid. Mozambique became a provider of prawns and prostitutes.

South Africa generated underdevelopment and exploitation in its own periphery and became itself a sub-metropolitan power. Mozambique was an important part of that periphery. Increasingly it was being drawn into a tighter regional rather than colonial economic nexus. This had serious future implications for the socialist development strategy which independent Mozambique wished to pursue, as we will demonstrate in the final part of the book.

Notes

1 F. Wilson, *Migrant Labour in South Africa*, South African Council of Churches and SPRO-CAS, 1972, p. 4.

2 R. Leys, *Lesotho: Non-Development or Under-Development?* Institute for Development Research, Project Papers D731, Copenhagen, 1973.

3 C. Bundy, *The Rise and Fall of the South African Peasantry*, London, 1979.

4 See P. Richardson, 'The Recruiting of Chinese Indentured Labour for the South African Gold Mines, 1903–1908', in *Journal of African History*, xvi, 1, 1977.

5 Centre of African Studies, *The Mozambican Miner: a Study in the Export of Labour*, Instituto de Investigação Científico de Moçambique, Maputo, 1977, p. 3.

6 This periodisation is accepted by several writers on South Africa. See, for example, M. Legassick, 'South Africa: Capital Accumulation and Violence', in *Economy and Society*, iii, 3, 1974.

7 D. Innes, 'The Exercise of Control in the Diamond Industry of South Africa', in *Perspectives of South Africa*, T. Adler (ed.), Johannesburg, 1977.

8 Legassick, *South Africa*, p. 260.

9 O. Letcher, *The Gold Mines of Southern Africa*, Johannesburg, 1936, p. 199.

10 *Ibid.*, p. 419.

11 F. A. Johnstone, *Class, Race and Gold*, London, 1976.

12 Other factors also played a part: population growth, crop failure, stock decimation, soil erosion and the desire to acquire money with which to purchase guns and cattle.

13 Johnstone, *Class, Race and Gold*, p. 31.

14 See D. H. Houghton, *The South African Economy*, Oxford, 1976, p. 15.

15 Centre of African Studies, *The Mozambican Miner*, p. 24.

16 See M. Legassick and H. Wolpe, 'The Bantustans and Capital Accumulation in South Africa', in *Review of African Political Economy*, 7, 1976.

17 E. Cole, *House of Bondage*, London, 1968, p. 23.

18 L. Bowman, 'South Africa's Southern Strategy and Its Implications for the U.S.', in *International Affairs*, xlvii, 1, Jan. 1971.

19 R. First, J. Steele and C. Gurney, *The South African Connection*, London, 1972, p. 263.

4 Establishing the chains of dependency in Mozambique

Introduction

The sub-metropolitan nature of the colonial power and South Africa's domination of the regional sub-system were the two crucial influences shaping the political economy of Mozambique. We can see their impact clearly in the three distinct historical phases which emerged before independence. In the early colonial period (1880 to 1930), the centre and north of the country were leased to foreign chartered companies and the south became a labour reserve for the South African mines. Then in the middle colonial period (1930 to 1960), Salazar attempted to limit foreign economic influence and turn Mozambique into a direct rather than an indirect source of profit. Forced crop cultivation and forced labour were intensified in order to furnish raw materials for the sub-metropole's embryonic industries, and fierce labour-repressive policies fuelled the flow of temporary and semi-permanent migrations to neighbouring countries. In the late colonial period (1960 to 1974), there was the outbreak of an armed nationalist struggle in the face of Portugal's unwillingness to decolonise, itself the result of its inability to neocolonise. This obliged Portugal to open up the colonies once again to foreign investors in a bid to hold on to its African possessions, and the result was even closer integration into the regional sub-system.

The roots of underdevelopment

Over most of the African continent peasants were bought into wage work after the implantation of the colonial state: An array of tactics were employed, foremost amongst them being hut taxes, forced labour laws and land appropriation. Individually, and more generally in combination, these measures obliged the male members of the self-sustaining agricultural communities to work for a wage. In southern Mozambique, however, the process was somewhat different. Men began selling their labour for a wage before the final conquest and implantation of the colonial state. Three factors can be identified to explain why this should have occurred: the early impact of merchant capital; the Ngoni invasion; and the development of plantation agriculture and mining in South Africa.

The pre-colonial societies had been seriously weakened by the activities of the merchant traders. Several studies have traced the roots of Mozambique's underdevelopment back over many centuries.[1] This primitive accumulation by merchant capital can be divided into three time periods according to the commodity dominating each era: 1498 to 1693 that of gold; 1693 to 1785 that of ivory; and 1785 to 1870 that of slaves. It has been estimated that half a million slaves were shipped from Mozambique between 1810 and 1860 and, overall, nearly twice that number.[2] The slave trade served as the cutting edge for underdeveloping Africa. Massive social and economic disruption inevitably ensued with the removal of a large part of the able-bodied population. Walter Rodney observed that

> The Portuguese government was the first in Europe to ship captives from Africa and the last to let go of slave trading. Much of the profit slipped out of Portuguese hands and went instead to Britain and Germany, but the Portuguese slave trade nevertheless helped the Portuguese themselves to finance later colonial ventures.[3]

The slave trade increased the level of Portuguese intervention in Mozambique, and as a direct effect of the trade large parts of the country became impoverished. Slaves were sold instead of being used for agricultural work, and certain areas were depopulated. From originally being a food-exporting area, for most of the nineteenth century the Zambezi valley was threatened by famine.

Portugal operated the slave trade mainly in the centre and north of the country by obtaining a political *modus vivendi* with the Swahili sheikhs who ruled the coastal strip. The Portuguese literature officially pronounced a five-hundred-year presence in Mozambique, but this was undoubtedly a hollow claim. Apart from a few customs posts, Portugal's 'presence', as such, rested on the *prazos* along the Zambezi valley.[4] These represented Portugal's most serious attempt at colonisation up to the middle of the nineteenth century. Allen Isaacman has demonstrated how these originally European institutions became Africanised and were virtually independent fiefdoms.[5] The *prazos* were huge tracts of land ruled by a lord or *senhor*, with both a slave and a free African population (*colonos*). An observer at the beginning of the nineteenth century painted a telling portrait of the *prazos*:

> While the slaves, male and female, work in the mines, the African traders pass through the bush, and the *colonos* cultivate the land. The *senhor*, lazy and inert, not needing to devote the least thought or combination of ideas to his affairs, passes his days sleeping or smoking or drinking tea, or at other times leaves his house when the sun is setting, offering the public the fatuous sight of his stupid indolence and bogus grandeur, appearing lying in a *machila* and carried along by four miserable slaves.[6]

Theoretically, there was supposed to be a contractual relation between the *prazo* and the Crown, but the reality was somewhat different, because the Portuguese government was impotent militarily, politically and economically over its titular possessions. As an example of its economic powerlessness, by the 1870s British Indian traders were dominant all along the Zambezi, and the Indian rupee even circulated as legal tender.

Concurrent with the slave raids were the invasions from south-east Africa by the Ngoni people. Soshengana established his domination over the Tsonga in the south of Mozambique and formed the new Gaza state. His empire steadily spread, eventually stretching as far north as the Zambezi river. This Ngoni invasion led to a considerable restructuring of the indigenous societies of southern Mozambique.[7] Once Ngoni domination had been established, the ivory trade, which was still of importance in the south, became the exclusive monopoly of the Gaza kings. They claimed a tusk from every elephant killed in the area. The military organisation of the state facilitated hunting on a larger scale, whereas previously animals had been hunted only for individual family needs. Within three decades large hunting expeditions had made some species of animals extinct. In the 1860s, 50 000 kilos of ivory, rhino tusks and hippo bones were exported annually from Lourenço Marques (after independence renamed Maputo), and Inhambane, but by the 1880s these exports had almost disappeared. Similarly, hides and skins, which constituted 80 per cent of exports from Lourenço Marques in the 1860s, had ceased altogether by the 1880s. Game was considerably reduced through overkill and also by disease.

Royal control of cattle was probably at least as important to the economy as trade. The Gaza state differed sharply from its predecessor in the greater emphasis that it placed on warfare and raiding, and this also played a part in the disruption of the pre-colonial economies. Tribute demands and the need to feed the army led to overcultivation. The destruction of traditional controls on grazing and cultivation made 'gathering' no longer viable. Under the Gaza state there was an increasing social differentiation as rulers concentrated women and cattle into their households. A growing class of the dispossessed was created as the wealth coming from trade consolidated the process of internal differentiation. In sum, the transformation in the social relations of production broke down the equilibrium between production and reproduction, making these societies vulnerable to the penetration of a new form of capital.

The third and final reason for the integration of Mozambican peasants into wage labour before the implantation of the colonial state relates to the developments in South Africa examined in the last chapter. Sugar plantations in Natal required a labour force that could not be furnished from the immediate surrounding territory, and labour migration from Mozambique to South Africa began in the 1860s to meet these needs. This supply was so important that in the early 1870s attempts were made to annex Delagoa Bay and Inhaca Island in the south of Mozambique to Natal. These were largely motivated by the desire to secure a safe method of shipping migrant labour, and South African claims to this area continued into the early twentieth century. However, it was the mining revolution which really intensified and regularised the migrant labour flow. These, then, were some of the roots of the country's underdevelopment.

The pattern is established (1880–1930)

In this period the essential mechanisms of Mozambique's integration into the southern African regional sub-system were established, and the economic centre of gravity passed from north of the Zambezi river, where the slave trade was dominant, to the south. Migrant labour to South Africa and Southern Rhodesia, the building of a transport infrastructure to serve the export and import needs of these two countries, and the hiring out of the northern two-thirds of Mozambique to foreign chartered companies were the three main features of the political economy. Given the weakness of its own economy, Portugal became little more than a *rentier* state hiring out the labour force of its African colony both externally and internally. In other words, Portugal exploited the country's labour indirectly.

Mine labour

With the defeat of Gungunyana and the Gaza state in 1895, Portugal could claim 'ownership' of the Mozambican labour force, at least in the south of the country. Under the terms of a series of conventions signed with South Africa, Portugal was then able to 'sell' this labour to the mines. The flow of migrants was regularised, and Lisbon charged a hire fee on every one recruited. Under the terms of these agreements (made in 1897, 1901, 1909 and 1928) Portugal received the following benefits: in exchange for supplying labour, the port of Lourenço Marques was guaranteed 50 per cent of the Transvaal trade (Accord of 1909) with fees paid for the use of the railway; the migrants earned cash to pay their taxes; a percentage of their pay was deferred to be received in Mozambique, with the Chamber of Mines paying the Portuguese government in gold and the workers receiving payment in local currency; finally, a charge was levied by the state at various times for each man recruited.

The flow of men to the mines was further fuelled by other factors. A rinderpest epidemic of 1896–1898 decimated cattle herds. Forced labour began on a large scale with the construction of the railways and ports, and in 1899 the labour code obliging blacks to seek work was introduced. The mines not unnaturally appeared a better alternative to many Mozambican peasants, but, even so, there still remained some forcible recruitment. However, hut tax and the brideprice increasingly came to be paid in cash, thus obliging others to enter wage employment. The mine labour recruiting organisation, WNLA, was responsible for the regularisation and smooth operation of the migrant labour system. Apart from a brief period during the Depression, every year throughout the century (up to 1977) between 80 000 and 115 000 Mozambicans worked on the Transvaal mines.[8] The mine labour organisation had an extensive recruiting network enabling the following seemingly extravagant claim to be made: 'The organisation is so established throughout the territory that a native can reach a WNLA station within twenty-four hours of leaving his kraal, no matter where the latter is situated.'[9]

Mozambican labour was contracted for twelve- or eighteen-month periods, on average longer than that of migrants from other territories. This labour was re-contracted regularly, and thus an experienced labour force was created. A class of worker-peasants was formed in the south of Mozambique. Of the active male population in the south, 25 to 30 per cent were working on the mines every year. In addition to those recruited through official channels, there was much clandestine emigration, with Mozambicans working in various other sectors of the South African economy. Labour for the mines came from all over the country. Elders in the north of Nampula Province in the district of Ribáuè explained that the first white man they encountered was Francisco Chichico, a German recruiter for the mines, at the beginning of the century.[10] Records in the archive of the local administration confirmed that a Lieutenant Neutel de Abreu of the Portuguese army founded the post of Ribáuè only in 1909, and other sources verify this pattern of non-Portuguese recruitment over a wider area.[11] In spite of later recruiting restrictions in the north, illegal migrants continued to go to the Reef, some by way of Nyasaland.

The transit trade

The external migrant labour flow created internal problems of labour shortage. Labour was urgently required to construct the railway lines and ports to enable the Portuguese government to take further advantage of the growth of mines and plantations in South Africa and Southern Rhodesia by providing transit facilities for their export and import requirements. It was for this reason that the first widespread introduction of forced labour occurred. When the construction of the first rail line began in the 1880s, the south of the country still remained to be pacified and so the Portuguese were unable to secure sufficient African labour. Several thousand Cantonese workers were imported in 1887 to make up the shortfall.[12]

The railway line linking the Transvaal to the port of Lourenço Marques, begun in the 1880s, was completed in 1894. When the line was being built, the Boers still controlled the Transvaal Republic. Lourenço Marques was the natural sea outlet for the Transvaal, and the Boers had a clear preference for a line passing through the Portuguese colony rather than through the British-controlled port of Cape Town. Total tonnage handled in the port increased from a quarter of a million tons at the turn of the century to one million tons by the beginning of the First World War.[13] Coal provided the bulk of South African exports (over half a million tons). The railway also served to transport labour quickly and efficiently to the Transvaal mines.

South Africa's influence was so great that in January 1929 it could force the Portuguese government to nationalise the port and railway. This was done in an attempt to improve the functioning and efficiency of the system. These nationalisations did not include the stevedoring and freight handling companies, however, many of which were South African-owned.South Africa's dominance did not go unchallenged, and attempts to take over the port and railway completely met with a sustained and successful resistance by the Portuguese government.[14] Undoubtedly in the early part of the century the railways did not run at the height of efficiency. The system of *padrinho* (patron–client relations) ensured promotion on the basis of whom a person knew and what he was prepared to pay. In the annual report of the port and railways for 1923 there was a proposal to 'methodically reduce the staff, increase the number of salaried employees and pay them in conformity with their merits'.[15] The report continued in a sarcastic vein to say: 'Whosoever has no qualities to recommend them is almost guaranteed a place around the payments table.'

Further to the north, Cecil Rhodes had a railway built linking Rhodesia to the port of Beira; this was completed in 1899. The port of Beira was constructed with the financial backing of the British South Africa Company. As with Lourenço Marques, the function of this port was to serve the non-Portuguese hinterland. Fully 90 per cent of the 682 000 tons of cargo handled in Beira by 1928 came from, or was going to, non-Portuguese areas. A railway from Nyasaland to Beira was completed in 1922.[16] The British were hoping to further their interests in the area through their proxy, the Mozambique Company. Any concern about the actual development of Mozambique was completely subordinated to more powerful interests elsewhere. At the end of the 1920s the construction of a bridge over the Zambezi was approved to replace the existing ferry service, but the main motivation for this step appears to have been the desire to increase orders for the British steel industry which was stagnating at this time on the eve of the Great Depression. Exploiting the coal resources of the Moatize mine in Tete Province could have made the rail and bridge project financially viable, but this was prevented through fear of creating competition with the Welsh coal industry.

Mozambique had a 'transit' rather than a 'transport' system. Rail lines ran from east to west, and even today the best route from south of the Zambezi river to the north lies through Malawi. The three main rail lines linked Mozambique with South Africa, Southern Rhodesia and Nyasaland. The transport services provided for the neighbouring countries had a threefold impact upon the political economy: they were a major source of foreign exchange; they were the principal reason for the growth of the country's two major cities (Lourenço Marques and Beira); and finally they created a small, internal African working class.

The company states

Portugal did not have the capital to invest in Mozambique, and the bankrupt condition of its economy impeded heavy borrowing on the European money markets for the purpose of colonial development. Companies controlled by foreign, mainly British, capital were invited in to exploit two-thirds of the country and worked in close co-operation with

South African, Rhodesian and British interests in the area. They were to form virtual states within states. The incentive that Portugal had to offer foreign capital was super-cheap, at times even free, labour. Brito Camacho, an early High Commissioner of Mozambique, made no excuses for inviting in foreign capital, even though people complained at one point that he was selling Mozambique to an English firm – Sena Sugar Estates – and was therefore committing high treason. In reply to his critics he simply stated the facts, that Portugal had neither the economic nor administrative capacity to do otherwise.[17]

Of the three giant companies, perhaps the most important was the Mozambique Company, set up in the 1880s and occupying the whole of Manica and Sofala province and beyond. It was granted a fifty-year charter in 1897, and given full sovereign rights over this area and its population. Some infrastructural investment was made through sub-concessions (primarily the construction of the railway from Beira to Rhodesia), but stock speculation took pre-eminence over local investment. Labour recruitment for use outside the territory was initially prohibited, as labour was in short supply. Men had to work on the sugar plantations or on public works projects, whilst women were compelled to grow cotton to sell to the Company's agents. But in 1913 an agreement was reached allowing Southern Rhodesia to recruit labour in the Tete district and in Barué, which were also under Company rule. From as early as 1910, nearly every adult male was performing some form of labour. The labour and taxation demands were such that they soon provoked a massive revolt. By Mozambican standards the plantations were quite successful, as up to the mid-1920s this province alone was exporting more than the rest of the country put together. Gold was also being mined and exported.

In 1891 the Niassa Company was issued with a twenty-five-year charter over the provinces of Niassa and Cabo Delgado. The Company succeeded in its 'pacification' campaigns only by 1912, and then the area became a field of combat between Germany and Portugal in the First World War. The territory was exploited in two ways. Firstly, recruitment of labour to the South African mines began on a small scale in 1903. A renewed search for labour in 1907 led to the formation of a holding company, Nyassa Consolidated, whose shares were almost entirely controlled by South African mining capital. The miners brought in £20 000 in gold per annum until 1913, when recruitment north of the twenty-second parallel was prohibited.[18] The landlords then sold their shares to German capital. Secondly, and more profitably, the population was made to pay a hut tax. By 1927 hut tax accounted for 70 per cent and customs duties for 21 per cent of the Company's total revenue. After the 1914–1918 War a British company bought back the shares from the German consortium and tried unsuccessfully to negotiate an extension of the charter as nationalist sentiments were rising in Portugal. The Company thus adopted a short-term policy of making a profit by repeatedly raising the hut tax. It stood at 2 escudos per annum in 1921, but was raised to 85 escudos in 1928. The following year the charter came to an end. In addition to tax and customs revenue, the Niassa Company granted sub-concessions to control the trade in African agricultural produce. The Nyassa Rubber Company, dominated by South African capital, held a monopoly over the rubber trade in the Company's territory. Well into the twentieth century the Company also continued to profit from the slave trade.

Portuguese officials were paid very little, in order to reduce the administrative costs of colonisation. Instead, they were allowed to retain 4 per cent of all taxes collected and to establish their own plantations. People not paying taxes were compelled to do forced labour. Abuses were widespread, and one observer remarked in 1914 that 'so far as natives are concerned, this is a land of blood and tears, where the most brutal ill-treatment is no crime and murder merely a slight indiscretion'.[19]

In 1922 a report on labour conditions in Mozambique was prepared for the Transvaal Chamber of Mines, and this gives an unvarnished account of working conditions in Mozambique. It first stated that 'labour conditions and the treatment of natives become worse as the distance from Lourenço Marques increases'.[20] In the northern territories, where the future national liberation struggle was to start, conditions were alleged to be particularly bad. One reason given was that underpaid officials regarded their posts 'merely as opportunities to be turned to their own advantage'. Many officials engaged in private business, using their positions of authority to obtain the labour required: 'Agriculture, planting, trading, the collection of beeswax, rubber, etc. . . ., and [the] transport of merchandise to the coast occupy the attention of officials, and practically the whole of the native labour required is forced, unpaid, and barely fed.'

One estimate put the death toll of porters carrying plantation produce to the coast in Cabo Delgado Province at 1 500 people in one year alone. Little wonder, therefore, that the report warns: 'It is the destruction of a race that is in progress in Portuguese Nyassaland.' People attempting to resist forced labour met a particularly pernicious form of corporal punishment called the *palmatoria*. According to the report, this invidious instrument, shaped like a club with a flattened circular end pierced with holes, 'reduces a hand to a shapeless, swollen mass of lacerated and bleeding flesh.'

During the First World War, most able-bodied men in the north were pressed into service as porters and road-builders. The withdrawal of these men from the agricultural labour force, the demands made on the people and resources of Niassa, the devastation of the war and a drought in 1919 all contributed to the effects of widespread disease, especially influenza, and starvation.[21] In a post-war claim for financial reparations from Germany, Portugal declared that the war had cost 130 000 African lives.[22]

As a result of conditions under company rule, there was a general depopulation of the area and a migration to the adjoining territories. It was to be from amongst those Mozambicans living abroad that the nationalist movement was eventually to emerge and take an organisational form. Already before 1919, more than 100 000 people had fled from Niassa Province alone.[23] It has been estimated that the Yao and Makua population in British Nyasaland increased from 185 363 and 120 776 respectively in 1921, to 246 723 and 235 616 in 1931. In

Tanganyika, estimates of the Makonde population rose from 75 000 in 1921 to 144 170 in 1931. Most of these increases were accounted for by immigration from Mozambique.

The third of the giants was the Zambezia Company (the only one not to be chartered). It was formed in the 1890s, and occupied Quelimane and parts of Tete provinces. The Company inherited the vast majority of the *prazos* and was later to develop similar patron–client relations. Many companies worked sub-concessions within it, such as the Boror Company (German capital), Sena Sugar Estates (British) and Madal Company (French). A startling comment on the hatred that the early company rule inspired can be read in the Boror annual report of 1900: 'the blacks prefer to die of hunger in their houses or in the bush, to receiving a daily sustenance and a wage'.[24] Judy Head, in her detailed and comprehensive study of the centre of the country, has shown how the period between 1890 and 1930 was one of repeated failure from the point of view of the colonial regime.[25] Unable to administer Zambezia effectively, still less to develop production, the colonial state was forced to encourage the entry of foreign capital into the province in the hope that some agricultural development would ensue, thus strengthening both the sub-metropolitan economy and with it Portugal's claims to the colony. Most of the capital attracted was adventurist, and most enterprises failed. Yet again, sources of revenue were mainly taxes and labour export. Head has commented: 'the attraction of tax-collection, designed to offer the incentive necessary for infrastructural development instead acted as a deterrent. Most leaseholders were content to sit back and collect the tax.' The 1922 report on labour conditions said of the concession companies in Quelimane Province: 'every penny paid out to the natives is returned to the employer either as Hut Tax [collection] or for the purchases made in the stores'.[26] The labour export was both to the South African mines and to the coffee plantations of São Tomé. By 1916, according to Shubi Ishemo, half of the imported labour on the São Tomé plantations came from Zambezia and Nampula.[27]

Conclusion

Over this whole early period up to 1930, Mozambique was under the domination of foreign – that is, non-Portuguese – capital. It not only controlled the economy of the country, but it also exerted a powerful political influence. Although Portuguese administrators were present, they had little power and were largely left to their own devices by the colonial authorities in Lisbon. This governmental neglect stemmed largely from the state of the economy and from the fact that during this period, the Portuguese Republic found itself in a permanent political and financial crisis. The official *Jornal de Comércio e das Colónias* (Commercial and Colonial Journal) shamefacedly admitted that 'the financial situation of the province of Mozambique and the conditions in which the economic life takes place, are greatly embarrassing'.[28] It went on to implore that agriculture in the colonies should not be indifferent to the needs of the metropole; colonies must offer the best markets for the industry of the metropole as well as their 'primary' materials. The trade situation was no better. In 1927 Portugal provided only 16 per cent of Mozambique's imports, and England accounted for 30 per cent.[29] Only 11 per cent of exports went to Portugal compared with 34 per cent to South Africa and 28 per cent to France.

Alan Smith has well summed up the state of the Mozambican economy at the close of this early colonial period:

> With the exception of a few Portuguese financed enterprises, virtually the whole of the economy was turned over to British and South African interests. The large agricultural estates, the financing of the railways, the development of the ports, and the search for mineral wealth all came to be dominated by foreigners. In fact, the two principal commercial centres, Lourenço Marques and Beira, often appeared to visitors as more British than Portuguese.[30]

Notes

1 See, for example, E. Alpers, *Ivory and Slaves in East Central Africa*, London, 1975.

2 C. McEvedy and R. Jones, *Atlas of World Population History*, Harmondsworth, Mdx., 1978. p. 256.

3 W. Rodney, *How Europe Underdeveloped Africa*, London, 1972, p. 229.

4 The standard history is M. D. Newitt, *Portuguese Settlement on the Zambezi*, London, 1973.

5 A. F. Isaacman, *Moçambique: the Africanisation of a European Institution: the Zambezi Prazos 1750–1902*, Madison, Wis., 1972.

6 Villas-Boas Truão, writing in 1806, and quoted in L. Vail and L. White, *Capitalism and Colonialism in Mozambique*, London, 1980, p. 12.

7 S. Young, 'Changes in Diet and Production in Southern Mozambique 1855–1960', mimeo, undated.

8 Centre of African Studies, *The Mozambican Miner: a Study in the Export of Labour*, Instituto de Investigação Científico de Moçambique, Maputo, 1977.

9 O. Letcher, *The Gold Mines of Southern Africa*, 1936, p. 42.

10 Interview with Lazaro Mutampua and Basiano Malesiwa, Mutuwali, Nampula Province, 10 July 1976.

11 *Elementos Para A Inspecção. Ref. A/26*, Administração da Circumscrição de Malema.

12 *Informação Económica Sôbre O Império. IV Volume. Moçambique*, Edições da Exposição Colonial Portuguesa, Porto, 1934, p. xvi.

13 *Relatórios, Propóstas e Orçamentos do Porto e Caminho de Ferro de Lourenço Marques, 1915 a 1923*, Lourenço Marques, 1924.

14 For a detailed study of the economic relationships between South Africa and

southern Mozambique in this early period, see S. E. Katzenellenbogen, *South Africa and Southern Mozambique*, Manchester, 1982.

15 *Relatórios, Propóstas e Orçamentos do Porto e CFLM 1915 a 1923*, pp. 15–16.

16 The history of the railway and its hinterland can be found in L. Vail, 'The Making of an Imperial Slum; Nyasaland and Its Railways, 1895–1935', in *Journal of African History (JAH)*, xvi, 1, 1976; and L. Vail, 'Railway Development and Colonial Underdevelopment: the Nyasaland Case', in *The Roots of Rural Poverty in Central and Southern Africa*, R. Palmer and N. Parsons (eds.), London, 1977.

17 B. Camacho, *Política Colonial*, Lisbon, 1936, p. 20.

18 B. Neil-Tomlinson, 'The Nyassa Chartered Company: 1891–1929', in *JAH*, xviii, 1, 1977, 119.

19 L. Vail, 'Mozambique's Chartered Companies: The Rule of the Feeble', *JAH*, 3, 1976, p. 401.

20 'Report on Native Labour Conditions in the Province of Mozambique, Portuguese East Africa', republished in *South African Labour Bulletin*, ii, July 1975.

21 B. Neil-Tomlinson, 'The Nyassa Chartered Company', 120.

22 T. H. Henriksen, *Mozambique: a History*, London, 1979, p. 108; Neil-Tomlinson, 'The Nyassa Chartered Company', 121, cites conservative Portuguese sources giving a lower figure of 50 000 dead.

23 The statistics are taken from Neil-Tomlinson, 'The Nyassa Chartered Company', 125.

24 Quoted in L. Vail and L. White, *Capitalism and Colonialism*, p. 120.

25 J. Head, 'Sena Sugar Estates and Migrant Labour', in *Mozambique*, Centre for African Studies, University of Edinburgh, 1979.

26 'Report on Native Labour Conditions in the Province of Mozambique, Portuguese East Africa', 22.

27 S. L. Ishemo, 'Some Aspects of the Economy and Society of the Zambezi Basin in the Nineteenth and Early Twentieth Centuries', in *Mozambique*, 28.

28 *Jornal de Comércio e das Colónias*, 'O Problema de Moçambique', Lisbon, 1923, 13.

29 *Anuário Estatística 1928*, Imprensa Nacional de Moçambique.

30 A. K. Smith, 'António Salazar and the Reversal of Portuguese Colonial Policy', *JAH*, xv, 4, 1974, 656.

5 The effects of Salazar's nationalist policies (1930–1960)

Although Mozambique's dependence on foreign investment and its integration into the regional sub-system remained the dominant features of the political economy, after Salazar's takeover some significant changes did occur. Specifically, the country's economy became more directly oriented towards the needs of the colonial sub-metropole, and the intensity of labour exploitation increased enormously. This generated widespread grievances which the nationalist movement later harnessed. It also spurred on the emigration, and amongst the exiles and migrants in the neighbouring territories the first proto-nationalist movements appeared. Amongst the grievances they voiced, forced labour, forced crop cultivation and the labour and produce tribute of the *latifundio* system figured prominently.

Forced labour

Salazar did make a serious attempt to administer the colonies and utilise the labour force more effectively, and the *Regulamento do Trabalho dos Indígenas* of 1930 was introduced to achieve this end. It was a comprehensive piece of legislation covering every aspect of employment. With few exceptions, all able-bodied African men were expected to work for six months in every year for a wage, either for a private employer or for the state. This was the so-called contract labour. The only exceptions covered those Africans given *assimilado* status, the 'civilised' black Portuguese; those Africans in permanent wage employment; rich peasants; and those engaged in migrant labour abroad. Three other forms of forced labour were also to be found, but these were of lesser importance. The first was obligatory labour, levied by the government for public works projects. Second was correctional labour, punishment for breaking the Labour or Criminal code or failing to pay taxes, and this provided a lucrative alternative to the expense of keeping prisoners idle. The third form of forced labour, voluntary labour, referred to a contract between employer and employee without the mediation of the state. This, however, was something of a misnomer, as the threat of contract labour took much of the volition out of voluntary labour.

A system of close collaboration developed between the administration and employers. Indeed, increasing administrative efficiency and a more intensive use of African labour went hand in hand. The district administrator and *chefe de posto* (sub-administrator) would collect men together for the private recruiters. As one official noted:

> When I arrived here, recruitment was practically done by the authorities. Periodically, and on specific days, the native authorities brought to the headquarters . . . all the natives whose rest period had expired and who were eligible for another contract. The recruiters undertook their work amongst the mass of the natives gathered there.[1]

Those who experienced the system have many harrowing tales to tell. Duarte João reported on his experience in Zambezia Province:

> Those contracted were paid 100 escudos per month. They worked on the tea plantations in Vila Junqueiro near to Alto Molocue from 5.00 a.m. to 5.00 p.m. Only the men – but *all* the men except *assimilados* – worked on the plantations. People worked for six months. They were bound and forced to work. For running away from the plantations people were beaten and imprisoned.[2]

Saraiva Gomes, working in the same area, on the Cha Luso tea plantation, reported that the chiefs and *regulos* (senior chiefs) organised the people to go to the plantations: 'Those who recruited people to work received gifts from the white settlers. The *recrutadors* and chiefs received their gifts at the end of the year, in the final month, so that they would work harder at getting labour for the plantations.'[3] Arangatoni Mikiras, an agricultural worker, had lived and worked in the province of Tete. He told how

> People were put in chains and obliged to work – it was forced labour. It started when boys were fourteen or fifteen years old. They had to go every year. Some were sent to one place and others to another. The administrator sent *cipaios* (local police) to get the people and bind them, and after they would be brought to the administration. Then the *recrutador* would ask them if they wanted to go with him – and they were standing in front of him in chains! People were paid 100 escudos per month.[4]

He added finally, 'I have many sufferings in my heart and it would take a long time to explain all of them.' Contract labour was employed to work on the plantations and roads, as well as in railway and port construction in the urban areas. Henrique Galvão presented extensive evidence of forced labour and widespread abuses of African labour to Portugal's National Assembly in his famous report of 1948, but no improvements were made either then or subsequently for some considerable period of time.[5]

The administration profited greatly from its role in the recruitment system. Recruiters had to buy a licence and pay a fee for each man they received. The legal wage in force was closely related to the tax – indeed, a certain ratio was legally maintained between the two. Frequently, after working a contract a man would have barely sufficient to pay his *imposto* (tax).

Forced crop cultivation

The major economic impact on the colonies of the coming to power of the Salazar regime was felt in the field of agriculture. Under the new 'nationalist' policies the rule of the old charter companies was slowly terminated, although foreign sub-concession companies continued to operate. But the emphasis was changing. The colonies were now to provide raw materials for the industries of the sub-metropole. Forced crop cultivation was gradually introduced and in particular the growing of cotton. Rice was the other major cash crop, with maize, copra, peanuts and cashew also being produced.

Cotton came to be by far the most important crop. National production increased annually from 1 000 tons at the beginning of this period to 46 000 tons near the end.[6] The number of peasants brought into cotton production was enormous. By 1944 it had reached 791 000 and afterwards, with some oscillations, stabilised at around half a million.[7] Not only did it produce cotton for export to Portugal, it also provided cash for the peasants to pay their head tax. At certain times of the year there would be cotton markets in a particular district and the field agent of the cotton company would travel around to do the buying. He would always be accompanied by the administrator's agents collecting the *imposto*.

In Morrumbene district of Inhambane Province cotton cultivation began at the end of the 1930s, coinciding with the setting up of the Cotton Export Board in 1938.[8] Initially there was one cotton plot in each *cabo*'s* area, measuring 50 metres. This was intended as an experiment to see if cotton could be grown in the area. It was the *cabo*'s job to organise his people to work the fields. From 1942 onwards, however, each married couple was obliged to cultivate a cotton field of 8 metres. Wives of men in the army were exempt, as were those of the cotton *capatazes* (overseers), but the wives of migrant labourers or those doing *chibalo* (forced labour) were not exempt. Cotton cultivation occupied eight months of the year, from January to August. In this particular area people were obliged to work three days per week on their cotton field, and it was the task of the *capataz* to enforce this. The *capitão*, head of the *capatazes*, would be carried around the fields on a type of sedan chair overseeing the cotton growing. If the land was not suitable and the cotton did not grow, then the peasants could be imprisoned. Punishment was harsh; Shabani Panu, up in Niassa Province, said: 'If the crop failed, I was always beaten.'[9] João Marariha, who lived in an area with plantations in the north, told how 'The old people who could no longer work on the plantations were forced to grow cotton'.[10]

Twelve Portuguese companies received monopolistic concession rights over huge areas of Mozambique, and within each one's territory peasants were obliged to produce the cotton in conditions, according to Professor Harris, of 'modern serfdom'.[11] Resende, Bishop of Beira, commented on the effects of the forced cultivation as follows:

> Since the beginning of the cotton production, stretches of fertile land
> had stopped producing food for the population and there had been

*The *cabo* was a junior chief at the lowest level of the administrative hierarchy.

acute hunger in the region. In one of my dioceses the spectre of death had fallen over the population, because of lack of food. I know some districts where the Africans got for their harvest fifty to ninety escudos. In the same regions and localities, if the Africans had cultivated crops other than cotton, the same plots of land would have yielded a harvest of which they would have got two to four thousand escudos.[12]

Even Spense, an apologist for the old regime, was forced to admit that as a result of the cotton, the Africans' food crops had 'reached almost famine production figures in the north of the colony'.[13]

The Latifundio system

From the time of the Salazar takeover, Portuguese settlement also began to take place in both urban and rural areas. Settler agriculture was not based on free wage employment; instead, it relied heavily upon pre-capitalist social relations of production. A settler would claim an area of land, and the African peasants living upon that land would then come under various obligations to their new landowner. They would have to pay both a labour and a produce tribute.

Along the fertile river valleys of the coastal strip, a number of *latifundio* settlers established themselves. The story of one in particular, Senhor Manuel Rocha, may serve to illustrate how the system operated.[14] He arrived in January 1942, and occupied most of the territory of six *cabos*. Under the colonial administrative hierarchy, below the district administrator there was the *chefe de posto* (two or three per district), *regulos* (the senior African chiefs) and *cabos* (the junior chiefs). The *latifundio*'s 'ownership' of the land provided the legitimacy for the extraction of a labour tribute, and the colonial administration provided the necessary support to ensure that this was carried out. Three *cabos* would provide labour on the *latifundio*'s plantations for the first half of the week, and the remaining three *cabos* would furnish the labour for the other three days. Each *cabo* divided the people in his area into two groups, and in this way peasants furnished three days' labour every fortnight. Anyone missing their labour obligation was caught and sent to the district administration, which then obliged the culprit to work *gratis* instead of receiving the normal low wage (this was the so-called 'correctional' labour). The wage was £3 for men and £1.50 for women, for every completed thirty days worked. Frequently, however, payment would be made in cloth or in credit to be redeemed in sugar cane alcohol produced on the plantation.

Inhambane was one of the three provinces in the south of the country furnishing migrant labour to South Africa. Under the law, work on the mines exempted men from forced labour obligations, but people in the Cambine area of Rocha's plantations testified that men returning from the mines would be expected to fulfil their labour service to the *latifundio*. The people of the area were emphatic that 'there was not a person who failed to go and work upon his *machamba*'. Not surprisingly, this encouraged men to return to the mines as soon as possible. Given the absence of much of the Mozambican labour force abroad, the forced labour laws, *chibalo*, were intended to secure labour requirements internally, but they tended to have the contrary effect of fuelling the external migrant flow.

Under the pre-colonial system the peasants offered a tribute, *xicaba*, to the junior and senior chiefs. The *latifundios* became a further recipient of *xicaba*. Thus from the small harvest of the peasant *machamba*, the *cabo*, *regulo* and the *latifundio* would each receive a share. Anyone failing to deliver the produce tribute to Manuel Rocha had to pay 40 escudos or three chickens, and if they failed to provide either of these then additional labour on the plantation was required.

The economy

In the short term Salazar's policies had some success, and the colonies became more efficient suppliers of raw materials for the sub-metropole. 'Nationalist' economic policies, however, meant that there was only a comparatively small growth in the number of new agricultural enterprises over this period, as a result of Salazar's restrictions on foreign capital. This was to cause a stagnation in the production of the main plantation crops of sugar cane and copra. It was partly as a result of this that in the early 1940s cotton (produced by peasant forced cash cropping) replaced sugar (a plantation product) to become the most important export product. In 1940 cotton brought in 11 million escudos and sugar, 48.1 million escudos. Only three years later the figures were 131 million and 57 million escudos respectively.[15]

Salazar's determination to use the colonies more directly for the benefit of the sub-metropole began to produce dividends. By the mid-1940s Portugal had increased its share in Mozambique's trade fourfold and accounted in total for a half of all trade. In the early 1930s, by comparison, a half of all Mozambique's imports were coming from Britain and the British empire.[16]

Before the Salazar takeover in Portugal there was hardly any industry in Mozambique apart from a little sugar and sisal processing for export. By the 1930s there was a discernible but small-scale development of internally-oriented industries – cement, mineral water, beer, maize flour, rice, pasta, cigarettes, soap, butter, cordials and bricks.[17] The level of Portuguese investment was small, however, reflecting the underdeveloped nature of sub-metropolitan capitalism. Also, according to the Salazar plan, the colonies were not supposed to develop industries in competition with those of the sub-metropole. However, it is possible that the 25 000 settlers already in Mozambique by 1939 had sufficient power to push through the internal production of some of their needs. This certainly happened elsewhere in Africa where there was a significant settler population. Industrial development in its turn increased the capacity of the colonies to absorb more settlers. Industry provided both jobs and the commodities which settlers needed to be encouraged to stay and raise their families. Between 1900 and the Second World War, more than one million Portuguese emigrated to Brazil, the United States and the Argentine, but Angola attracted only 35 000 settlers and Mozambique even fewer. If the policy of encouraging settlers was to succeed, then a more drastic effort was required on Lisbon's part. Industry remained dominated by the export sector, which accounted for more than half of the total value of production.

The vulnerability of dependent countries on the periphery is particularly evident in times of economic crisis. The Great Depression had an important impact upon the transit trade, and this can be well illustrated with evidence from the port of Lourenço Marques. The port's most important cargo was coal. The vulnerability of a country strongly dependent on transit earnings, with a substantial amount of these based on one commodity from a single foreign country, is all too obvious. When, for example, India opened new coal mines, South Africa lost one of its principal buyers, and this coincided with the Depression. In the first four months of 1929, Lourenço Marques handled 167 000 tons of coal.[18] A mere 65 000 tons were handled during the equivalent period in 1932. Unemployment, a reduction in wages, a large surplus capacity in the port and no possibility of finding alternative cargoes were just some of the consequences of Mozambique's dependence on South Africa. The entire growth of the port was determined by South Africa's requirements. Later in the 1930s, for example, early mechanisation of South African agriculture increased that country's food exports, and refrigeration plants had to be built in the port of Lourenço Marques to handle this new cargo. Throughout the 1930s between 80 and 90 per cent of the total cargo handled in the port came from or went to the Transvaal. After the Second World War, although the Transvaal's percentage of traffic was some-what reduced it still represented more than two-thirds of the total.

Salazar had undoubtedly introduced some significant changes, but the basic pattern of underdevelopment and dependency remained. Mozambique was on the periphery of a regional sub-system dominated by capital accumulation in South Africa, the peripheral centre. Southern Rhodesia was a sub-peripheral centre. The south continued to furnish a third of its able-bodied men annually to the mines, and the fortunes of the cities of Lourenço Marques and Beira continued to centre on the ports and railways, which were at the mercy of Western economic fortunes in general and those of South Africa and Southern Rhodesia in particular. Although many Mozambicans chose mine labour as a preferable alternative to forced labour at home, conditions in the mines were still appalling. Between 1936 and 1966, no fewer than 19 000 miners (93 per cent of whom were black) died as a result of accidents in the mines, and earlier the toll was even heavier.[19]

The migrant labour system did not always continue with Mozambique's other neighbours as it did with South Africa. For example, in Tanganyika the system changed from one of oscillation to one of permanence. In 1944, the Tanganyika Sisal Growers' Association established its own labour bureau called Silabu (Sisal Labour Bureau). This recruited workers locally as well as from the north of Mozambique and elsewhere, but in the late 1950s it ceased recruiting outside

Tanganyika and in 1965 closed down altogether. A major reason for this was that many workers, whose families were transported free of charge, settled locally instead of accepting repatriation on completion of their contracts. On Kigombe Sisal Estate for example, in the Tanga region of Tanzania, half of the six hundred workers (in 1975) were Mozambican Makondes who had settled permanently.[20]

The contradiction in the policy

Forced cultivation of crops was a major grievance amongst the Mozambican peasantry. After the Second World War the intensity of exploitation increased considerably. A law in 1946 gave the concessionary companies, which held a monopoly over the purchase of the crop, greater responsibility for its actual production. Over the fourteen-year period to 1960 the tonnage of cotton produced was more than doubled, its selling value increased more than fivefold, the area cultivated increased only slightly and the number of peasant producers fell by one sixth or more.[21] Forced cultivation of crops with an increasing level of exploitation made a decisive contribution to the development of a revolutionary situation. Increasing hardship was felt, especially in the north, and people fled in vast numbers to neighbouring countries. In the face of forced crop cultivation and forced labour, people 'voted with their feet' and either left the country or chose the least odious employment alternatives open to them. It was the underdeveloped nature of Portuguese sub-metropolitan capitalism which led to a policy of extreme labour coercion with the widespread use of forced labour and forced crop cultivation. Forced labour ended in the British colonies of Africa in the 1920s, and in the French colonies in the 1940s, but continued in the Portuguese colonies into the 1960s.

Portuguese capital could not compete on an open market for labour; it therefore employed the mechanisms of the colonial state to ensure compulsive compliance. Thus was set in motion one essential contradiction in Portuguese colonial policy: economic conditions forced people to go abroad at the same time that the corporate state hoped to isolate its colonies from the nationalist sentiments and independence campaigns burgeoning throughout the rest of the continent; but the 238 900 people who migrated from Mozambique to Zanzibar, Tanganyika, Nyasaland, Southern Rhodesia and South Africa between 1952 and 1954 alone could not fail to be influenced by the political ideas and mass ferment that surrounded them in those territories.[22] To give some comparative indication of the size of this migration, it was almost equivalent to the combined migrations for the same period from the Sudan, Uganda, Kenya, Tanganyika, the Congo, Northern and Southern Rhodesia, Nyasaland and Bechuanaland. It was to be from amongst the ranks of these migrants that the first proto-nationalist parties would emerge.

Notes

1 Quoted by J. Head, 'Sena Sugar Estates and Migrant Labour', in *Mozambique*, Centre for African Studies, University of Edinburgh, 1979.

2 Interview with Duarte João, a textile factory worker, Vila Pery, Manica and Sofala Province, 28 April 1975.

3 Interview with Saraiva Gomes, a textile factory worker, Vila Pery, Manica and Sofala Province, 28 April 1975.

4 Interview with Arangatoni Mikiras, Sussendenga, Manica and Sofala Province, 1 May 1975.

5 See H. Galvão, *Santa Maria: My Crusade for Portugal*, New York and Cleveland, Ohio, 1961, pp. 57–71, for excerpts from the report.

6 N. S. Bravo, *A Cultura Algodoeira na Economia do Norte de Moçambique*, Lisbon, Junta de Investigações do Ultramar, Estudo de Ciências Políticas e Sociais, 66, 1963, p. 64.

7 *Ibid*.

8 Information on Murrumbene district is drawn from field research in 1977, which included interviews with a former cotton *capataz*. This provided the data for the subsequent section on the *latifundio* system.

9 Interview with Shabani Panu, Messauize, Niassa Province, 20 July 1976.

10 Interview with João Marariha, Ribáuè, Nampula Province, 5 July 1976.

11 See M. Harris, *Portugal's African Wards*, New York, 1958.

12 Quoted by E. Martins, *Colonialism and Imperialism in Mozambique*, Copenhagen, n.d., pp. 123–24.

13 C. F. Spense, *The Portuguese Colony of Mozambique*, Cape Town, 1951, p. 54.

14 The research on the *latifundio* was carried out in July and August 1977, in connection with the study of migrant labour carried out by the Centro de Estudos Africanos (Maputo).

15 See *Anuário Estatística 1943*, Imprensa Nacional de Moçambique.

16 *Informação Económica Sôbre O Império. IV Volume, Moçambique*, Edições da Exposição Colonial Portuguesa, Porto, 1934, p. xxvi.

17 The information on industry is taken from two unpublished papers presented at the Eduardo Mondlane University: J. M. Brum, 'Manufacturing Industries in Mozambique: Some Aspects', 1976, and D. V. Wield, 'Some Characteristics of the Mozambican Economy Particularly Relating to Industrialisation', 1977.

18 All the statistics on the port are taken from the *Relatório Anual de Administração dos Serviços Dos Portos, Caminhos de Ferro e Transportes de Colónia de Moçambique*.

19 M. Shope, 'Black Gold', *Sechaba*, viii, 6, June 1974.

20 Private communication with D. V. Wield based on a study, *The Transfer of Technology in Tanzania*, Institute of Development Studies, Dar es Salaam, 1976.

21 See N. S. Bravo, *A Cultura Algodoeira*.

22 P. Anderson, 'Portugal and the End of Ultra-colonialism', *New Left Review*, 16, 1961.

6 War and the economy

The outbreak of wars of national independence in the Portuguese African colonies forced the Lisbon government to change its former policies. Although transformations within the sub-metropolitan economy had enabled Portugal to put considerably more investment capital into the colonies, this proved to be woefully insufficient to help finance the rising costs of the wars. The earlier 'nationalist' economic policy was therefore reversed, and foreign investment was encouraged once more. The hope of Salazar, and of his successor Caetano, was that this would also ensure the diplomatic support of the Western powers; to a large extent their assessment proved correct.

Belatedly, several legislative changes were made in an attempt to divert mounting international criticism of Portugal's colonial rule and practice. This was in an effort to remove the spotlight from Portugal itself and to ease the embarrassment of its allies. Though Portugal had ratified the two International Labour Organisation (ILO) conventions against forced labour in 1956 and 1959, Ghana made an official complaint to the ILO concerning Portuguese Africa in 1961. An ILO Commission was appointed to investigate the complaint and presented its findings in February 1962. After spending only one week in Mozambique it rejected many of the allegations.[1] However my own research and that of others has confirmed the fact that forced labour continued in parts until the early 1970s. In Angola, a secret government report made in 1969 by the Director of the Labour Institute (the bureau which regulated the entire labour system throughout the country), clearly showed that widespread abuses were still common.[2] In spite of the repeal of the Rural Labour Code, which was intended to end forced labour in all of the Portuguese territories, there was certainly no overnight change on the ground. This is perhaps hardly surprising, as like so much of Portuguese 'human rights' legislation it was intended for external consumption.

From the middle of the 1950s, Portugal's economic activity in the colonies became more dynamic. The first five-year plan (1953–1958) and subsequent plans concentrated on increasing the numbers of Portuguese settlers and building up the infrastructure, besides increasing investments in agriculture and industry. Stabilisation of the colonial occupation became an urgent requirement with the rising nationalist threat, and much time, energy and money was spent on establishing settler *colonato* schemes.

Settlement schemes

Half of all the expenditure from the development budget of the second plan (1959–1964) went on settlement schemes and expanding infrastructure.[3] Most of the settlers came from the thousands leaving the poor rural areas of Portugal after 1950. Hence consolidating the Portuguese hold on Mozambique went hand in hand with relieving the pressure inside Portugal caused by the huge numbers of unemployed, although most preferred to go to other European countries. The largest *colonato* scheme was on the Limpopo river in the south, but others were in Revué, Manica and Sofala Province, and at Montepuez in the north.

The *colonato* schemes were by no means a great success. By the 1970s only 3 500 white and black families were living on the Limpopo project, and far fewer on the others. Many abandoned the schemes altogether and drifted to the cities. Although in Mozambique the settlement schemes did increase agricultural production, this hardly warranted the vast amount of governmental expenditure. It was the same in Angola, where more than $100 million was spent on planned rural settlement in two decades of colonialism, but by 1969 only 840 European *colonos* had been successfully settled.[4]

If we focus in some detail on one of the schemes operating in Mozambique, we shall reveal some of the reasons for the general failure of the settlements. On the Revué *colonato* there were seventy-two white farmers with an average plot of 100 hectares (considerably larger than those on the Limpopo) and, in addition, one hundred and twenty African farmers with much smaller landholdings.[5] Each *colono* was given a house, 200 hectares of land with about 40 of these hectares cleared, all the equipment necessary to cultivate the land, 1 500 escudos per month for the first year, two tobacco stores and one for the food harvest, plus eight workers paid for and fed by the administration.[6] The Chief Engineer directing the scheme would tell the farmers what to grow, and their produce would be sold to the co-operative, which was run by the engineer and five farmers chosen by him. The co-operative would sell its produce to the *grémio*.

Repayments began after the second year; then the *colonos* had four years to pay back their running costs and a further fifteen years to repay fixed costs. It was officially estimated that after all repayments had been made, each *colono* would have 100 000 escudos per annum. However, the calculations were based on a small pilot scheme at 1/40th scale, on fertile land where productivity was high. Furthermore, the settlers did not have a sufficient market for their produce. Very few farmers were even able to meet the repayment deadlines, but because the problem was so widespread they were not expelled from the scheme. However, those farmers selling their produce outside the co-operative (and thereby receiving higher prices) were forced to leave.

The intention was that these schemes would be similar to, and indeed modelled upon, the kibbutzim of Israel.[7] The labour for the Revué scheme was provided by contract workers from the north; the local people tended to go to Southern Rhodesia to work, where pay was higher and conditions were better. Contract labourers were distributed to the farmers by the *Grémio de Produtores de Cereais do Distrito da Beira*, and they received a wage of slightly more than £3 each month.[8] Many plans were announced to try and improve the settlements, and one advocated the use of demobilised soldiers, following the successful experiences of Israel, Brazil, Colombia and Venezuela.[9] The most ambitious settlement plan revolved around the Cabora Bassa dam hydro-electric scheme on the Zambezi river, and there was talk of bringing in up to a million white settlers, thus forming a human wall against the Frelimo advance from the north; but these plans were never implemented.[10] Settler farmers in Southern Rhodesia, who also acted as police reservists and intelligence gatherers, made a major contribution to the counter-insurgency effort in that country, and their relative absence in Mozambique was a contributing factor to the rapid spread of Frelimo's influence in the rural areas.

Although the agricultural settlement schemes were not a great success, the number of urban settlers increased dramatically. The white population stood at under 50 000 in 1950, and by 1973 there were well over 200 000 settlers, concentrated in the cities.[11] The proportion of women increased, indicating a more stable and settled European presence, but the roots of the vast majority of settlers did not go deep.

Changes in agriculture

Between 1960 and 1970 the land areas of the white-owned farms and estates rose from 1.6 million to 2.5 million hectares, and the number of agricultural enterprises doubled.[12] As a consequence, the African peasants were squeezed further out of the fertile lands and there was an increasing rural proletarianisation. According to the 1970 Agricultural Census, 4 200 estates owned half the cultivated land, whilst 1 258 000 peasant families working *machambas* of less than two hectares per family occupied only 23.7 per cent of the cultivated land. Much land still remained uncultivated, but the best land was expropriated by the settlers and this provided a major grievance for the African population. A further important change in agriculture in this period was the increasing significance of plantation production, which can be explained in part by changes taking place amongst the peasants. The forced cultivation of crops, employing extreme levels of coercion coupled with unequal exchange between the colony and sub-metropole, brought forth increasing levels of protest. The uprising in Angola in February 1961 with the subsequent massacres on both sides, along with increasing international pressure, finally pushed the Portuguese government into making belated reforms, and forced labour and forced cultivation were abolished in law. The effects on peasant cash-crop cultivation were spectacular. In Morrumbene District of Inhambane, for example, production fell by five-sixths between 1959 and 1963.[13] Production of cotton nationally fell from 139 000 tons in 1960 to 87 000 tons in 1963. The other main peasant forced cash crop, rice, declined from 22 100 tons in 1960 to 8 400 tons in 1967.

The government found a twofold solution to the problem. Soon after the war started in 1964, it began constructing protected villages to isolate the population from the guerrillas. Once the peasants were inside these, under guard, it was not difficult to resume the old policy. The President of Frelimo, Samora Machel, explained the process thus:

> The needs of the concession companies, which in the final analysis controlled the government, rapidly reasserted themselves and started again the system of compulsory crops within the framework of the (*aldeamento*) concentration camps, set up to isolate the population from Frelimo. As a result, more than a million and a half Mozambicans (about one-sixth of the population according to government statements) were interned in such camps, where under threats of colonialist arms, they were forced to produce these products later acquired at low prices by the companies which enjoy a purchasing monopoly.[14]

The second part of the solution to the problem of declining cash-crop production amongst the peasants, once legal and ultimately coercive measures were 'officially' removed, was to expand production on plantations and settler farms. By 1970 this 'modern' sector was producing more than half of the rice and a third of the cotton.

Three fairly distinct zones emerged within the country during the colonial period, with the north predominantly a peasant economy, the centre a plantation economy and the south an industrial reserve army of labour for the mines.[15] It has been estimated that of total agricultural production (in 1970), 55 per cent was subsistence and the remainder was marketed, with the latter split evenly among plantation, settler and peasant production (15 per cent each), but there were marked regional differences.

In the north the peasants produced mainly cotton, cashew and other food crops that were marketed through the Portuguese *cantineiros* (shopkeepers/traders) and concession companies. Peasants in the centre of the country were mainly subsistence producers furnishing migrant labour to the plantations both of their own region and also of Southern Rhodesia. The plantations inside Mozambique produced tea, sugar and copra. In the south there was a certain development of settler farming which provided food for the towns, especially the capital, Lourenço Marques. However, the peasants of the south were not transformed into a rural semi-proletariat for the settler farms; instead, as we have seen, they provided the labour for the South African mines. The colonial system, therefore, operated on the countryside in two major ways. Firstly, it institutionalised a system of migrant labour. Externally this was to the Transvaal, Southern Rhodesia, the tea plantations of Malawi and the sisal plantations of Tanzania, and internally it was to the foreign-owned plantations in the centre of the country. Secondly, it forcibly transformed African cultivators into a peasantry producing cash crops.

Foreign investment and western support

Faced with the vast expenditure of fighting three colonial wars, Portugal was obliged to seek the assistance of other Western powers. Already by the mid-1960s Portugal's military expenditure was about 6.5 per cent of gross national product, twice the level before the start of the war in Angola and accounting for 48 per cent of total current government expenditure. From the beginning of the 1960s onwards, Salazar was forced to ease the restrictions on foreign investments in order to finance the wars. Then in 1965 a virtual 'open-door' policy was adopted, reversing the 'nationalist' policy pursued for decades. Tax holidays were granted, profits and capital could freely be repatriated, there was no obligatory association with Portuguese companies, investment procedures were simplified and guarantees were offered to all foreign firms.[16] As a result of these measures, foreign capital flowed into Mozambique. When Portugal announced its five-year development plan for 1968–1973, European and American corporations were expected to provide $171.7 million of investment in Mozambique compared with $78.5 million from Portugal.[17] Actual foreign private investment increased moderately, from $23 million in 1968 to $28.5 million in 1970.[18] This helped finance the wars both directly and indirectly, especially as the colonies were increasingly expected to assume a greater burden of the military expenditure, amounting to almost half the total cost by 1970.[19]

In addition to increased investment, Portugal drew on other forms of support from the West. President Nixon signed an agreement in December 1971 authorising the United States Export-Import Bank to extend a credit loan of $436 million to Portugal for the use of the Azores base. United States military aid also increased, with $14.5 million worth of helicopters and aircraft being exported to Mozambique between 1969 and 1972.[20] American exports of herbicides to Mozambique also rose in a spectacular fashion. Generally, under the Nixon and Ford administrations, military aid to Portugal was more forthcoming than in the mid-1960s, when military support had been less open.

The ex-CIA intelligence officer Victor Marchetti revealed that his former employers provided B–26 bombers to Portugal for use in the African colonies.[21] There is overwhelming evidence that North Atlantic Treaty Organisation weapons were being used by the colonial army,[22] although this was always denied officially.[23] Military delegations from the West held consultations on the wars during visits to the colonies. The Central Intelligence Agency of the United States had strong links with the Portuguese secret police, PIDE[24] (International Police for Defence of the State) and British Intelligence services also offered their co-operation. They had an agent, for example, who was the harbour master in the southern Tanzanian port of Mtwara, and he would check on the arrival of armaments for Frelimo.[25]

Even closer co-operation developed between Portugal, South Africa and Southern Rhodesia, which together formed the remaining 'white bastion' on the African continent (the Spanish and French enclaves apart). The most spectacular form of collaboration was that between Portugal and the Zamco consortium headed by South African capital (in particular, the Anglo-American Corporation), with a plan to dam the Zambezi river at Cabora Bassa. It is clear that the final criterion for building the dam was political rather than economic. Briefly, the plan was that the hydro-electric energy produced would feed into the South African grid. Thus one more chain integrating the southern African regional sub-system would be laid. The dam would form a lake, cutting the province of Tete in half. In 1968 the guerrillas re-opened the Tete front after an abortive earlier attempt in 1964, and the lake was supposed to provide a physical barrier preventing the spread of insurgency. Lake Kariba on the Zambia–Southern Rhodesia border was intended to fulfil a similar role for the Rhodesian settlers. The final cost of the Cabora Bassa dam was estimated to be £340 million, and without massive foreign assistance Portugal could never have tackled such a project.[26] It was hoped that an undertaking of this kind would ensure increased support for Portugal's military effort.

Speeding up the pace of economic development was deemed to be essential to maintain the war effort, but, as in the nineteenth century, Portugal was forced to rely on foreign capital; this time, however, the transnationals replaced the concession companies of earlier years. By 1970 there was an estimated $70 million invested in the Portuguese colonies by foreign countries. South Africa was by far the most important of these investors, accounting for more than one-third of the total. Britain and the United States had 15 per cent each, West Germany 11 per cent, Spain 6 per cent, Belgium 5 per cent, Switzerland 3 per cent and France 2 per cent.[27]

Trade and manufacturing

Portugal was forced to abandon some of its special trading privileges with Mozambique as a result of the grossly distorted system of foreign currency payments. By 1971, 10 000 million escudos awaited settlement.[28] The reasons for Portugal's fears of foreign competition soon became all too apparent and confirmed the continuing sub-metropolitan nature of the economy. In 1973 South Africa replaced Portugal as the main exporter to Mozambique, selling machinery, spare parts, fertiliser, iron and steel, wheat, potatoes and coal. After Portugal and the United States, South Africa provided the third largest export market for Mozambique's products. The relative importance of Portugal as a trading partner declined dramatically, and the increasing importance of South Africa served to demonstrate further Mozambique's increased integration into a southern African sub-system dominated by South Africa. In the 1970s, Mozambique derived 42 per cent of the gross national product and between 50 and 60 per cent of foreign exchange earnings from the rand.[29]

Mozambique's general trading situation was similar to that of all underdeveloped countries. The price of raw materials fluctuated constantly, while prices of imported industrial goods continued to rise, leading to a serious deterioration in the terms of trade. Although this position naturally militated against the efforts being made by the colonial administration to improve the economic situation, more significant was the increasing trading importance of the regional centre in the southern African sub-system and the reduction of the colonial power's trade with Mozambique, reflecting its sub-metropolitan situation.

Mozambique's invisible earnings continued to be of great importance. In addition to migrant labour and the transit trade, tourism grew rapidly, becoming a major earner of foreign currency. By 1971 there were almost one million visitors to Mozambique, compared with 150 000 in 1964;[30] 63.1 per cent were South Africans and 27.3 per cent Rhodesians. Nevertheless, the other two invisibles, migrant labour and transit trade earnings, were still of greater importance. Up to independence, income from the provision of railway and port services to the hinterland countries furnished approximately 40 per cent of Mozambique's budgetary revenue. The manufacturing sector grew considerably over this period, but it was the settlers who benefited, as the greatest increase was in the production of luxury goods. The African population was beginning to feel the adverse consequences of the rapid changes, and the index of retail prices in Lourenço Marques (baseline 1956/57 = 100) shot up from 115 in 1969 to 163 in the first half of 1972.[31] That same year the provincial government of Mozambique launched its four-year action programme which aimed to encourage local and foreign capital to invest in the manufacturing sector. The balance of payments crisis with the sub-metropole meant that the development of local import substitution industries took on a renewed importance. However, development in manufacturing certainly did not produce any increased wealth for the mass of the African population which might have induced them to lessen their support for the nationalist struggle. Excessive bureaucracy, the scarcity and inaccuracy of published statistics and the lack of any solid research all hampered the success of colonial planning. The economy remained severely distorted and dependent – an inheritance which would tax to the full the resourcefulness of Mozambique's post-independence government.

An overview and summary of changes in the political economy

Portugal, the colonising country, was itself dependent on the larger industrial powers, and, given the weakness of the sub-metropolitan economy, Mozambique's dependency took a very particular form. Within the whole southern African region South Africa was dominant and the neighbouring states were to a greater or lesser extent brought under its influence. Their economies were subordinated to the rapid process of capital accumulation which took place in that country, resulting in a grossly unbalanced pattern of regional development. The economic dependency of Mozambique took three main forms: at the level of the labour force, contracts were made to furnish Mozambican workers to

Rhodesia and South Africa; at the level of investments, there was the installation of privileged monopoly companies dominated by foreign capital; at the level of infrastructure, there was the construction of railways and ports to serve the needs of Nyasaland, Rhodesia and principally, of course, South Africa. These three features were established in the early colonial period (1880s to 1930). Portugal, without the necessary capital to valorise the Mozambican labour force, was obliged to rent it out in two different ways: south of the twenty-second parallel it hired the labour to the Transvaal; north of that line, it invited foreign companies in to use the labour and pay a rent for so doing. Portugal's own direct exploitation of the colony began later, after Salazar took power, with the widespread introduction of forced cash-crop cultivation.

The extreme labour coercion employed encouraged extensive migration and generated widespread discontent. This second period (1930–1960) saw a slowdown in the rate of foreign investment. Industrial development, widespread settler immigration and the growth of the two major cities began only in the final period of colonialism (1960–1974). Portugal was obliged to make certain legislative changes regarding forced labour and forced crop cultivation, but the general situation for the peasants did not improve. Portugal remained a weak capitalist power unwilling to decolonise because she was unable to neocolonise. Salazar was forced to reverse his former policy and open up the colonies to foreign capital. Foreign investment increased enormously as a result. The main stimulus for these final changes came from the wars of national liberation being fought in the African colonies, but these changes both failed to buy off African support and to make the colonial position secure. In spite of Portugal's persistent attempts to dominate the economic exploitation of Mozambique, in the end this was a failure. Mozambique's political economy remained dominated by South Africa, the peripheral centre of the regional sub-system. In Part Two we examine the effects of these processes on the history of resistance.

Notes

1 ILO, *International Labour Office Official Bulletin*, xlv, 2, Supplement II, April 1962.

2 *Petition by the Angola Comité Concerning the Report by Mr Pierre Juvigny Regarding the Implementation of the Abolition of Forced Labour Convention, 1957 (No. 105) by Portugal*, Amsterdam, 1972.

3 J. Duffy, *Portuguese Africa*, Cambridge, Mass., 1959, p. 334.

4 G. J. Bender, *Angola under the Portuguese: the Myth and the Reality*, London, 1978, pp. 130–31.

5 Interview with Father Miguel Perez, a priest for many years near the *colonato* scheme, Vila Nova de Vidigueira, Manica and Sofala Province, 30 April 1975.

6 Interview with Joaquim Fornelas de Aranjo, a *colono* farmer in Revué since 1964, Sussendenga, Manica and Sofala Province, 1 May 1975.

7 V. Faria, *Colonização Relatória de uma Missão de Estudo a Israel*, Direcção de Agricultura e Florestos, Província de Moçambique, 1960.

8 *BTFPR (Grupo de Agronomia) 1° Relatório Anual*, Moçambique, 1959, Annex II, p. 14.

9 C. S. da Costa, *A Fixaçao do militar desmobilizado como factor de valorização do pouamento agrário na província de Moçambique*, Agência-Geral Do Ultramar, pp. 48–50.

10 See K. Middlemas, *Cabora Bassa: Engineering and Politics in Southern Africa*, London, 1975.

11 *Anuário Estatística, 1973*.

12 The relevant figures in this section are taken from *Estatística Agrícola* (1960); and *Estatísticas Agrícolas de Moçambique* (1970).

13 A. A. de Souza Andrade, *Relatório Anual. Administração do Morrumbene 1963*, Archive of the District Administration of Morrumbene, Inhambane Province.

14 S. Machel, *O Processo da Revolução Democrática Popular em Moçambique*, Lisbon, 1975, pp. 33–34.

15 For an important analysis of these three zones, see M. Wuyts, *Peasants and Rural Economy in Mozambique*, Centro de Estudos Africanos, Universidade Eduardo Mondlane, Maputo, 1978.

16 Banco de Formento Nacional, *Investments in Portugal*, Lisbon, 1973, pp. 192–95.

17 J. Davies, 'Allies in Empire. Part I', *Africa Today*, xvii, 4, July–Aug., 1970.

18 M. A. El Khawas, 'Foreign Economic Involvement in Angola and Mozambique', *The African Review*, iv, 2, 1974, 12.

19 United Nations, *Document A/8023/Add 4*, p. 41.

20 B. Cohen and M. A. El Khawas, *The Kissinger Study of Southern Africa*, Nottingham, 1975, p. 18.

21 V. Marchetti and J. D. Marks, *The CIA and the Cult of Intelligence*, London, 1976, pp. 172–73.

22 S. J. Bosgra and Chr. van Krimpen, *Portugal and NATO*, Angola Comité, Amsterdam, 1972.

22 See, for example, M. Caetano, *Portugal Belongs to Us All, We All Go to Make up Portugal*, Secretaria De Estado Da Informação e Turismo, Lisbon, 1970, p. 7.

24 *Weekend Telegraph*, 1 Jan., 1972.

25 D. Martin, *General Amin*, London, 1974, p. 178.

26 Middlemas, *Cabora Bassa*, p. 211.

27 *Província*, 12 April 1971.

28 *Portugal: an Informative Review*, No. 25, July 1972.

29 J. H. Mittleman, 'Mozambique: the Political Economy of Underdevelopment', *Journal of Southern African Affairs*, iii, 1, 1978, 44.

30 *Ibid.*, 45.

31 *Economist Intelligence Unit*, 'Portugal and Overseas Provinces', *Quarterly Economic Review*, Annual Supplement, 1973, 29.

PART TWO

Resistance and emerging nationalism

---

7 Colonisation and resistance

Having charted the major changes taking place in the political economy of Mozambique, it is now possible to focus on the history of African resistance. Colonialism and the expansion of the capitalist mode of production on the periphery went hand in hand, and opposition to colonialism was expressed in resistance to forced labour, forced cash cropping, compulsory taxation and other such impositions on the indigenous population. Transformations in the economy produced changes in the social structure, with a dual process of proletarianisation and peasantisation taking place. This in its turn was to affect both the form and the content of African resistance.

War and conquest

The visible effects of the Portuguese presence in Africa by the middle of the nineteenth century were negligible. Duffy has commented: 'The occupation of territory and control over African peoples scarcely extended beyond the sight of scattered forts and towns. Legitimate commerce was modest. Capital investment in the colonies was insignificant. Communication was uncertain. Educational and health services did not exist. The missionary programme had collapsed into oblivion.'[1] Fierce armed resistance as well as negotiation, diplomacy and collaboration were practised by the African polities from the second half of the nineteenth century up to the 1920s, as they attempted to maintain their independence or relative independence in the face of Portugal's military and administrative conquest. In part these wars were fought in defence of the privileges of the traditional ruling classes. The spearhead of the resistance to the colonial occupation in the south was the Ngoni leader, Gungunyana. Effectively there was a clash between two raiding systems: one African and the other European.[2] After many years of exercising diplomacy in an attempt to maintain the independence of his empire, in 1895 Gungunyana was eventually defeated militarily and exiled to the Azores. Undoubtedly this struggle was in no small part an attempt by the Ngoni aristocracy to maintain their privileged position as tribute takers.

Antonio Enes and Mousinho de Albuquerque, who led the victorious Portuguese armies in 1895, were to become national heroes and symbols of Portugal's colonial presence. Their victory was achieved in a relatively short period of time because of the earlier penetration by merchant capital, enabling the Portuguese to enlist African support for their military ventures. As Rodney has pointed out, 'many Mozambicans were to serve as porters, front-runners and expendable soldiers, because they as individuals were already tied to the export-oriented trade economy and because the social formations in which they lived had not been [internally] integrated to the extent of forming a barrier to foreign penetration'.[3] The effects of the slave and ivory trades, coupled with the Ngoni invasion, facilitated the Portuguese conquest in the south. Military occupation and pacification were essential if Portugal was to extract any benefit from the migrant labour flow and construct a railway to profit from the South African transit trade. The struggle of the Ngoni was not a battle to prevent integration into a wage economy, as men were already migrating to the mines; rather, it was a struggle to maintain a certain freedom and independence of choice *within* given structural constraints.

Until the conquest of the Gaza state, Portuguese control of the south was extremely weak, with the Portuguese able to tax only a small area surrounding Lourenço Marques.[4] In 1895, when the Portuguese prohibited labour migration, probably because recruits were supporting the Gaza state, this had absolutely no effect on the number of miners recruited. It was only when Gungunyana recalled his men to fight in the war later that year that there was a disastrous labour shortage on the Rand. Only with the defeat of the Gaza state could the labour needs in the south of the colony be met.

The north of the country was not finally conquered until the First World War, and it was some time after that before the peasantry were prevailed upon to produce a significant volume of cash crops. Both the Yao and the Makonde people put up a spirited resistance. The Makonde were a segmentary society, with each village offering its own guerrilla resistance. In the centre of the country, the *prazos* – supposedly representing the Portuguese presence – had in fact become an Africanised institution independent of the alleged sovereignty of Portugal. *Prazeros* had adopted many of the values of the African belief system, including the importance of ancestors, and there was a fusing of indigenous ceremonies with certain Catholic rituals to create syncretic religious forms. Allen Isaacman's work has shown how extensive and bitter resistance to the imposition of colonial rule shattered Portugal's self-perpetuated myth that the Zambezi valley had been an integral part of the empire for centuries.[5] Between 1885 and 1902, more than fifteen major military campaigns were initiated in the region, and there were only two years when the Portuguese were not embroiled in at least one major confrontation.

The Barué revolt of 1917 was perhaps the most important of the primary acts of resistance and has been portrayed as a forerunner to modern nationalism. The resistance was co-ordinated by local spirit mediums and encompassed people of different ethnic groups and racial composition. The Barué occupied the territory allocated to the

Mozambique Company, and it was only with the pacification campaign of 1902, led by Coutinho, that the area was finally brought under European control. The policy of the military commander aimed at 'the preservation of the native as ... [the] principal producing element'.[6] Forced labour became widespread; then with the First World War and the heavy demand for porters, pressures on the Barué built up. Just before the rebellion, 5000 males were forcibly recruited. Brutalities, the poll tax and control of the movement of labour were further grievances amongst the peasants. This huge pan-ethnic revolt was a mass rebellion against colonial capitalist penetration, with 100 000 Africans fleeing to take refuge in Nyasaland, Northern Rhodesia and Southern Rhodesia. Men already brought into the wage nexus were involved, and the guerrilla commanders included a waiter from the Commercial Hotel in Salisbury and a former member of the colonial police. An appeal to the grievances of both peasantry and workers produced a widespread level of popular support. It was not only the agents and property of the Mozambique Company which suffered in the revolt, as several posts of the Zambezia Company were also burnt down. In addition to the larger revolts, there were numerous small-scale acts of resistance by social bandits such as Dambukashamba, as well as tax avoidance and migration to escape forced labour.[7] One estimate, based on figures from the official British Blue books, says that 50 000 Africans from the regions of Tete, Milange and Massingire sought refuge in the surrounding British territories between 1895 and 1907.[8]

Acts of armed resistance both large and small were all eventually overcome. The first important lesson later drawn by Frelimo from these early battles was graphically expressed by Soko Saulula, a Frelimo guerrilla fighter: 'Our ancestors let a snake enter their house and it grew up there. But they never united together to take the stick that would kill the snake. Today we can see that they failed because they lacked unity.'[9] The pan-ethnic resistances were the exception rather than the rule. Like virtually all other African countries, Mozambique is made up of a variety of ethnic groups. In the far north are the Makonde, Yao and the Islamic coastal peoples; then, coming south, is the largest of the groups, the Makua-Lomwe and a smaller group known loosely as the Maravi in northern Tete Province. The peoples of the lower Zambezi valley defy any single categorisation. To the south of them are the Shona, and farther south still are the Tsonga, Chopi and Tonga. There are scattered pockets of Ngoni both in the south and in the north and an enclave of Nyanja on Lake Niassa. These groupings should not be seen as coherent unified entities themselves; rather, they represent clusters of smaller groups. There was clearly no unified resistance to colonial occupation by these various peoples, and the primary task of the nationalist movement was to weld them into a single struggle and forge a national identity. Colonial authorities, on the other hand, did all that they could to foment ethnic divisions and avert the threat of a co-ordinated nationalist opposition.

Proletarianisation, control and resistance

In Mozambique there were several constraints in operation preventing a full and rapid proletarianisation. First, there were those features of the country's political economy that Mozambique shared with other countries on the periphery: because Mozambique was an exporter of raw materials to the industries of the sub-metropolis and the metropoles, its own secondary sector was tiny, and the need for a manufacturing working class was therefore small. Secondly, the primary sector (mines and plantations) operated a migrant labour system creating a semi-proletariat or class of 'worker-peasants' rather than a permanent proletariat. Thirdly, Portugal, an underdeveloped capitalist colonising power, was unable to compete for Mozambique's labour on an open market; hence it employed a *chibalo*, or forced labour system. The ability to call on labour for a compulsory fixed period each year arrested tendencies towards a more permanent and widespread proletarianisation. This clearly affected the development of workers' organisations and the growth of a class consciousness – in particular, given the quasi-military control exercised in the mine compounds. However, a small working class did grow up around the ports and railways. A careful distinction needs to be made between the 'external' proletariat (those workers of Mozambican nationality whose point of production is outside the territorial boundaries of the state) and the 'internal' proletariat (those working inside the country).

The external proletariat

Migrant mine labourers were kept under a tight and extremely rigid form of social control whilst on the mines. A whole battery of extra-economic measures were employed to ensure the ultra-cheapness and subservience of non-white labour. Every miner had to sign a contract for a minimum period of twelve months, and the Master and Servant Laws of South Africa made the breach of such a contract punishable by imprisonment. Any strike or insubordination was illegal. Even so, the resistance to bad conditions of work was such that by 1910 there was a desertion rate of 15 per cent.[10] Pass laws were introduced in 1911, under the Native Labour Regulation Act, in an attempt to halt the flow of deserters. All African mine workers, including foreign migrants, were subject to the pass laws. Compounds housing the migrants were constructed like prisons, being surrounded by high galvanised iron fences with barbed wire on top. Arms and ammunition were kept in the manager's office, and there was strict supervision over entry and exit. Compounds permitted the maximum control to be exercised over the workforce, who were isolated from society and divided internally. Each compound was kept separate from the others. Disturbances could easily be dealt with by sending troops or police to surround a compound; and in the case of a dispute, the management could always tell the miners of one compound that the others had gone back to work, thus destroying their unity. Similarly, inside each compound miners from different ethnic groups were kept separate, and frequently an immediate supervisor would be from another 'tribe'.

The strong repressive control exerted within the mine compounds tended to dampen the growth of an active and militant workforce. Nevertheless, it would be incorrect to assume that resistance was absent; instead, workers' discontent must be sought in the nooks and crannies of the day-to-day work situation where various forms of passive resistance took place.

Although the South African mines were by far the most important employers of Mozambican labour, a significant number of workers also went to the Southern Rhodesian mines – 36 000 by 1920. Over the first twenty years of the century, 2 000 workers died from accidents and 18 000 died from diseases in the compounds.[11] According to official statistics, on the South African mines between 1902 and 1914, 43 484 Mozambicans died from accidents and disease.[12] Some mines were far worse than others, so clearly the choice of mine was a life or death decision. Van Onselen has shown how workers developed their own intelligence system as a response to this danger. The Bonsor Mine in particular had a bad reputation for accidents, and workers refused to go there. Mozambicans were brought in, but they soon declared it to be 'bewitched' and left the mine. The fear of the mine had a real cause, the high death rate. But the miners could not provide an explanation for the fatalities other than in witchcraft: this furnished an explanation of the otherwise inexplicable. Traditional beliefs in witchcraft provided here the form in which miners expressed their resistance to dangerous working conditions. This in no way detracts from the value of the example in demonstrating working-class resistance, albeit reflecting the continuing influence of pre-capitalist ideology. The form of resistance remained pre-capitalist, but the content was most definitely a struggle of labour against capital.

Another expression of 'worker' consciousness was desertion. Given the appalling conditions in the mine compounds, the choice of employer was vital, and a rapid and efficient system of market intelligence developed about employment prospects throughout southern Africa. Miners generally preferred to work in South Africa where conditions were better, and van Onselen concludes that worker strategy can best be understood 'within the context of the functioning of a regional economic system embracing all of southern Africa'.[13]

Ethnic, dance and mutual aid societies were also formed amongst the migrant workers in their compounds, and provided a further expression of resistance to the new-found wage labour situation. Many of the mutual aid societies were involved with funeral expenses, which, given the high mortality rates on the mines, was hardly surprising. The organisational hierarchy in these societies is well evidenced in the case of the Port Herald Burial Society, at Shamva Mine in Southern Rhodesia. The majority of its membership came from Mozambique, and the society had its own king, governor, prince, general, commander, doctor, bishop, lord and king's servant.[14] Through their compound associations Africans were responding as workers, and societies were frequently not restricted to people of any one tribe or even country of origin. The compound associations preceded the trade unions, and, although forming an important component in the spectrum of resistance, they had their limitations, with funding a permanent problem. Little is known about participation by Mozambican migrants in Clements Kadalie's Industrial and Commercial Workers' Union, but there is evidence that Mozambicans did participate in strikes on the mines.

The penetration of capitalism, in particular the growth of mining, led to the creation of a migrant proletariat and to attempts by the newly 'transformed' peasants to make sense of industrial experience in a colonial society. A variety of methods of resistance were offered to the exploitative relationships in which they found themselves, but they met with little success. Alongside the internal weaknesses of these organisations there was also the hostile external context within which they had to work. The mining companies and the colonial state were quick to repress the slightest challenge to their power. Although mutual aid associations might be tolerated, as they had the potential for being used as an instrument of social control, trade unions, and even the religious Watch Tower movement, were soon suppressed when they were seen to pose a threat to white power. But it was the migrant labour system itself which was the key mechanism for stunting the growth of a permanent and class-conscious proletariat: 'The perpetual rotation of Africans under intensive police surveillance has a crippling effect on African labour and political organisations. The fear of being "endorsed out" of towns has been a major deterrent to mass action against apartheid. Labour migration accordingly delays the processs of consolidating Africans into a class-conscious proletariat.'[15]

Although the South African migrant could be removed from the cities or mines back to the 'homelands', the situation was even more difficult for the development of working-class consciousness amongst Mozambican migrants. Their point of production was outside the nation-state boundary. When they returned from their contracts on the mines, migrants disappeared back to isolated peasant homesteads. Their resistance did not, directly at least, pose a threat to the Portuguese colonial state.

The internal proletariat

Inside Mozambique a small working class was growing up around the ports and railways of Lourenço Marques and Beira. Among black workers, forms of resistance such as those found among the migrant miners also appeared: crime, desertions, avoidance and even strikes. A clear example of avoidance of the worse-paid jobs and choice of the better paid was the labour shortage in Lourenço Marques at the end of the first decade of the century.[16] Men were going to the mines of South Africa rather than work for an absolute pittance in the city.

In the pre-Salazar period, the greatest organised militancy was expressed by the white workers. With the onset of the Republican period in Portugal (1910–1926), there was a broad upsurge of workers' struggles in the sub-metropole, and these were reflected among the white workers in the colonies. On 6 June 1917, a general strike of all European personnel in the port and railways was called in Lourenço Marques, and a state of seige was declared in the city. A particularly bitter strike occurred in 1925–1926, which included sabotage of the railway track. Severe repression was used to crush the strike. After a derailment, a group of the workers' leaders were bound and placed in a carriage attached at the front of a 'phantom' train, as a severe warning against further acts of sabotage.[17] Wives of striking workers carrying black flags held a hunger march which was violently dispersed by mounted troops and police.[18] This strike had a similar importance to that of the white miners on the Rand a few years earlier. Whether intentional or not, when Salazar came to power repression of all workers increased, but the privileges of white workers over black workers were consolidated in the colonies.

With the overthrow of the Republican government in 1926, workers' rights to organise and strike were severely curtailed, and state-run *sindicatos* replaced trade unions. During this early period there was not one major combined struggle of white and black workers. Despite colonial mystique to the contrary, racial divisions existed in the work-place, mirroring colonial society at large. White workers monopolised the skilled jobs, had rights to organise which were never conceded to blacks and, under the stimulus of radical political movements in the sub-metropole, they entered into co-ordinated and extended periods of industrial action. Even so, African workers were not entirely quiescent, and there are several instances of their taking strike action.[19]

The first recorded incident took place on 18 January 1904, with a strike in the Lingham Timber and Trading Company in Lourenço Marques. At issue was a cut in wages; the strikers managed to win, and the former wage was regained. Again it was a cut in wages which prompted a work stoppage on the wharf on 11 July 1910, but this time it was unsuccessful. The following year, wagon drivers in the capital won the confrontation in a strike over a small wage rise. Even outside the capital there were examples of overt and organised workers' resistance, with a walkout at the Incomati Quarry over beatings and poor food (March 1904) and a commercial work stoppage in Chai Chai (April 1908).

The upsurge of strikes among white workers provided an example for Africans of the power of combined workers' action. Following the stoppage in the port by European workers in January 1919, black workers on the wharf attempted a strike in May to secure for themselves the 20 to 30 percent wage increase being demanded by whites. But the administration was keen to discourage such a trend, and three of the strike leaders were sentenced to forced labour. Given the increasing economic chaos and, in particular, massive inflation, African workers were obliged to press ahead with their claims for more money if only to halt the tremendous decline in their real wages. These actions were therefore mainly defensive. In all, there were twenty-seven reported incidents (so far recorded) over the first twenty-five years of the century involving white or black workers, but never both together.

The unequal but parallel growth of resistance

The early colonial period to 1930 saw the beginnings of an unequal but parallel growth of resistance. It was unequal in the sense that by 1917 the Makonde were experiencing their earliest contact with the Portuguese; the Barué were in revolt against colonial/concession rule; migrant miners in Southern Rhodesia were forming burial societies and choosing the safest and best-paid mines on which to work; white workers in the capital were in revolt, and a state of siege was declared; and black dock workers were soon to go on strike to try and secure for themselves a similar 20 to 30 per cent wage rise to that which was being demanded by whites. Even this was not all. There began to emerge the glimmerings of nationalist ideas amongst the tiny grouping of educated Africans. *Assimilado* groups with members drawn from the different colonies were formed in Lisbon, and they hosted the Pan-African Congress in 1923. Inside Mozambique, *assimilado* groups started a series of newspapers and formed their own organisation, *Grémio Africano*, which pressed for African rights.

Salazar rapidly suppressed these early overt flowerings of elite protest, but they refused to become totally submerged. Of greater portent in hampering the growth of the nationalist movement was the almost complete hiatus between the protest of the educated few and that of the illiterate majority of the population after Salazar took power. What is significant is that elite protest paralleled in time the wars of resistance, the labour boycotts using witchcraft and the formation of the burial societies with their kings, princes, governors, bishops and generals as title-holders of office. The essential reason for this unequal but parallel growth of resistance was the uneven penetration of colonial capitalism documented in the first part of this book.

A disjointed and incomplete process of class formation resulted. The structural growth of the Mozambican working class (and of working class struggles therefore) was both slow and partial, with a large section of the working class being based outside the national boundaries. A migrant labour system was widely employed both externally and internally, and this ensured the retention of a peasant base for most workers. Because forced labour rather than the 'free' sale of labour power was a further limitation on the creation of a working class, only a partial proletarianisation occurred. These structural constraints limited the growth of a strong class consciousness. Nevertheless, there were signs of an emerging worker consciousness among both the internally and externally based proletariat.

In the countryside, in the centre and north, the wars of pacification and the implantation of chartered company rule were intimately connected. In the south, men were already integrated into the wage economy, but they fought to retain their 'freedom' within the structural constraints of the situation, both economic and political. Active and passive resistance, armed revolt and massive migrations provided an entire spectrum of opposition to the penetration of colonial capitalism in the rural areas. The Barué revolt employed spirit mediums but mobilised people against forced labour and taxation. In this early period old forms of resistance (witchcraft and spirit mediums) appeared with a new content (labour boycotts and opposition to forced labour and taxation) in response to the penetration of capitalist relations of production and exchange. Over the following period from 1930 to 1960, new conditions – both internally and externally generated – would ripen, culminating in a new form of resistance in the shape of the nationalist parties.

Notes

1 J. Duffy, *A Question of Slavery*, Oxford, 1967, p. 1.

2 See D. L. Wheeler, 'Gungunyane the Negotiator: a Study in African Diplomacy', in *Journal of African History (JAH)*, ix, 4, 1968.

3 W. Rodney, 'The Year 1895 in Southern Mozambique: African Resistance to the Imposition of European Colonial Rule', *Journal of the Historical Society of Nigeria*, iv, 4, June 1971, 535. The bracketed insertion is mine.

4 P. Harries, 'Labour Migration from the Delagoa Bay Hinterland to South Africa: 1852–1895', *Collected Seminar Papers on the Societies of Southern Africa in the Nineteenth and Twentieth Centuries*, University of London, Vol. 7, 1977, p. 5.

5 A. Isaacman, *The Tradition of Resistance in Mozambique: Anti-colonial Activity in the Zambezi Valley 1850–1921*, London, 1976.

6 T. O. Ranger, 'Revolt in Portuguese East Africa: the Makonde Rising of 1917', *St Antony's Papers*, Oxford, 15, p. 61.

7 See A. Isaacman, 'Social Banditry in Zimbabwe (Rhodesia) and Mozambique 1894–1907: an Expression of Early Peasant Protest', *Journal of Southern African Studies*, iv, 1, Oct. 1977.

8 Isaacman, *Tradition of Resistance*, p. 107.

9 *Mozambique Revolution*, 47, May–June 1971.

10 F. A. Johnstone, *Class, Race and Gold*, London, 1976, p. 37.

11 C. van Onselen, 'Worker Consciousness in Black Miners: Southern Rhodesia 1900–1920', *JAH*, xiv, 2, 1973.

12 M. Harris, 'Labour Emigration among the Mozambique Thonga: Cultural and Political Factors', *Africa*, xxix, 1959.

13 Van Onselen, 'Worker Consciousness'.

14 C. van Onselen, *Chibaro: African Mine Labour in Southern Rhodesia 1900–1933*, London, 1976, p. 201.

15 H. J. and R. E. Simons, *Class and Colour in South Africa 1850–1950*, Harmondsworth, Mdx., 1969, p. 616

16 Direcção do Porto e Caminho de Ferro de Lourenço Marques, *Relatório Anual dos Serviços da Exploração*, Lourenço Marques, 1909, p. xxxi.

17 See A. P. de Lima, *História dos Caminhos de Ferro de Moçambique*, Vol. 1, Edição da Administração dos Portos, Caminhos de Ferro e Transportes de Moçambique, Lourenço Marques, 1971, p. 231.

18 Interview with Gilberto Varegilão, Carlos Sousa Coelho, José Francisco Madeira, Nassone Mulate Suleimane E. Juma, Farinha Lopes, Benjamin Wilson and Abdul Magid Hassangy, all senior officials of the railway, Maputo, 1 March 1978.

19 See J. Penvenne, 'Preliminary Chronology of Labour Resistance: Lourenço Marques', mimeo, 21 April 1977.

8 The weaving of the nationalist tapestry (1930–1960)

There was an extension of the uneven but parallel growth of resistance in this second period, from 1930 to 1960, creating the conditions for a qualitative leap in the form of struggle which occurred from 1960 onwards. A nationalist political programme replaced the witchcraft, and political commissars the spirit mediums of earlier years, although the path proved both uneven and difficult. Mozambican nationalism was born after a gestation period of colonial occupation which Eduardo Mondlane explained quite simply thus: 'The source of national unity is the common suffering during the last fifty years spent under effective Portuguese rule.'[1]

Frelimo, the Mozambican nationalist movement, was formed exactly half a century after the African National Congress of South Africa (founded in 1912). The reason for the late development in Mozambique can be accounted for in the main by lack of educational facilities for Africans, censorship and heavy repression. In addition, Portugal's non-participation in the Second World War obviated the necessity of levying colonial troops to serve in foreign lands. New insights and a comparative perspective gained by British and French African troops during the war acted as a powerful stimulus for their own indigenous nationalist movements. The first wave of struggles for African independence, for example, occurred in what had been the North African theatre of war. This input was lacking in the case of the Portuguese colonies, a factor acknowledged to be of importance by Frelimo's sister movement in Angola, the MPLA (Popular Movement for the Liberation of Angola).[2]

Various disparate trends of resistance were apparent in the 1930–1960 period. Resistance among the non-Catholic churches, popular cultural resistance, 'anti-fascist' activity amongst the white settler population, protest in the rural areas, and activity among the internal and external working class were all to provide the threads with which the nationalist tapestry was woven. One key ingredient was the role of the educated few. Only they could surmount the barriers erected by the colonial system, gaining an education, broadening their horizons and developing a nationalist perspective.

Colonial education and the Roman Catholic church

In the early colonial period the country was virtually bereft of missionary work of any kind. By 1910 there were only sixty-seven Roman Catholic missionaries and fewer than two thousand people taking confession.[3] However, this was soon to change. The Catholic church was given a central role in the 'civilising mission' by Salazar. Indeed, under the 1940 Missionary Accord with the Vatican, the marriage of the Catholic church with Portuguese colonialism was made complete. Funds cut off under the Republican period were now forthcoming, and there was a general expansion of missionary activities.

Nevertheless, this proved to be a thin veneer. Those children receiving any education whatsoever attended one to three years of 'education for adapting' – namely, adapting to Portuguese language, culture and colonialism with a Catholic halo. Official government statistics gave the percentage of illiteracy in 1958 as being 97.8 per cent. In the Lourenço Marques district in 1950 only 1 per cent of the African male population could speak Portuguese and only 1 per cent of those could write it.[4] For women, the respective figures dropped to 0.1 per cent. Those attending Catholic mission schools complained of little education and much unpaid labour. One particularly horrifying story concerned the Roman Catholic church and forced labour for women. Lucia and Martha Ngulele described how the Portuguese 'picked up 13-year old girls from the streets of the capital and brought them to the *administração do conselho*, where a lady examined the girls to see if they were virgins. If they weren't they had to pay two hundred escudos'.[5] The majority of the girls could not possibly produce the money and had to pay off the fine with their labour, helping to construct the cathedral, and two Catholic churches in the area.

The miserable record on education was no mere by-product of a general neglect; it was in many ways a conscious and actively pursued policy. A dual education system existed, one for the *indigena* (native) and another for the whites, coloureds and *assimilados*. For the mass of the population, according to the Missionary Statute, education was 'essentially nationalist and practical', aimed at 'curing laziness and preparing future rural workers and craftsmen'.[6] Although the number of African pupils receiving rudimentary or functional education rose from 95 444 in 1942–1943 to 385 259 in 1960–1961, most of those leaving school could barely speak Portuguese and certainly could not write it. Professor Silva Regio of the Institute for Overseas Studies was forced to concede in 1964, 'the partial but undisputed failure of the church' in education.[7] When viewed as an educational exercise the school system was clearly a failure; but when seen as an *anti-educational* exercise, as we would argue, then it was clearly a success, as it hampered the development of the nationalist movement.

Those few who did achieve fluency and literacy in Portuguese could be eligible for *assimilado* status. The official criteria for one possessing this status were to be over 18 years of age; to have fluency in Portuguese; to earn a salary from a trade or profession; to have possession of property adequate to provide for the person and his dependants; to be of good character; to have a good educational background and habits, for the purpose of full liability to Portuguese public and private law; and not to have avoided military service or to have been posted as a deserter. The intention was to create black Portuguese, forced to deny their African culture in its entirety. *Assimilado* status brought many benefits, exemption from forced labour and forced crop cultivation not least among them. Assimilation, it was hoped, would keep the educated few tied to the coloniser and prevent any emergence of a mass nationalist movement. This strategy, though, was doomed to work for only a limited period, because of the growing resentment among those who had been forced to struggle against all the odds to achieve their education.

The educated few

The sub-metropolitan power was unable and unwilling to produce a fully fledged dependent class to serve its interests in a neocolonial setting. Many of the incoming settlers were illiterate, and occupied even the skilled working-class jobs within the existing social/technical division of labour of colonial society, which acted to suppress the emergence of an African petty bourgeoisie. Yet among the tiny group of educated and assimilated Africans, nationalist ideas and organisational forms were to emerge. The process was to be both slow and tortuous, as a result of the isolation imposed by the colonial system and the secrecy required when confronted with a repressive and authoritarian state (the Portuguese colonies were the only ones in Africa where the independence struggle never acquired a legal character). It was only from among this group that the vision and potential could come to supersede the limitations of the disparate and unco-ordinated forms of resistance existing amongst the peasants and workers.

The one crucial problem was how to overcome the barriers between the few assimilated, educated Africans and the vast mass; barriers created as a deliberate act by the colonisers. The writings of Amilcar Cabral help to explain the transformations which took place among the few.[8] They centre on the theory that culture provides the seed of opposition born among peoples when imperialist domination removes their natural historical process. Although the mass of the people retain their culture – for, with few exceptions, the era of colonialism was not sufficiently long to destroy it – the coloniser attempts to assimilate the petty bourgeoisie culturally. Cabral considers this class to be 'marginalised', being prisoners of their social and cultural reality. They develop a frustration complex which leads them to contest their marginal status in the search for an identity. Only a small section of this class, however, goes through a threefold process of rejecting the coloniser's culture, re-Africanising themselves and finally becoming integrated within the national liberation movement, which is for Cabral the organised political expression of the culture of the oppressed people. This process can be seen at work with the formation in Lisbon in 1948 of a Centre for African Studies and can be traced in the poetry of a number of *assimilado* intellectuals.

One young Mozambican poet destined to play an important role in the nationalist struggle was Marcelino dos Santos. He studied in Portugal and Paris alongside other future leaders of the lusophone nationalist movements. Dos Santos, with other *assimilado* intellectuals, was involved in an important debate with the Portuguese opposition movement in exile in Paris. This movement still held an ambiguous position concerning the colonial question, and dos Santos and others, including the Angolan Lucio Lara campaigned vigorously and successfully for the autonomy of the nationalist movements *vis-à-vis* the anti-fascist opposition movement. Previously the Portuguese opposition had held that the colonial questions could be resolved only after the overthrow of the Salazar regime, and that an anti-fascist rather than an anti-colonial struggle should therefore be waged by all. This victory by the re-Africanised intellectuals was an important one, and they formed the *Movimento Anti-Colonial* in Paris in 1957. This was the forerunner of later international organisations uniting the nationalist movements of the Portuguese colonies.

Inside Portugal, African students gathered in the Casa dos Estudantes do Império, and there – in closely guarded discussions – nationalist ideas began to crystallise. These students established links with sailors from the colonies and also with dockers, through the Club dos Marítimos. The anti-fascist Portuguese underground used this club as a front. Black students came into contact with the Movement of United Democratic Youth, and some joined a clandestine Centre of Marxist Studies. Ironically, it was to be in Lisbon that nationalist and even Marxist ideas first began to take shape. With education, the few could gain access to the ideas and organisational forms which could break the *impasse* of resistance back home. At the turn of the 1960s, a number of Mozambican students fled from Portugal to France, and there they created, in 1961, the *Union Nationale des Estudiantes de Mozambique* (UNEMO).[9] This was soon to become the student wing of Frelimo, and several of its members were destined to play an important part in the nationalist movement.

Inside Mozambique, the educated few were also making halting steps towards nationalist ideas. The *Grémio Africano* evolved into the *Associação Africana*, with its paper, *O Brado Africano*. The stress placed on the African nature of this association and journal was important, as under colonialism there was a strict racial hierarchy of whites, mulattoes, assimilated and indigenous blacks. Mulattoes had a greater access to education and were trapped between the two worlds of their black mothers and white fathers.[10] Some asserted their Africanness through the association and the journal, and worked together with blacks to overcome the racial divide. The authorities perceived the danger of this unity, implying a much clearer definition between coloniser and colonised, and they manoeuvred to create a black breakaway from the *Associação Africana* called the *Instituto Negrófilo*, later renamed the *Centro Associativo dos Negros de Moçambique* (CANM). Similar dangers were perceived by the authorities in allowing mixed sports. Mulattoes and blacks were forbidden to box against whites, but mulattoes were permitted to enter the white football club, the *Associação de Futebol de Lourenço Marques*. However, the majority of mulattoes joined the *Associação Africana de Futebol*, which was a further expression of their Africanness and, as such, became an act of resistance. In 1962, after the formation of Frelimo, it was considered too dangerous to allow Africans a separate football organisation, and all were incorporated into a single one, with close white scrutiny of the (still racially separated) African third division.[11]

Until the end of the 1950s, the colonial authorities managed quite successfully to keep the various social and racial groups apart. The *Associação Africana* was mainly for mulattoes, the *Centro Associativo dos Negros de Moçambique* was for blacks and in particular for the assimilated. The educated few who could formulate and spread nationalist ideas and organisational forms were kept separated from the mass of the 'native' population. The CANM tended to be dominated by a few petty bourgeois *assimilado* families.[12]

A group called NESAM, the Nucleus of Mozambican Secondary Students, was to breach in part this hiatus between the educated few and the illiterate many. On his return from South Africa in 1949, Eduardo Mondlane helped found the student movement, and NESAM spread across racial and ethnic divisions, acting as a focus point for young people. Mondlane tried at that early stage to press for unity among the associations, but only in the young did he find the necessary openness and willingness.[13] Through the CANM (in the late 1950s), NESAM members gave lessons to ordinary Africans and they began to go beyond the former elitist thinking. Future leaders of Frelimo played an important part in NESAM: Armando Guebuza, Joaquim Chissano, Marianho Matsinha and Pascoal Mocumbi all taught in the school set up within CANM. The establishment of the school was an important breakthrough, and for this reason, no doubt, the secret police closed it down. The younger intellectuals of NESAM were to prove far less reluctant than their older counterparts in the associations to join the revolution. Writing in 1964, Mondlane was to comment that the *Associação Africana* and the CANM 'are at best bourgeois social clubs . . . [which] no longer serve any visible social or political purpose for the masses of the oppressed African population'.[14]

After the Second World War there were many small groups which sprang up all over the country; some tried to revive cultural traditions, but as a whole they did not possess a clear understanding of Mozambican nationalism. The people concerned in these groups lived mainly in the towns and worked in the government administration, in commerce, teaching and nursing. Under conditions of Portuguese colonialism, Mozambique's African intellectuals were also wage earners and tended to have at most a few years of secondary education. However, the intellectual leadership for the nationalist movement, small though it was and working under extreme difficulties, was slowly being formed – inside the country, in Portugal and, for a handful, in the Western metropoles.

The non-Catholic churches

Much acrimony was directed by the colonial authorities against the Protestant missionaries, and centred in particular upon their active educational programme. The flow of migrant labourers had spread the

Protestant word in the south and centre of Mozambique from the mining compounds of South Africa. Many people in the north of Mozambique also became converted to Protestantism while working as migrant labourers in Nyasaland and Tanganyika. Under the Salazar regime, discrimination against non-Catholic missions increased. In 1928 the Portuguese administration withdrew the rights of Protestant missions to have schools outside their properly registered centres. One missionary at Cambine in the Inhambane region has written of 'countless instances of discrimination, harassment, intimidation, suppression of worship even to private meetings in homes for prayer, hand beatings (in the Zavala area, all pastors were thus beaten for attending Annual Conferences), imprisonment, and exile of our Christians, particularly our pastors'.[15] Under Salazar, the Protestant missions came to be regarded as the advance guard of African nationalism. They were essentially centres of resistance in that they opposed the colonial policy of denying education to Africans. Several of the future nationalist leaders received their education from Protestant missions: Eduardo Mondlane, Daniel Mbanze and Graça Simbine all at the mission of Cambine. They suffered persecution and discrimination as a result of their religion.

The colonial authorities were particularly worried by the emergence of an Africanised Protestantism. By the end of the 1950s there were thirteen Ethiopian and eleven Zionist churches in Mozambique.[16] These Africanist churches were a typical manifestation of the secondary resistance which sprang up all over Africa. Traditional religious beliefs were still dominant in the country, but Islam also had a hold along the coastal region and the old slaving routes. Both were regarded with contempt by the ruling Catholic church, and adherence to these beliefs was an important implicit rejection of colonial culture by the African population.

Popular cultural resistance

Amilcar Cabral argued that people were able to create and develop the liberation movement only because they kept their culture alive, in spite of continued cultural repression. Cultural resistance takes over when early political military resistance is destroyed. Portugal's cultural impact was limited in time, because the colonial era lasted only three generations and not the self-proclaimed five hundred years, and was limited in its effectiveness because of the weakness of the sub-metropolitan power. Culture is a bond of solidarity within social structures, a method of identity which becomes of particular importance in confrontation with an outside force – in the case of Africa, with colonialism. Cultural resistance in African societies acted in two ways.[17] First, it resulted in a doubling of the colonial authority's administrative system by an unseen but effective traditional one. Often, if a chief was not amenable to co-operation with the Portuguese, he was replaced; but the authentic chief who maintained the link between the dead, the living and the yet unborn would retain his authority in a dual form alongside the colonial appointee. This is clearly expressed in a song of the Chopi people who live in Inhambane Province: 'You, the elders must discuss our affairs. For the man they have appointed is a son of nobody.'[18] In a more indirect but no less effective way, cultural resistance was expressed by emphasising traditionalism. Cultural separation was used with great strategic skill to retain a separate identity. This is what Frantz Fanon referred to as maintaining 'co-existence' as a form of conflict and latent warfare.[19] Repression of cultural and religious forms gives them a political content where none may have existed previously.

A more ostensible passive resistance was expressed through various cultural media such as music and wood carvings. The words of one Chopi song were as follows:

O-oh, listen to the orders,
Listen to the orders of the Portuguese.
Men! The Portuguese say, 'Pay your pound'.
This is wonderful father!
Where shall I find the pound?[20]

The 'pound' referred to was the money earned on the mines which went to pay the taxes. Two of the most serious grievances felt by the migrant miners were that the South Africans sent the miners deferred pay in gold, which the Portuguese authorities exchanged disadvantageously into escudos (paying the miners less); and secondly, that most of their money would go to pay the tax. The *paiva*, sung on the Zambezian sugar estates, expressed a similar cultural resistance. As Mondlane has recorded: 'A simple psychological rejection of the colonizer and his culture was very widespread but it was not a conscious, rationalised stand; it was an attitude bound up with the cultural tradition of the group, its past struggles with the Portuguese and present experience of subjection.'[21]

White resistance

After the Salazar takeover, white working-class struggles lessened and an intensified racism consolidated the privileged position of whites, thereby encouraging their acquiescence in the *Estado Novo*. Trade unions were smashed and incorporated into the state structure, and the once-militant white railway workers, no doubt sharing in a measure of prosperity, provoked no further state of siege. Nevertheless, a white anti-fascist opposition certainly existed. Just prior to Salazar's show elections in 1949, the detention of some 'democrats' was announced.[22] The group was accused of using the cover of a number of associations to further its ends, and these included the Society of Studies, Art Nucleus, 1st of May Sporting Group, and *Associação Africana*. The group was called the Movement of Young Mozambican Democrats, and according to contemporary press reports, it aimed to propagandise against the state and existing social injustices, promote the union of all Africans and spread democratic ideas. A small group called the Communist

Organisation of Mozambique worked within it and was linked to the Portuguese Communist Party.[23] The newspapers reported with shocked relish that people were enticed to join the Democrats irrespective of race, age or sex. Attempts were made to set up cells in the secondary schools and in other associations.

Strong support for General Delgado, the opposition presidential candidate was also registered among Mozambique's settlers in the 1958 election. At the end of the 1950s there was a further ripple of white resistance centring in part on the *Associação dos Naturais de Moçambique* (ANM), a club for Europeans of Mozambican origin. A small group managed to take over the management of the association, which until that time had been open only to whites.[24] They opened up the association to people of other races, and by the time of its banning in 1961 there were 10 000 members,[25] including Indians, whites and a majority who were black. Armando Guebuza attended a typing course, and Marianho Matsinha received a bursary from the association to study in Portugal. Both were to become future leaders of Frelimo. In mid-1960, ANM was refused permission to open a night school, but the *Associação dos Antigos Estudantes de Coimbra* was permitted to start one for high school students, and it was here that Samora Machel attended fifth class.

Apart from isolated protests by a handful of white democrats, once the nationalist struggle started the majority of white opinion appears to have swung towards Salazar, in the face of what was perceived as the greater threat of black nationalism. Elections were always a total sham. In 1961, there were only 29 587 registered voters out of a population of 6 750 000.[26] In the 1973 elections, 91 per cent of all registered voters cast their vote, a total of 111 000 people;[27] but they represented only 2 per cent of the adult population of the country. Africans had little voice in what were essentially white elections. Even for whites, however, the elections had little meaning, as the result was never in doubt.

The significance of the white opposition movement for our purposes was that it provided a few future members of Frelimo. These courageous few, who were regarded as traitors by so many of the white settlers, were to play an important role in reinforcing the non-racist line pursued by the Frelimo leadership. There were whites within the country who collaborated with the guerrillas during the war, and the revived democrat movement played an important role in gaining the acceptance of Frelimo in the towns after the April coup of 1974.

Rural protest

Many of those forms of rural protest existing in the first period, to 1930, were carried over into the second. Africans would try to maximise their limited opportunities and escape from the harsh rule of forced labour and forced cultivation of crops, both of which were intensified with Salazar's 'nationalist' policies. Migration continued to be the dominant expression of this protest. Many of the Lomwe-speaking people of Mozambique, for example, preferred the tea plantations of Malawi to the alternative prospects in Mozambique. At the turn of the century none of these people had been in Malawi, but their number had reached an astonishing 380 000 by the end of the Second World War[28] and 476 300 by 1966.[29] In Tanzania also, there were 123 316 Lomwe-speakers to be found by 1957. Forced labour was at its most intense from the end of the 1940s into the 1950s. Many in the centre and south of the country fled to South Africa. Jermia Nhanombe, a Protestant pastor, who was in South Africa at this time, remarked, 'When you were there, you would not think there were any people left in Mozambique.'[30] Even men working on the mines, who were officially exempted from forced labour for six months after returning home, slept in the bush at night during their rest period to avoid being taken. Among the hundreds of thousands of Mozambicans who fled to the neighbouring countries of East Africa, Malawi, Southern Rhodesia and South Africa a fertile base was laid upon which the first nationalist movements would be able to draw.

In this second period the nature of African resistance to labour began to change. 'Forced labour' was avoided wherever possible, but no longer labour *per se*. People 'volunteered' in order to avoid recruitment and thus sought out the best wages and working conditions. Absenteeism, a further expression of resistance, was frequent. The known readiness to flee certainly operated to restrain the forced labour policy. Absenteeism and migration obliged the companies to move to a waged system of migrant labour as they were unable simply to levy the amount of labour that the plantations required. Although an organised and official migrant labour system had operated with South Africa, other areas had relied for their labour on uncontrolled flows of migrants and refugees. Gradually, however, the other 'host' territories evolved more organised systems of recruitment.

Those unable to flee from the forced cultivation of cotton would sometimes be fortunate enough to get away with cooking the seeds and claiming that the ground was infertile. However, a more organised and social response to the forced cultivation emerged in the 1950s. Co-operatives began to be formed in certain areas, notably in the provinces of Gaza and Cabo Delgado. The authorities at first permitted this development, thinking no doubt that they acted as a safety valve. People in the Guiza area of the Limpopo river formed a co-operative in 1957, with capital put up by the local *régulos*, but the scheme lasted only a year.[31] Co-operatives in Cabo Delgado had a longer life. In 1957 Lazero Kavandame, a traditional Makonde leader, received permission to set one up; it was called the *Sociedade Agrícola Algodoeira Voluntária dos Africanos de Moçambique*.[32] By 1958 the co-operative had 1 000 members and was flourishing. The cotton company which controlled the north offered Kavandame a salary to work for them, a mark of the co-operative's success. By July 1959 there were more than 1 500 members, and the company then started putting pressure on the government to intercede, worried no doubt by a potential rival. People were sent round to destroy the co-operative's fruit trees under the pretence that they interfered with the production of good cotton. Some of the members of the co-operative were obliged to carry out forced labour on sisal or cotton plantations. Then in September of that year,

Kavandame and others were imprisoned. He was later released, and this time set up a co-operative under Portuguese auspices, profiting personally by hiring out a tractor to those who wanted it.[33]

Kavandame was to become an important leader of Frelimo, but as we shall see, he opposed the revolutionary direction that the movement increasingly adopted. He was at the centre of the movement's crisis when his entrepreneurial activities in the 'liberated areas' became an issue. The existence of co-operatives in Cabo Delgado at this early stage, when they were prohibited elsewhere, poses a certain question. Were the authorities content to let the co-operatives continue because they had faith in Kavandame? Conclusive evidence is not yet available to provide an answer, but the doubt must remain. Whatever the intentions of its leader, with or without the complicity of the colonial authorities, it would be entirely wrong to undermine the importance of the co-operatives. There were several young militants who used them as a means to politicise the peasants. They were an important step forward in rural African self-assertiveness and organisation. The co-operatives were also to furnish future members of Frelimo and provide a base for the movement's clandestine organisational structure.

Rural protest, then, was not restricted to popular cultural forms, although these had an important part to play. When the armed struggle started, it was to be based on the rural areas, spreading slowly from the north and feeding on the widespread discontent. Because there were no functional channels for the political articulation of rural protest under the colonial system, there was a simmering rural discontent, which only the colonial culture of violence and the lack of new ideas and organisational forms among the peasantry prevented from boiling over even earlier than it eventually did, on 16 June 1960.[34] If any single day marks the end of an old and the beginning of a new era in the country's history, it was this. Six hundred people were killed at the massacre of Mueda in Cabo Delgado. It was a testament to the futility of peaceful rural resistance. One of the early proto-nationalist parties, the Makonde African National Union, was behind this mass peasant protest. It proved to the peasants that peaceful requests for reform would meet only with repression. It also threw a first challenge to the Mozambican nationalist movement to find a strategy to meet the violence and intransigence of the colonial power to any discussion of change. It was a measure of the success of Salazar's censorship policies that hardly any word of the massacre reached the world's press.

The emerging working class

With the consolidation of the corporate state, repression and control in the workplace increased. During the depths of the Depression in the early 1930s, the ports and railways cut African pay, precipitating a strike, but all those involved were soon arrested and forced to return to work. Informers were present in the workplace, enabling most 'agitation' to be prevented at an early stage. Racial barriers were strictly applied, entrenching white workers in their privileged and supervisory position over blacks. The continuing and reinforced racial division amongst the workers successfully prevented the development of any combined struggles.

At the end of the Second World War there is evidence of increasing discontent among African workers, with sharp declines in productivity on the docks, eventually building up to a major strike wave around the capital in 1947. Following the strike by dock and plantation workers, in 1948 there was an abortive rising in the capital of which little is known, but more than 500 were exiled to the coffee plantations of São Tomé as a consequence.[35] In 1956 there was a further revolt on the docks, exacerbated in part by the increased need for labour as a result of expanding South African trade and the opening up of the Rhodesia link-line to the port of Lourenço Marques. Stevedores were employed on a casual basis; they gathered each morning at the gates of the port, and the numbers required for the day were then chosen. The exact numbers required were never known beforehand, as the work of the port varied greatly from day to day. By maintaining a large pool of labour, wage rates could easily be depressed. To ensure that there was always the large pool of labour necessary, each stevedore had a card which was supposed to be stamped every day at the dock gates, whether a man worked or not. In order to meet the extra labour needs of 1956, one morning the police swooped and arrested all those stevedores who had no stamp for the previous day.[36] They were then obliged to do three months' forced labour on the docks and were housed in the *pousada* (the boarding house) of the railways. Those stevedores not arrested were encouraged by this incident to make an appearance every day at the docks. *Chibalo* labour was also brought in from the north (Macuas from Nampula), which was an unusual practice.[37] There was a large-scale riot over poor food served in the *pousada* and a demand for improvements. Police and dogs were used to break up the disturbance, and many *chibalos* were injured with up to fifty killed.[38] There were also reports of fighting against the *chibalo* labourers from the north.[39] Colonial policy successfully divided the workforce, creating divisions between the forced labourers and the wage employees. Although this served the interest of the colonial state generally, on occasions such as this the situation could get out of hand.

Although workers in the port had the longest and most dynamic history of resistance amongst the blossoming Mozambican proletariat, other workers also made their protest felt. In 1957, nurses from the Lourenço Marques hospital struck for better wages, and the leaders of the strike had their hands beaten with the *palmatória,*[40]. Samora Machel was a nurse in Lourenço Marques Province throughout the 1950s, and could not fail to be influenced by the strike. Not all workers' responses took the more spectacular form of strike action. There were many small craft brotherhoods or guilds existing in the capital at this time. Mutual assistance organisations existed over many parts of the country, in Beira and Chai Chai, as well as in the capital; they too provided many future leaders of Frelimo. From the 1950s onwards, under the stimulus of a larger settler presence, Portugal's own belated industrialisation, South Africa's outward expansion and the opening up of the sub-metropole and colonies to foreign investment, Mozambique's manufacturing sector grew from 8.6 per cent of the total workforce in 1950 to 14.9 per cent in 1966.[41]

The Mozambican working class had five basic structural characteristics. First, there was little stability and much fluctuation in its membership, as a result of the *chibalo* and internal migrant labour systems. A second characteristic was the racial division of the working class, with whites occupying the well-paid skilled and semi-skilled jobs and blacks the low-paid unskilled jobs. Thirdly, industry tended to be labour-intensive with a low level of technology and, therefore, little need for a large and skilled workforce. A fourth feature was the small scale of the manufacturing enterprises: the 1973 statistics indicate that three-quarters of them employed forty-nine workers or less. This contrasts markedly with the large concentration of workers in the transit sector. Finally, there was a massive regional distortion, with Lourenço Marques Province accounting for 40.5 per cent of the manufacturing working class and three provinces accounting for 73.6 per cent. The nature of the Mozambican working class was an extremely important consideration for Frelimo's attempted socialist transition. The weakness of the class, mirroring the dependency of the economy as a whole, had many implications, as we shall see later.

In addition to these five structural characteristics which acted to constrain the development of the manufacturing sector of the internal working class, there was a further feature of great importance – the illegality of free trade unions and political organisations for black workers. A strong working-class consciousness did not therefore emerge. Although African trade-union organisation was absent in the Mozambican experience, workers' struggles were not. The transport sector in particular was the forum for many of these struggles and thus warrants closer study. Not only was this the most militant, it was also the oldest and one of the largest sections of the working class. It was not a unified whole, however, and a careful distinction needs to be drawn between its constituent parts.

Port workers, even though they were the most militant part of the internal working class, never developed beyond a sense of group consciousness to one of collective class consciousness. Class formation is a slow process; it is the ever-increasing unity of organisation in defence of common interest. This interest has as its base a common relationship to the means of production.

An examination of the labour process is crucial for an understanding of the formation of group and class consciousness, as this creates technical and occupational divisions within the working class and can promote or impede the development of class consciousness, as can the system of labour control. The labour processes within the ports and railways were very different, and this was a major contributing factor to the differential development of group consciousness and its overt expression in the form of strike action.[42] An analysis of the labour processes and systems of labour control helps explain why the most militant workers were the stevedores, followed by the dockers and finally the railwaymen. The railways were organised in a number of different and separated sections, within each of which there was a strict and highly differentiated work hierarchy. In the *secção do movimento*, for example, there were twenty-seven separate grades of workers. Ten of these (the lowest ten) were reserved for blacks. Occupational differentiation did not correspond with the technical division of labour; for example, there would be first-, second- and third-class firemen, station auxiliaries and servants. Different rates of pay, authority and prestige were attached to the different job categories. Workers in the railway were thus not only divided into clearly demarcated sections, but they were also hierarchically divided within each section, making unity very difficult. Loyalty tended to be towards the job and the section, rather than a group consciousness developing of being railwaymen. Voluntary self-help associations, for example, were organised on a section-by-section basis. In addition, promotion resulted from long and faithful service as well as the *padrinho* system, and anyone aiming at promotion would be wary of being seen to be organising his fellow workers.

The strict hierarchy within the railways reached almost military proportions. Heads of sections were treated like gods, and the slightest criticism of superiors met with immediate reproof. As a punishment, Europeans were fined and Africans were frequently beaten with the *palmatória*. As a more 'serious' punishment, they were immediately dismissed. The greatest form of control was exercised structurally through the presence of the reserve army of labour. A worker knew that he could easily be replaced, and given that the railways provided the most prestigious and stable jobs this was a very serious threat.

Permanent employment has always been assumed to be one of the important objective criteria for developing a militant worker's consciousness. In fact this was not the case in the Portuguese colonial context. African dock workers were recruited on a casual basis from a registered pool. Their history of militancy under Portuguese colonial conditions indicates that they felt they had less to lose by taking militant action than the more quiescent railway workers. The black railway worker had the possibility of promotion from, say, a third-class to a first-class 'assistant', with an extra few escudos' earnings per week. Port workers had no such promotion prospects.

In the port (as with the railway), a strict racial division existed in the occupational hierarchy. Within the African workforce, a clear distinction has to be made between those working on the quay (dockers) and those who go on to the ship (stevedores). The highest level of militancy was found among the stevedores. *Chibalo* workers as well as casual dockers were employed in large numbers on the quay, but they were not used on the ships; hence the stevedores did not always have hanging over them the permanent threat of *chibalos* being able to take over their jobs. *Chibalo* labour was strictly controlled, not only at the point of production but also at the *pousada* where they were housed. However, control over the casual dock workers could not be as tightly exercised as in the railways. There were no strict compartmental divisions, with workers being permanently placed in different sections. Neither was there a massive and complex hierarchy of job categories. Most of the black workers were *carregadores* (carriers) and *arrumadores* (stowers), and every day they would have different workmates. This enabled a certain group consciousness to emerge, but militancy was diluted, as already indicated, by the presence of large numbers of *chibalo* workers.

Stevedores congregated at the port gates every morning, when the numbers required for the day were chosen. They worked in gangs with a membership varying from day to day, in stark contrast to the compartmentalised sections in the railways. Working under appalling conditions in the holds of the ships, a close solidarity developed. Only a minimum technical division of labour existed within a gang, and this was not complicated by an occupational hierarchy as on the railways. Possibilities of promotion for Africans were virtually non-existent. The labour process and absence of occupational hierarchy helped to cement the growth of a group consciousness undiluted by fear that *chibalo* labourers would replace them. This group consciousness was reinforced by a certain ethnic and regional unity, with recruits coming from certain specific districts.

The entire history of strikes in the port and on the railway in the twentieth century demonstrates that the stevedores were involved in the most militant actions, followed by the dockers. The mechanisms of daily control were harsh. Each morning when the workers gathered at the dock gates to try and obtain work, there was a contingent of *cipaios* present. A strong police presence was 'required' to maintain order, given the arbitrary and anarchic system of work distribution. Police would stand behind the throng of stevedores and beat workers in the general *mêlée* which ensued as the work tickets were distributed. The general competition for work caused fighting among the men, with those at the back of the crowd pushing towards the front. This inter-worker conflict was probably viewed positively by the private stevedoring companies. The sheer physical struggle in the crowd was to the disadvantage of the old and weak. Not infrequently men were severely injured when they fell and were trampled by the throng. Such a system of recruitment was dehumanising and brutalising and was itself an aspect of control in its intention of breaking the collective spirit of the workers. Nevertheless, this strategy did not entirely succeed.

The stevedores working on the ships naturally made contact with sailors, and the news of the better wages and working conditions abroad, as well as the successful independence struggles in many African countries, could not fail to have been transmitted by word of mouth. In August 1963, the stevedores of Lourenço Marques went on strike yet again and those of Beira and Nacala followed suit. These were to be the most significant strikes of all, not for what they achieved but for what they did not achieve. More than sixty strikers were arrested in Lourenço Marques, and both police and troops were called out. The first issue of the Frelimo publication *Mozambique Revolution*, which came out soon after the strike, made an appeal not to waste more time striking as the time had come for workers to join the nationalist movement.[43] There were clearly severe limitations to the potential for strike action and working-class organisation. Without trade unions or a legally operating nationalist party and given the tight control exercised in the workplace, as we have shown, a different way forward had to be found. Those migrant workers abroad who were not under the same tight constraints were to help provide a solution.

Mozambicans in some of the neighbouring British colonies had the right to join such trade unions as existed in those countries. As we have seen, this differed markedly from the situation inside the Portuguese colonies. Gaining the experience of trade-union organisation was important for those who founded the proto-nationalist parties. The point can be illustrated through the lives of individuals such as M. Mallinga, who became the General Secretary of the Mozambique African National Union (MANU). He had worked in the labour unions of East Africa with the dock workers in Mombasa and the cotton workers of Uganda. The full extent of the involvement of Mozambican migrant workers in trade-union organisation and strike action is as yet unknown, but it was undoubtedly significant. However, the limitations of this kind of action are readily apparent. Even strikes in the neighbouring territories did little to change Portuguese colonial rule in Mozambique, and still less to end it. However, as we shall see, the early nationalist parties were formed from among the migrant workers, in the territories of Tanganyika, Nyasaland and Southern Rhodesia.

Under the repressive conditions of sub-metropolitan colonial domination, the nationalist movement was to form in exile and then confront the problem of its return. All conventional forms of working class and peasant organisation to resist labour-repressive policies met with complete failure. Figueiredo has pointed to a major reason for this. After 1945 the regime at home and abroad 'passed from the arbitrary, but casual stage of repression, to the development of a scientific system which in its basic laws and operative methods was tantamount to a Neo-Inquisition'.[44] From the lessons of these failures, and those even earlier failures of the ethnically or even regionally based primary wars of resistance, grew the need for a united nationalist movement.

The old ideologies and methods of organisation proved impotent to meet the colonial challenge, but those with education were able to learn and assimilate new ideas and organisational forms – in Lisbon, Dar-es-Salaam, Blantyre, Salisbury, Paris and New York. Nationalism in its totality sprang from the combination of struggles that emerged with the uneven penetration of colonial capitalism into Africa. The development of resistance was, therefore, both parallel and uneven, but the various strands that we have outlined were eventually woven into the nationalist tapestry.

Notes

1 E. Mondlane, *The Struggle for Mozambique*, Harmondsworth, Mdx., 1969, p. 101.

2 *Angola: M.P.L.A. First Congress*, Mozambique, Angola & Guinea Information Centre, London, 1979, p. 4.

3 A. da Silva, 'Ocupação missionária de Moçambique', in *Moçambique*, Curso

de Extensão Universitário, Ano Lectivo de 1964–65, Instituto Superior de Ciências Sociais e Política Ultramarina, Lisbon, 1965, pp. 681–82.

4 See M. S. Alberto, 'The Native Population South of the Sabi River, Lourenço Marques District. I. The Ronga of Maputo', *Boletim de Sociedade de Estudos de Moçambique*, xxvi, 101, Nov.–Dec. 1956.

5 Group interview with people from Chamanculo Bairro, Maputo, Centre of African Studies Archive, Mozambique.

6 E. de Sousa Ferreira, *Portuguese Colonialism in Africa: the End of an Era*, UNESCO, 1974, p. 67.

7 *Ibid.*

8 See A. Cabral, *Unity and Struggle*, London, 1980.

9 *Africa Report*, x, 5, May 1965, 20.

10 I am grateful to the Mozambican poet, José Craveirinha, for his help in understanding this period.

11 See *Mozambique Revolution*, 1, Dec. 1963.

12 *Tempo*, 14 July 1974.

13 Interview with Sansão Mutemba, a former leader of CANM and member of the early Frelimo underground, Maputo, June 1976.

14 E. Mondlane, 'The Development of Nationalism in Mozambique', in *Emerging Nationalism in Portuguese Africa Documents*, R. H. Chilcote (ed.), Stanford, 1972.

15 M. V. Kemling, *A Chronicle of Events in the Life of Methodist Missions in Mozambique, particularly in Relation to Mission Schools*, Oct. 1962. Archive of the Former Mission School of Cambine, Morrumbene District, Inhambane Province.

16 J. J. Gonçalves, *Protestantismo em África*, Vol. I. Junta de Investigaçoes de Ultramar, Lisbon, 1960, fn. p. 175.

17 See G. Ballandier, *Political Anthropology*, Harmondsworth, Mdx., 1970, p. 160.

18 Quoted in Mondlane, *Struggle for Mozambique*, p. 103.

19 F. Fanon, *A Dying Colonialism*, Harmondsworth, Mdx., 1970, p. 33.

20 H. Tracy, *Chopi Musicians*, Oxford, 1970, p. 14.

21 Mondlane, *Struggle for Mozambique*, p. 102.

22 *Notícias*, 9 Oct. 1949.

23 Interview with João Mendes, a former member of the Communist Organisation of Mozambique, Maputo, 15 June 1976.

24 Interview with Maria da Natividade, a former official of the ANM, Maputo, May 1976.

25 *New York Times*, 22 June 1961.

26 D. W. Wainhouse, *Remnants of Empire: the United Nations and the End of Colonialism*, New York, 1964, p. 33.

27 K. Middlemas, *Cabora Bassa: Engineering and Politics in Southern Africa*, London, 1975, p. 265.

28 T. H. Henriksen, *Mozambique: a History*, London, 1979, p. 132.

29 E. A. Alpers, 'Ethnicity, Politics and History in Mozambique', *Africa Today*, xxi, 4, 1974, 43.

30 Interview with Jermia Nhanombe, Inhambane Province, 25 July 1977. Jermia had actually cut the rope he was bound with after being taken to do forced labour, and had run away to South Africa.

31 Information supplied by Salamão Nhantumbo, Maputo, June 1976.

32 See Frelimo, *Bulletin d'Informação du Frelimo*, Algiers, Oct.–Dec. 1966.

33 I am grateful for this information supplied by Aquino da Bragança, Director of the Centro de Estudos Africanos in Maputo.

34 The fullest account of the massacre is to be found in W. Burchett, *Southern Africa Stands Up*, New York, 1978, pp. 128–32.

35 D. J. Mabunda and J. Sakupwanya, 'Brief History of Moçambique', in *Emerging Nationalism*, Chilcote (ed.), p. 388.

36 Interview with thirteen long-serving stevedores, Maputo, 28 March 1978. Corroboration of this incident may be found in *Emerging Nationalism*, Chilcote (ed.), p. 389.

37 Interview with Marrulane P. Mondjane, 'Contramarca de 1° classe' at the port of Maputo, Maputo, 2 March 1978.

38 R. H. Chilcote, 'Mozambique: the African Nationalist Response to Portuguese Imperialism and Underdevelopment', in *Southern Africa in Perspective*, C. B. Potholm and R. Dale (eds.), New York, 1972.

39 Interview with Marrulane P. Mondjane, *op. cit.*

40 Report of the United Nations Special Committee, 'The Situation in the Territories under Portuguese Administration since January 1961', *Presence Africaine*, xvii, 45, 1st Quarter, 1963, 184.

41 See *Terceiro Plano de Fomento*, Part 1, Vol. 3.

42 The following analysis emerged from research undertaken by the author as a part of a project carried out by the Centro de Estudos Africanos in Maputo. This involved extensive interviewing and archival work (for complete referencing see the author's Ph.D. thesis, *'Frelimo and the Mozambican Revolution'*, University of Manchester, 1980, ch. 4).

43 *Mozambique Revolution*, 1, Dec. 1963.

44 A. de Figueiredo, *Portugal: Fifty Years of Dictatorship*, Harmondsworth, Mdx., 1975.

PART THREE
From nationalism to revolution

---

9 The search for unity

Although the Portuguese colonial authorities tried to insulate their territories from the decolonisation process which was advancing rapidly over most of the continent, this proved to be an impossible task. The economy of the country was such that at any one time there were hundreds of thousands of Mozambicans working abroad. Almost inevitably they were in contact with the nationalist movements and independence struggles in the British territories where they worked. Furthermore, when the migrants completed their contracts and returned home, they came clutching a small bundle of possessions in one hand and a prized radio in the other, enabling them to follow news of the nationalist victories spreading across Africa. The independence of the Congo in June 1960 and of Tanganyika in 1961 made a particularly noteworthy impact on Mozambicans, as did the Indian invasion of Portuguese Goa in December 1961. Because many had worked in English-speaking territories, enough could be understood of the foreign broadcasts to ensure that the news would be spread by word of mouth along the trails and alleyways of the bush and shantytowns. Tears were at last appearing in the curtain of silence that Salazar had thrown around Portugal's colonial possessions.

However, given the total ban on all political activity inside Mozambique and the large number of migrants working abroad, the early parties were formed in exile and mainly operated from outside the country. The first and perhaps the most influential was the National Democratic Union of Mozambique (UDENAMO). It was profoundly influenced by the nationalist movement in Southern Rhodesia, where it was formed in 1960, and the structure of UDENAMO closely followed that of Joshua Nkomo's National Democratic Party. Recruitment for UDENAMO was mainly among peoples from the centre and south of the country. It was headed by Adelino Gwambe and the Rev. Uria T. Simango, who was destined to play a major role in the unfolding drama of the Mozambican nationalist struggle. It operated mainly, but not exclusively, among the community in exile.

A second party, the Mozambique African National Union (MANU), was formed in 1961 in Mombasa, Kenya. This organisation emerged from a coalition of smaller groups, the most important of which was the Makonde African National Union. The Makonde people live on both sides of the Rovuma river which marks the border between Mozambique and Tanzania. That MANU was modelled upon the Kenya African National Union (KANU) and the Tanganyika African National Union (TANU) is illustrated by the similarity in their acronyms. Indeed, it was a Kenyan politician, C. Chockwe, who organised the movement's opening conference.

Finally, there was the National Union for Mozambican Independence (UNAMI). This group, based in Malawi, drew its support mainly from the people of Tete Province. It is thus evident that all the proto-nationalist parties had a predominantly ethnic or regional base, so disqualifying them from any claim to leadership of a genuinely 'nationalist' movement. Their membership was also confined mainly to migrants and exiles in the neighbouring territories, and a good deal of their energy was spent on petitioning the United Nations. Nevertheless, the pressures were building up inside Mozambique, especially among the younger people, to form a single party that was genuinely nationalist.

Of greater importance than the parties working in exile were those small groups operating clandestinely inside the country. These were in closer touch with the mood of the people and knew the realities of the situation better than those living abroad, who were subject to the familiar exiles' syndrome. By 1961, many of these political activists, operating in cultural associations, co-operatives or student groups, had heard of the existence of the nationalist parties and left for Southern Rhodesia, Nyasaland and Tanganyika wishing to join. They soon pressed for the creation of a united movement.

This need for unity was apparent to all those who had reflected on earlier defeats, stretching back to the wars of 'pacification'. A single movement was necessary if the efforts of all the people were to be directed towards the overthrow of Portuguese colonialism, and it seemed that anything less than that would be doomed to failure.

There existed a climate of mistrust amongst these early parties, as they had been heavily infiltrated by the Portuguese secret police. Adelino Gwambe, President of UDENAMO, had been a self-confessed former member of PIDE, sent to spy on workers and exiles in Rhodesia. Many believed that he continued to operate as such.[1] In October 1961, the Portuguese consulate in Tanganyika was closed, accused of running a spy centre. Three Africans in high places within MANU and UDENAMO were revealed to be linked with the centre.[2] This climate of mistrust inside the proto-nationalist parties served only to reinforce the need to form a new united nationalist movement.

With the arrival of Tanganyikan independence in 1961, all three proto-nationalist parties moved their headquarters to this first independent African country bordering on Mozambique. Frelimo was indeed fortunate that one of Africa's great statesmen, Julius Nyerere, was to become the President of that country. His support throughout the whole course of the nationalist struggle was to prove invaluable. With Tanganyika now the base for all the Mozambican movements, Nyerere was in a useful position to urge the formation of a genuine nationalist front. The problem, however, was to find someone capable of leading this initially somewhat fragile coalition of forces. It was doubtful whether members of one of the proto-nationalist parties would be prepared to accept the leadership of a member of another party. In fact the future leader, Eduardo Mondlane, was not to be associated with any of these parties.

Mondlane was born in Gaza, the home of Gungunyana, and had studied at the Protestant mission school in Cambine, Inhambane Province.[3] The school was situated next to the *latifundio* estate of Senhor Manuel Rocha (mentioned in an earlier chapter). There was plenty of opportunity for the young Eduardo to examine at first hand the workings of the colonial system, both the labour migration to South Africa and the forced labour and labour tenancy mechanisms operating inside Mozambique. Later he continued his studies in South Africa at a time when the Congress Youth League was blossoming, and on his return to Mozambique helped to form the Nucleus of Mozambican Secondary Students. (This group, as we have seen, was one of the first real attempts to organise people irrespective of their tribe or region of origin.) Mondlane went on to study briefly in Portugal but soon obtained a scholarship to the United States. He later became a university lecturer before being offered a position at the United Nations.

Given his successes internationally, the Portuguese government made several attempts to attract him back to work for the state, thus hoping to provide a cosmetic lift to their colonial image. Although he refused all these offers, he did take advantage of his UN diplomatic immunity to return home in 1961. News of his achievements had already filtered back to Mozambique, and many made efforts to see him. The denial of education to blacks and keeping it as the preserve of the settlers helped to create a sense of dependence amongst Africans and a concomitant lack of confidence in their ability to achieve anything alone. If the national struggle was really to be waged in earnest, then this mental barrier would have to be overcome. According to those present at the time of Mondlane's visit, both his own example and the message he was able to convey in his speeches helped in this respect.[4] Harassed by the secret police and prevented from discussing politics openly, he still managed to convey to people that they should prepare for the impending struggle. He had won himself a reputation as an advocate of unity both by forming NESAM in 1949, and later, by refusing to join any of the proto-nationalist parties given their regionalist biases. Mondlane thus provided a figurehead around which the united Mozambican independence movement could be built.

The formation of Frelimo

On 25 June 1962, as a result of the increasing pressures building up both internally and externally, the Front for the Liberation of Mozambique (Frelimo) was founded. The first Congress, held in September of that year, was attended by eighty delegates and five hundred observers, and Mondlane was elected President. The event marked a qualitative leap in the long history of resistance to colonial rule. People from the north, centre and south of the country were present. Peasants, teachers, ministers of religion, manual workers and office workers, students and chiefs all met together to discuss the common theme of independence.

Frelimo was a 'front' in two senses. Firstly, it was the product of the unification of the three proto-nationalist parties. Secondly, and of greater importance, it was an alliance of different classes: workers, peasants and the petty bourgeoisie, although the interests of these classes obviously varied and at a future stage were to come into conflict. Frelimo's platform for creating unity was quite simple: opposition to colonialism and the demand for national independence. Such a stand was sufficient to bring the various classes and parties together within the front, but unity had still to be made concrete and tangible. The first Congress laid down only the broadest outline of an economic policy for an independent Mozambique – namely, the ending of all colonial and foreign economic domination.

In fact no consensus could have been reached at this early stage of the struggle for independence as the task of maintaining unity with any more specific programme would have been impossible. In this, Frelimo was little different from African nationalist movements all over the continent. Indeed, it seems likely that if the armed struggle had not occurred, permitting as it did the active participation of the people and the development within the front of a hard core of cadres committed to socialism, independent Mozambique would not have been any different from the rest of neocolonial Africa.

All the proto-nationalist movements had structures largely based on those of the independence parties in the British territories. This heritage was passed on to the newly formed Frelimo. The front was organised on the following levels: nation, province, district, area (locality) and cell.[5] Each cell was to have a secretariat, and each province, district and area an assembly electing an executive committee. Congress was the supreme organ at the national level, electing a National Council which in its turn elected a Central Committee. Executive committees at every level were responsible to their respective superior organs for the carrying out of resolutions and political directives.

The crucial problem associated with this structure was that Frelimo had to achieve goals significantly different from those of the nationalist movements in the British colonies, where that structure originated. Frelimo eventually had to fight an armed struggle in a protracted people's war. The British committee system, with its chairmen and absence of grassroots participatory democracy was soon to prove inadequate for this task.

Democratic centralism was adopted as a guiding principle, and this certainly helped in creating an effective unity within the movement. Work methods and more general orientations were also clearly stipulated: a democratic and collective spirit, unity in action, criticism and self-criticism, and mutual help. The eventual success of Frelimo in making a revolution owes a great deal to the emphasis always placed on these principles. Those within the leadership either incapable of or unwilling to make the changes necessary to accompany the rapid transformation in the movement's ideology often exposed themselves by their unwillingness to follow these methods of work. Effectively, the latter acted as a measure of how far the movement's ideology had been absorbed by each member. Much of the credit for maintaining the early unity among such an ethnically, ideologically and educationally heterogeneous group must go to Mondlane.

The debate over strategy

As the independence struggle progressed, a series of critically important decisions had to be taken. Was there to be an armed struggle or only peaceful protest? If the former, then what kind of military strategy should be adopted? If it was to be a protracted war with the development of whole areas under Frelimo's control, how were these to be organised and administered? The first Congress programme could not provide the answers to these and other problems that the movement as a whole would sooner or later have to face. These issues were resolved only after a painful but necessary period of internal crisis. But the programme of the first Congress did create the conditions enabling the independence struggle to be set on course. It established the basis for unity, and that was its achievement.

At the Congress the option of an armed confrontation with the colonial power had been left open. Opposing views were held within the leadership.[6] Some expected independence to come as a result of international pressure on the colonial power, and argued against a military confrontation. Others pointed out that the evidence would seem to go against this hypothesis. They cited in particular the massacre of hundreds of unarmed civilians at Mueda in Cabo Delgado Province. For many this event heralded the end to all hope of peaceful change. Some still remained unconvinced or were opposed to armed struggle for other reasons, but Portugal's military preparations showed clearly that there was no intention of decolonising. A vast reorganisation and strengthening of the administration's military and intelligence systems took place. The secret police, PIDE, created new specialised sections based on the experience of the French in Algeria. A Centre for the Co-ordination and Centralisation of Information was established, along with a Psycho-Social Action unit. Within a year of the start of the Angolan anti-colonial uprising in 1961, Portuguese military forces in Mozambique were increased from 3 000 to 12 000. The military budget for educational and psycho-social work rose by an incredible 2 000 per cent in 1961 over the previous year.[7] This was to be doubled again in 1962. New riot police units and a special civil volunteer force were organised. Displays of napalm bombing, intended to intimidate the population, were staged in front of large crowds.[8] A tough new governor was appointed with both civilian and military powers. Regulations were altered to permit the wholesale purchase of arms by Europeans. Property owners were issued with printed 'anti-sabotage' instructions and ordered to collaborate in defence measures.[9] Immediately after the formation of Frelimo, thousands were arrested, imprisoned and killed for carrying the movement's card or being sympathisers.[10] In October 1962, a top secret circular was sent out to the District Administrators telling them to establish an information network.[11] It suggested the use of traders, hunters, farmers, *capatazes*, people in public services, chiefs and the Catholic missions.

All offers of negotiation with the Portuguese government were refused, and there remained very little room for doubt about the colonial power's intentions. Frelimo thus made preparations for the ensuing military confrontation. Groups had been sent for training in Algeria soon after the first Congress, but armed struggle was not actually launched until September 1964. In the meantime, 'those Mozambicans who were not psychologically prepared for an armed struggle (and who were a majority of the founding members of Frelimo) deserted the organisation'.[12] Expulsions and desertions from the leadership were frequent, and this reflected the difficulties of exile politics. Once the fighting began there was less time for mutual recriminations, and all were then implicated in the membership of a movement using arms to defeat the government.

Some of those who left both before and after the war began went on to form or join one or other of the multitude of tiny Mozambican exile movements. These were to have only nuisance value to Frelimo in the nationalist war. Most of the energy of these groups was directed towards making hostile criticisms of Frelimo rather than fighting against the colonial government. These groups never had a base inside the country, and only COREMO, the Mozambique Revolutionary Committee, was ever to put even a handful of guerrillas in the field.[13] Many of those who left had been members of the three original proto-nationalist movements and remained unable to make the necessary transition from exile politics. As Machel later recorded:

> These elements had lived for a long time outside of Mozambique without direct contact or real knowledge of the existing situation. Their political experience was acquired in close association with nationalist organisations of Rhodesia, Malawi, Zambia, Tanganyika and Kenya – organisations which through demonstrations, strikes, and other non-violent action created a situation which led the colonial power to negotiations resulting in an initial phase of internal autonomy and ultimately independence.
>
> These elements confused the situation of a developed colonial power like Great Britain with the situation in Portugal, an under-developed, non-industrialised country with the status of a semi-colony. They ignored the distinction between a bourgeois democracy – where, after all, national and public opinion play a role, where issues can be seriously raised in parliament – and a fascist country where censorship and political repression prevent any display of opposition.[14]

However, the movement readily agreed that it turned to an armed solution only after diplomacy had failed.[15]

Among those prepared to take up weapons, a fierce debate developed over the form which the armed struggle should take. Three different lines emerged. The first propagated the idea of a putsch in the capital, and thought that it could be started by as few as fifty men.[16] But against this it was argued that only a tiny proportion of the population lived in the city and colonial control was there at its strongest. An uprising in the Angolan capital of Luanda, in February 1961, had been easily crushed.

A second group proposed a general armed insurrection in which the people would be encouraged to take up whatever arms were available in an all-out assault on the settlers, with guerrilla soldiers having only a minor role. This spontaneous insurrection would bring independence rapidly, so it was argued, because of the favourable international situation. Opponents pointed out that it was a gross fallacy to think that the colonial army would flee after a few shots: this was a serious underestimation of the enemy's strength. Again, the Angolan experience proved illuminating. The other nationalist party in that country, the UPA (Union of Angolan Peoples), headed by Holden Roberto, had encouraged just such a spontaneous insurrection. Tens of thousands had been killed and hundreds of thousands made refugees, and yet nothing had been achieved. The colonial resolve had remained firm, and Portugal's Western allies had prevented the implementation of effective international action following the massacres carried out by troops and settlers. One of the most serious implications of this strategy concerned the movement's definition of the enemy, always the central political question. An attack on the settlers would mean a racial war, in which the enemy was defined by the colour of his or her skin. This was fiercely opposed by those who saw the colonial system rather than the whites as the oppressive force.

A third group believed that guerrilla warfare was the only possible way to win independence in the face of the total intransigence of the colonial power. Those who had trained in Algeria, including Samora Machel and Alberto Chipande, had digested the lessons of that bitter struggle, and others had read and studied the classics of peoples' warfare by Mao Tse-tung and General Giap (of Vietnam).[17]

Mobilising the people and preparing for a protracted guerrilla struggle appeared to them to be the only possible strategy within the Mozambican context. Digesting the experience of other armed struggles was obviously important, though, as Paulo Freire has observed, 'Experiments cannot be transplanted; they must be reinvented.'[18]

There was no conclusive end to the debate before the fighting actually started, though both those who rejected any form of armed struggle and those proposing one or other of the rapid military solutions did share one common perspective. They did not want the organised mass of the people to be the principal force in the struggle, for if this were to happen then perhaps the people would require too large a voice in the government of an independent Mozambique. In the event it soon became clear that only one strategy could hope to succeed, though it would require intensive preparation.

Notes

1 R. H. Chilcote, *Portuguese Africa*, Englewood Cliffs, N.J., 1967, p. 121.

2 A. Ehnmark and P. Wastberg, *Angola and Mozambique: the Case against Portugal*, Roy Publications, 1963, p. 159.

3 For biographies of Frelimo's first leader, see Pan Af, *Eduardo Mondlane*, London, 1972; J. A. Marcum, 'A Martyr for Mozambique', *Africa Report*, xiv, 3 and 4, March–April 1969. A concise autobiography may be found in *Emerging Nationalism in Portuguese Africa Documents*, R. H. Chilcote (ed.), 1972, pp. 411–14.

4 Interview with Sansão Mutemba, Maputo, June 1976. (See Chapter 8, note 13.)

5 See Frelimo, *Documentos Base da Frelimo*, 1977.

6 See *Mozambique Revolution*, 51, April–June 1972, for an exposition of these views.

7 Região Militar de Moçambique, Quartel General, 2ª Repartição, 3ª Secção, *Acção Educativa e Psicosocial do Exército em Moçambique. Relatório dos Activadades em 1961*, Lourenço Marques, 1962, p. 25.

8 *Christian Science Monitor*, 8 May 1961.

9 *Observer*, 2 July 1961.

10 *Mozambique Revolution*, 15, Feb. 1965.

11 Província de Moçambique, Serviço de Acção Psicosocial, *Círcula Muito Secreto No. 404/A/3, Porto Amélia, 29 de Outubro 1962*. Archive of the District Administration of Namuno, Cabo Delgado.

12 *Mozambique Revolution*, 43, April–June 1970. The phrase in parentheses was included in the original text.

13 R. Gibson, *African Liberation Movements*, Oxford, 1972, p. 288.

14 S. Machel, *O Processo da Revolução Democrática Popular Em Moçambique*.

15 *Boletim Nacional*, 13, Oct. 1964.

16 Interview with Samora Machel in *Tempo*, 200, 21 July 1974.

17 See A. de Bragança, 'La Longue Marche de Samora', *Afrique-Asie*, 18 April–1 May, 1977, for the influence of their thinking on Samora Machel.

18 P. Freire, *Pedagogy in Process: the Letters to Guinea-Bissau*, London, 1978, p. 9.

10 The war begins

The date 25 September 1964 saw the opening of the armed struggle, and Frelimo was initially overwhelmed by the chain of events it had unleashed. The original idea was to have a widespread uprising, and cadres were despatched to seven of the nine provinces, covering the south, centre and north of the country.[1] The South African, Southern Rhodesian and British police (operating in Swaziland) clamped down on the Mozambican nationalists, making the supply of weapons to the south extremely difficult. Then, only three months after the start of the war, most of the southern underground network was uncovered and dismantled, with 1 500 Frelimo sympathisers (including many workers and students) being arrested. In the centre of the country the movement fared no better. Guerrilla units started operating in Tete and Zambezia provinces, but by the end of the year these fronts were forced to close. It had been thought in 1964, with the coming of independence in both Malawi and Zambia, that access would be granted to the Mozambican forces, but this was not to be. Zambian independence was still being consolidated, and the government of Hastings Banda in Malawi was openly collaborating with the Portuguese authorities.[2] The implications of neocolonialism were brought home to the Mozambican nationalists, and a few drew the relevant conclusions. With supplies unable to get through, there was no alternative but to halt all military operations in this region also. The following year the Unilateral Declaration of Independence by the white settlers in Rhodesia made the problem of access even more difficult, ending as it did all hopes of a friendly nationalist party coming to power.

By 1965, the war was continuing only in the north, in Cabo Delgado and Niassa provinces, bordering on Tanzania. What kind of war this was to be, and how long it was to last were dictated by the final setback. In 1965, Salazar was forced to take action over the precarious state of the sub-metropolitan economy. Because he was faced with three wars – in Angola, Guinea and Mozambique – some of the nationalists felt that financial considerations would force an early capitulation. They had not analysed the situation sufficiently to realise that another option existed. Salazar opened the doors to foreign capital, allowing a 100-per-cent repatriation of profits. This was the single most important transformation in the political economy in this final period. Military co-operation with the Portuguese by the North Atlantic Treaty Organisation, South Africa and Rhodesia increased, and all hopes of an early victory faded. Those who had looked to the United Nations to bring an early end to the war were also disappointed. Portugal had long expressed its secret contempt for the UN. As one author close to the regime announced:

> Should an ancient civilised nation like ours submit to the resolution of
> an assembly dominated by a majority which is Communist and
> Afro-Asian – more or less savage and biassed, and making no secret of
> its antagonism to Portugal?[3]

Although this body would prove useful in the campaign to isolate
Portugal diplomatically, it was incapable of delivering independence to
the nationalists. There was no alternative to the prospect of a long
struggle. Though this was eventually to prove a successful strategy, its
adoption created a whole new series of problems.

The training camps

To engage in a struggle of this nature there were many preparations to be
made. It meant that Frelimo

> needed a sound and consistent programme and this presupposed both
> a detailed study of the country and of the control established by the
> enemy and at the same time, a survey of the political and social traditions
> of each region.[4]

In the first Frelimo camp at Bagamoyo, Tanzania, endless discussions
took place. Each recruit spoke about his personal experience of colonial
oppression and exploitation in his home region, and also of the culture
and traditions of his people.[5] In this way people were able to pool their
knowledge and gain an over-all view of the country and the colonial
system. If guerrillas were to fight in different parts of the country, then
they had to understand and win the support of the local people wherever
they were operating. As one early editorial of the movement's journal
commented: 'Without the support of the people, the fighting
programmes of Frelimo would be condemned to failure.'[6] In a war of this
nature, national unity had to become more than a slogan; men drawn
from many different tribes and regions would have to fight side by side. A
guerrilla fighting far from his family and home had to realise that these
could be defended only if the whole country was free. Thus every effort
had to be made to weld together a truly national army.

When the main training camp at Kongwa, Tanzania, was created in
1965, the instructors were all too aware of the importance of their tasks.
The movement was fortunate in having Samora Machel and Joaquim
Chissano as the instructors in the camp. Samora Machel was a trained
nurse who had worked in Lourenço Marques. A man of exceptional
political and military ability, he was to become future President of the
People's Republic of Mozambique. Joaquim Chissano had been a student
until he entered the nationalist movement. Once again a man of
enormous talent, he was soon appointed secretary to the President. Later
he was placed in charge of security and was made chief Frelimo
representative in Tanzania. After independence he became the first
Foreign Minister. It was in this training camp that Frelimo first

introduced collective production methods, and the army was to be at the forefront of their later implementation in the liberated zones. The seeds of Mozambique's future progressive development strategy were to be found here. But the importance of the camp was more than just this. As Samora Machel later commented: 'When we arrived here in 1964, we came divided, and it was the unity which we managed to obtain here that permitted us to win in Mozambique.'[7]

Political preparations

In the two years before the start of the armed struggle, political preparations were made all over the country. It was above all crucial that the reasons for taking up arms were fully explained before the bullets actually began to fly, otherwise the uprising could degenerate in just the same way as the revolt inspired by Holden Roberto in Angola. Frelimo's aims had to be explained and the people mobilised around its programme. If this movement was to be any different from those preceding it, then it had to establish its roots inside the country and avoid the sterility and isolation of exile politics. But in the early stages, those Mozambicans living in exile provided an easier target for political mobilisation. Mondlane estimated that there were 100 000 Mozambicans per year working on the Rand gold mines, 200 000 Mozambican workers in South African plantations, farms, homes and secondary industries, 150 000 in Northern and Southern Rhodesia, and 100 000 in Tanganyika, Zanzibar and Kenya. He drew the conclusions that: 'We Mozambicans, therefore, have the largest number of people working outside of their national boundaries in the whole of Africa.'[8] His estimate of the number involved appears on the whole to be fairly accurate. According to the official Southern Rhodesian census, the number of Mozambican workers varied between 107 000 in 1961 and 122 600 in 1966.[9] Mondlane's estimate for the number in East Africa, however, appears to be on the low side, as there were 100 000 migrant workers and settlers from Mozambique living in Tanganyika alone.

Many of these migrants and refugees were to join Frelimo, and the constitution made special provision for organising emigrants into proper sections of the movement. These developed first in Tanganyika, then later in Northern Rhodesia, Swaziland and Malawi. However, after the war started, an agreement with the Tanzanian government in 1965 regularised the conditions under which Mozambicans living in the country could contribute to or partake in the nationalist struggle. This became doubly necessary because after the start of the fighting many more refugees appeared. They could either go back to Mozambique, join the liberation army and be trained outside Mozambique, be full-time Frelimo staff members, settle in one of the Mozambican refugee camps or apply to become citizens of Tanzania contributing to the independence struggle through TANU. It was agreed that Frelimo would no longer carry out political mobilisation among the emigrants living in Tanzania, and all branch offices were closed. This marked an important change of emphasis from outside to inside Mozambique, and the movement grew in strength as a result. It was far more important to establish branches of Frelimo inside the country. Existing co-operatives, mutual aid societies and cultural groups provided the necessary fertile terrain for implanting the movement's structures. It was from among these groups originally that many of the young militants who had fled the country to join the nationalist movement had emerged.

Frelimo propaganda focused on the need for the independence struggle to overcome abuses of human rights and exploitation of the people. One of the movement's early publications complained about the occupation of the most fertile land by the colonialists, and explained its effects: 'Deprived of all means of gaining a living we are obliged to go to work in a factory, commercial enterprise, a white's house or some other area where our labour makes more money, and in comparison they pay us a miserable salary each month.'[10] Appeals were made to all the strata of society that were affected by this same discrimination. This particular text continues: 'good farmers are exploited on the plantations because they do not have a farm or land, artists because they do not have money to buy materials or get a small office, clerks because they don't have money to take a course in book-keeping or whatever else they want, police because they don't go to school and take a colonial course, etc., etc.' However, the decisive political work took place in the rural zones among the peasantry. These areas were relatively free from the administration's control, and in the early phase every effort was made to win over the traditional chiefs. However much the authority of the chiefs had been weakened by the colonial power, they still held the allegiance of the people. For the movement to go against both colonial and traditional authorities at the same time, before it had established its own credibility and claim to popular allegiance, would have been political suicide. To win the support of the chief was to ensure the support of his people. Some religious authorities, too, had the allegiance of the people and could use their influence in support of the nationalist cause.

Frelimo cadres frequently adopted a very imaginative approach. One militant involved in the earliest mobilisation work was Adelino Siculava, a Makonde from Mueda, in Cabo Delgado. At the time he was recruited by Frelimo, he worked overseeing fishing boats in the small coastal town of Mocimba da Praia.[11] He was given the task of mobilising the people of that town, and explained the difficulty of his assignment:

> Even I didn't know what I was doing. There were two main problems, an inter-tribal dispute between the Mwanes (of the coast) and the Makonde, and religious differences because the Mwanes are Mohammedan.

He soon found a solution to the problem as he went on to reveal: 'To win the confidence of the Mwane I adopted their religion, previously I was a Christian.' Slowly he began to gain the confidence of the town's religious leaders and then began to politicise them. Through them the politicisation permeated downwards. Before long most of the people in the town had been won over. Not only did he alter his religion to facilitate his political work, as he went on to explain:

I adopted the disguise of a carpenter. Thus I could move freely around, see the Portuguese and talk to the people whilst doing my work. This gave me the opportunity to get to know about everything in Mocimba da Praia, particularly the enemy's fortifications.

Early organisation

Many of the chiefs became members of Frelimo in those early days. As the enemy was forced out of certain parts of the countryside, the movement had to replace the political and administrative structure, and the traditional leaders were best equipped, at this stage, to provide an alternative. Although the first Congress had carefully laid out the various tiers of the movement's structure, this could not possibly begin to function in the early stages. In the first phase, a group of people tended to gather around a guerrilla unit for protection after being forced by the activities of the colonial army to flee from their villages. People in these new war zones would initially be organised by the military. Later, power would be handed over to a person responsible for organising the civilian population, known as the chairman. It was no accident that the English word 'chairman' was employed; it was an inheritance from the structure of the nationalist parties in the British colonies. In many cases the chief became the chairman and ruled without a committee, having only an assistant. In a petition presented to the UN, the movement freely admitted that in the liberated areas it left the people to manage their own affairs.[12] Effectively, this meant that in the earliest liberated zones the colonial power had been removed only to be replaced by the old traditional authorities. The tasks of the chairmen included the distribution of clothing arriving from the exterior, organising food contributions for the combatants and setting up the village militias.

All the political structures of Frelimo at this time were the responsibility of the Department of Interior Organisation (DOI). It took several years before a fully operational hierarchy linking the grassroots with the leadership could be established. The organisation of a district committee could not take place until sufficient locality committees had been set up in an area and effective lines of communication established between them. Members of the district committee were then elected by the lower organs. However, the pace at which these political structures were set up varied considerably from one area to another, density of population and the local state of the war being the most important determinants. In eastern Niassa, for example, the proper functioning of structures from base to district level began only in 1968.

The guerrillas were organised within an entirely separate structure, the Department of Defence. But the DOI was the senior partner, and following the 'hallowed' British tradition, the military wing was not intended to have a political role of any kind. However, once it became clear that the colonial power was determined to hold on and the front was faced with fighting a protracted people's war, the idea of a politically impotent guerrilla force grew more and more absurd. This contradiction became increasingly apparent as time went on, but there was to be stiff opposition to any encroachment by the 'military' on the preserve of the 'political' cadres inside the liberated zones.

Armed struggle and production

The armed uprising in Angola in 1961 shocked the Salazar government into making hasty and belated legislative changes. The forced cultivation of cotton and forced labour were abolished in law; forced labour continued in practice, however, for some time.[13] Fear of the spread of armed resistance to all the Portuguese colonies was clearly a major incentive to implement those belated paper reforms, and it was only the beginning of the war inside Mozambique, in September 1964, which made the authorities comply more readily with the law.

The immediate effect of Frelimo's military actions was the disappearance of colonial authority in certain rural areas, and with it the *palmatória* and the predatory activities of the *cepaios* who frequently stole crops and livestock, and abused the local women. The dreaded *imposto* (tax on all adult males) was abolished, and straight away the people began to see some benefits from the war. Frelimo's army (later called the FPLM – Popular Forces for the Liberation of Mozambique) aimed to contrast sharply with the *cepaios* in its behaviour towards the population. A standing order given to all militants was this: 'Respect the people, help the people, defend the people.'[14] People's war demands the closest relationship between the guerrillas and the population in a symbiosis of mutual support. Abuses of power by the guerrillas would quickly result in the betrayal to the colonial army. Although there were inevitably exceptions to this rule, the very success of the movement in winning substantial support would seem to verify that the code was broadly adhered to.

Between production and the armed struggle there existed an intimate and reciprocal relationship, but this relationship was only developed slowly and unevenly and not without setbacks. Though they shared many similar problems, significant differences existed between the liberated zones of Cabo Delgado and Niassa. The reasons for this are not apparent from the available literature, but by interviewing those who actively participated in the life of the liberated zones, it has been possible to uncover them.

Niassa

This province covers 129 056 square kilometres, just under one-fifth of the total surface area of Mozambique. With a population in 1970 of 285 329 (3.5 per cent of the total population) it had the lowest density of inhabitants in the whole country, 2.2 per square kilometre.[15] This was substantially the result of mass migrations to escape the labour-repressive policies, which were probably at their zenith in the north. The land is not fertile, and there are relatively few rivers; as a result, agricultural output was the lowest in the country. Production for the market was carried out only in certain specific and closely controlled areas within the province. These were the western lakeside region and the south, where the majority of the population was to be found. Liberated areas, therefore, had to be set up in the interior of the province where there was a sparse population, poor soil and little water. The sheer problems of survival were enormous.

In addition to the difficult natural conditions, there were also problems of a political nature. Early mobilisation work had not always been carried out satisfactorily. Because of this, as well as a general fear of fighting, there was an exodus to the neighbouring territories once the armed struggle began. Thousands fled across the border, and even amongst those who stayed, because of deficiencies in the political work there persisted an illusion that victory would come rapidly and no attempt was made to cultivate the fields.

In the first two years of the war, guerrillas entering Niassa carried out sabotage operations, destroyed bridges, interrupted commerce and laid ambushes. Their weapons were unsophisticated: Mausers with only five-round magazines; the Mati, firing thirty rounds but with a short range; grenades, mines and a few machine guns. However, these activities were sufficient to restrict the movement of the colonial army and create the conditions for the people to leave the government-controlled areas and move to the Frelimo bases. Hunger was widespread. The people, first expecting a quick victory and later imagining that everything would come from Tanzania, did not continue their work in the normal agricultural cycle.

The story of Asani Ali helps convey the flavour of this early period:

I first became aware of Frelimo whilst I was working for the Administration in Vila Cabral, the provincial capital. I was then earning 200 escudos a month (about seven U.S. dollars). One day I overheard the *patrão* (the boss) say that fighting had begun in the west.[16]

Soon after hearing this he returned to his home in Mutaca. On his arrival he found that his father already knew of the struggle, even though the guerrillas had not yet entered the district. His father, who was a tax collector, soon left to tell people from a neighbouring area to flee to Frelimo, but the authorities heard of this and he was imprisoned. Asani then went to the Administrator: 'I told them that if my father died no-one would pay their taxes.' The Administrator was sufficiently impressed by this to release the old man.

Together we returned to our village but left shortly afterwards to find Frelimo. We eventually met up with the guerrillas who took us to a place in the bush where there were others like ourselves. Soon afterwards Portuguese troops arrived at our old village, but Frelimo had laid an ambush and they destroyed four vehicles carrying the soldiers.

The crops had been left in the fields, and after the rains the people returned with the guerrillas to take in the harvest. But others were not so fortunate. Destruction of crops in reprisals against the front's sympathisers was widespread.[17]

Two observations may be made on this early phase. First, the people did not cultivate when they entered the bush; rather, they expected their daily necessities to be supplied from Tanzania. This was clearly impossible because of Frelimo's limited financial resources and the huge distances involved. Moreover, if supplies were to be brought in, armaments had priority, and food had to go primarily to the orphans and those guerrillas in bases that could not receive food from the people. Secondly, Frelimo cadres in this province did not prepare the people for the necessities of a protracted struggle which would demand fighting on the economic as well as the military front. Production was not yet seen as an integral part of the struggle. Famine and great hardship were widespread in the first few years, with many of the people and guerrillas dying of hunger. It was a bitter lesson. They were obliged to live off the land as best they could, collecting wild fruit, hunting and fishing.

The liberated areas were subjected to continuous Portuguese attack, and houses and *machambas* were frequently burnt down. Proper housing was virtually impossible to construct, because people had to be prepared to move hurriedly when threatened by the enemy presence. The makeshift *palhotas* (huts) were extremely vulnerable in the rainy season, which exacted a heavy toll. Shortage of clothing was another serious problem, and even the guerrillas suffered from a lack of boots and uniforms. Very little soap, salt or sugar arrived from Tanzania, and local production could not furnish these basic commodities. There were no schools in many areas, but at least in every guerrilla base there was a health post. Finally, for the guerrillas the low population density meant difficulties with transportation. There were fewer people available to help carry supplies. The liberated zones were slow to develop in Niassa and as one commander fighting in this zone put it: 'The liberation of an area signified an increase of suffering'.[18]

In the front line of the struggle, armed groups penetrated deep into enemy territory, keeping their presence secret and collecting whatever information they could. As the war escalated, people were somewhat belatedly moved into *aldeamentos* (strategic hamlets), similar to those established by the British in Malaya and the United States in Vietnam. The government's aim was to try and separate the people from the guerrillas. Their *machambas* were frequently a long way from their homes, and when they went to the fields they had to carry identity cards. As control of the population intensified, it became increasingly difficult to get supplies to the guerrillas, and food became an ever-scarcer commodity. Nevertheless, however many difficulties there were on the Niassa front, stemming from inadequate political preparation, low population density as a result of migrations, and the relatively inhospitable natural environment, there were still some positive results for the nationalist movement. The shared suffering appears to have promoted a firm bond between the people and the guerrillas. Later, when the confrontation arose between the 'traditional' authorities and the new political structures being proposed (in particular by the commanders), that bond was to prove of great importance to the eventual victors.

Frelimo's leaders, realising the seriousness of the situation, took rapid measures to correct its earlier shortcomings. At the important Central Committee meeting of 1966, the order of the day was sent out: 'Develop production.'[19] Slowly the people themselves had begun to study the problem of food shortages and had come to the conclusion that they had to be self-sufficient. Under Frelimo's guidance, they began to cultivate their *machambas* once again. This was organised on the basis of individual families working their own fields. These were widely dispersed and thus presented more difficult targets for enemy bombers. But given all the difficulties, it proved impossible for Frelimo to establish a trading network within the province. Three commercial posts were set up on the Tanzanian border to serve the liberated zones throughout the province. However, there was very little surplus produced with which to trade, in marked contrast to the situation in Cabo Delgado where a large surplus was produced, and the whole question of exchange in the Frelimo shops was to play a decisive role in the internal crisis of the movement.

Cabo Delgado

Cabo Delgado had a population of 546 113 according to the 1970 census. The province covers an area of 82 625 square kilometres. Density of the population (6.6 per square kilometre), although still low in comparison with other provinces in the country, was considerably higher than in Niassa. With an urban population of only 10 070, this province, like Niassa, was overwhelmingly rural: 80 per cent of the active population were non-salaried subsistence cultivators. There was not only a greater population density than in Niassa, but also more fertile terrain and high agricultural production. Whereas in Niassa's liberated zones the main problems facing the movement stemmed from the vastness of the province and scarcity of the population, in Cabo Delgado the problems stemmed from the greater intensity of the war. It was also here that the decisive political battle concerning the ideological orientation of the nationalist movement was to be fought. The production of a relatively large agricultural surplus and the substantial numbers living in the liberated zones brought sharply into focus the questions of how production was to be organised and the surplus distributed, as well as of how the people were to organise themselves politically.

Mobilisation had been more thorough in this province. The people had not needed as much convincing of the need to stay and fight. In the wake of the Mueda massacre, many people believed that the only remaining course of action was to take up arms. Therefore, when Frelimo first arrived in the province, people flocked to the bush to give their support. From the very beginning people began producing basic foods such as maize, cassava, millet, beans and groundnuts. With the removal of forced cultivation of cash-crops, people began to grow produce of more immediate benefit to themselves, which naturally stimulated production. Frelimo backed up its exhortations to produce with the provision of hoes and *pangas* (large knives). Slowly, new social methods of production were introduced, based on various forms of collective organisation.

The social organisation of production took different forms within the liberated areas. In some places people worked their own fields and gave a part of the produce to the guerrillas, whilst in others villagers worked one *machamba* co-operatively to produce a surplus for the army and for other groups unable to produce for themselves. In some areas production was organised collectively, though, as we shall see, 'collective' production in this early phase might not be what its name would imply. The chairman, who was in over-all charge of all aspects of the civilian population's life in the liberated zones, often gave the name 'co-operative' to a system of private enterprise where the peasants were working collectively for the benefit of the chairman's own pocket. Illiteracy could also be a problem. Book-keeping is an essential ingredient of co-operative production, and the number of days worked by individuals has to be carefully recorded. With such high levels of illiteracy, this was a serious handicap to the spreading of the co-operative system, and it was to take some time before Frelimo's educational programme was sufficiently developed to make this feasible on a broad scale.

Production of a surplus was essential not only to supply the army and areas where the war interrupted cultivation, but also to furnish exports. These were necessary to pay for the import of items which could not be produced inside the country. By 1966, Frelimo had already begun to export certain products. This involved large numbers of people carrying heavy loads over long distances up to the Tanzanian border. Attempts were made not only to increase exports but also to reduce imports. Salt began to be extracted in the north-east, and traditional crafts were encouraged to satisfy the immediate needs for agricultural and household implements. Research was carried out in numerous fields to promote import substitution. One experiment concerned ways in which soap could be made from oil, extracted from seeds. Nevertheless, it was still the case that everyday products had to be imported in carefully limited quantities, as foreign aid was by no means abundant. Shops were established inside the liberated zones as a way of distributing imported items in exchange for the surplus produced by the peasantry.

On the whole, by 1968, the material situation in Frelimo's liberated zones in both Niassa and Cabo Delgado had considerably improved, to the extent that Mondlane was able to report:

> not all the problems of organisation and administration have yet been solved, but in spite of difficulties and occasional shortages, conditions in the liberated areas are now such that the flow of refugees over the border has not only ceased but been reversed.[20]

Reports of the international refugee authorities confirmed this. According to the 1967 Tanzanian census, of the 240 000 foreign citizens in the country, 61 000 were Mozambicans.[21] This was not significantly higher than the 1963 estimates.

The consolidation of the Frelimo zones became an urgent necessity, as these provided the best evidence of success for the nationalists. But their mere existence was not alone to be sufficient, as Mondlane was well aware. He wrote:

> Frelimo faces a large and challenging task in proving to the people that a better life really is both possible and worth struggling for. This can be done only by supplying concrete evidence, through the provision in the liberated areas of schools, health centres, and the promotion of trade, internal and external.[22]

Although the worst period of material shortages was over, a new and potentially more menacing threat remained, as the battle lines began to form between the revolutionaries and those opposed to fundamental structural reform. The seeds of this same conflict were sown early on among the Mozambican students studying at the Frelimo school in Dar-es-Salaam, and it is to the field of education that we now turn our attention.

Education

The movement summarised its aims after the first Congress as consolidation and mobilisation; preparation for war; education and diplomacy. Given the policy of deliberate neglect by the colonial government of all but the most rudimentary education for Africans, education had to be given a high priority by Frelimo. It was essential for the success of the nationalist movement and for the development of Mozambique. Initially, education was constrained by a shortage of funds and options were dependent on foreign aid. There was no coherent over-all strategy, and educational policy was a matter of piecemeal expediency. The first steps taken by the movement were to send students to the Kurasini International Education Centre (KIEC) in Dar-es-Salaam. This was an organisation supported by the Afro-American Institute. The teachers there had no knowledge of Mozambican realities, and the classes were totally unsuitable for preparing the future cadres of a national liberation movement. Elitist notions and individualist aspirations underlay the ideology of the lessons, and Machel was later to refer to the school as 'a poisoner for our students'.[23] Moreover, there was no political selection of those who wished to be educated. Students graduating from the KIEC would go on to take up scholarships abroad and thus for long periods would be away from Frelimo's direct influence. This naturally presented a potential threat to the movement. It was then decided to set up Frelimo's own secondary school at the Mozambique Institute, but many of the students were dissatisfied with this move as they believed that scholarships for higher education would be easier to obtain from the KIEC. Only countries sympathetic to the national liberation struggle, so it was argued, would recognise the Mozambique Institute qualification. Thus was sown a seed of future antagonism between some of the students and Frelimo.

Many of those coming to study were primarily interested in their own personal advancement. Given the barriers existing inside Mozambique for Africans to continue their education, some saw in Frelimo nothing more than a golden opportunity for further study. A Catholic priest, Father Mateus Gwenjere, a teacher at a mission school on the banks of the Zambezi river, had recruited many of his pupils for Frelimo by promising the certainty of scholarships abroad once they reached Tanzania.[24] In 1967 he fled to Dar-es-Salaam and began teaching at the Institute. Gwenjere was to become the central figure in the ensuing crisis at the Frelimo Secondary School. He encouraged the elitist ideas already present among some of the students, arguing for example that lessons should be given in English and not Portuguese. Portuguese was the language of the coloniser, he said, and scholarships would be easier to obtain if students were fluent in English. He was also evidently anti-white. Gwenjere further proposed that as those receiving education were to become future leaders, their lives should not be put at risk by obliging them to fight inside the country after the completion of their studies. More damaging still, he tried to turn the students against the existing leadership by arguing that scholarships were being refused because leaders were afraid for their positions when highly qualified students returned. This whole approach to education helped provoke the ideological confrontation within the nationalist movement. These educational issues, however, were not only confined to the students in Dar-es-Salaam.

Some of those active during the 1950s in the secondary school students' union, NESAM, went on to study abroad, and in 1961 they founded UNEMO. By 1965 UNEMO's headquarters had been moved to Dar-es-Salaam, and the organisation had branches in Morocco, Western Europe and the United States. Attempts were made to integrate the members of UNEMO more closely into Frelimo and the liberation struggle, as often there was very little contact between them. But the gulf widened between the movement and some of the students abroad, and eventually a discontented caucus based in America began to agitate against Frelimo. They were opposed to any *white* Mozambicans having a place in the liberation struggle, and they blamed Mondlane for this. Using racism, they hoped to discredit the President and the line that he defended. If colour was to be the criterion for identifying the enemy, then the nationalist struggle was merely concerned with replacing whites by blacks within the given system. But if the whole colonial system and its imperialist support were defined as being the real enemy, then the nationalist struggle implied more far-reaching changes. Black racist ideas were in fact a concomitant of the elitist positions associated with neocolonial forms of independence.

By December 1967 events were coming to a head, and Frelimo published a condemnation of these students.[25] One of the principal complaints concerned those who had completed their first degrees and even their masters' degrees, but still insisted on continuing their studies when their participation in the struggle was urgently needed. The American branch of UNEMO published a reply in May 1968.[26] Mondlane was accused of being a traitor, of harassing students who might be his future rivals and of sabotaging the revolution. Thus the same sentiments that had appeared within the Mozambique Institute showed themselves again amongst a certain section of UNEMO. By the close of 1967 many of the leaders had accepted that they were engaged in a protracted struggle, with all that this required of their organisation. Frelimo had to provide the personnel to run the 'state within a state' that was swiftly growing up in the liberated areas. Doctors, agronomists, economists, diplomats and all the other skilled people necessary to operate a social and economic system had to be trained and then put to work in the Frelimo-controlled areas. If the armed struggle was to be a fundamentally political option with far-reaching socio-economic consequences, one of those consequences would have to be the active participation in the war of the movement's intellectuals.

The issue of the students in secondary and higher education was fought out in the exterior, but it was inside the liberated zones that the key developments regarding education were taking place. The first 'bush' schools sprang up in Cabo Delgado in 1965. By 1967, the movement had one hundred schools inside the country catering for about 10 000 children. Towards the end of 1967, ten teachers started work setting up schools in Niassa, and soon 2 000 children were also receiving education there. The beginning of the armed struggle in Niassa had caused a mass exodus of people escaping from the bombing and general hardships, and along the way many children were abandoned. One Frelimo cadre, on his own initiative, collected about twenty-five of these children and early in 1966 took them to Tunduru camp in Tanzania. Originally, this camp had been earmarked as a rehabilitation centre for the wounded, but the *de facto* presence of these children halted this development and instead it became a 'children's camp'. Towards the end of 1966 it was formally placed under the Department of Education and National Culture, and primary school classes then began. First-year classes already existed inside Niassa, but there were very few second- and third-year classes, so children completing their first-year primary school were permitted to attend the Tunduru school. In addition, places were also provided for children of Mozambicans temporarily resident in Tanzania but not living in the refugee camps. Educational work was not solely confined to children; members of the army and adults also took literacy classes.

All these developments inside the liberated zones highlighted the question of whether scarce resources should be used primarily for educating a small number to the highest levels, thus leaving a large, passive, illiterate mass of the peasantry, or whether most effort should be placed on raising the general educational level of the people. As Frelimo saw it:

> The problem which is posed today is whether the progress of our country is the task of the few or whether it must be the result of the efforts of the whole people. The answer which springs from the practice of our liberation struggle is obviously the latter. Without the active and responsible participation of the masses what could the few dozen Frelimo militants have done?'[27]

By the middle of 1968, it was becoming obvious that a reassessment of educational priorities was in order, and the movement's journal reported: 'We must train our youth in our schools and abroad in those fields of knowledge which can be of direct and immediate use in the liberation struggle.'[28]

Notes

1 Interview with Joaquim Chissano, Dar-es-Salaam, April 1972.

2 Interview with Political Commissar Alfredo Wassira, M'temangão, Manica and Sofala Province, 5 May 1975. He was with the first guerrilla group in Zambezia Province. When they were forced to flee back into Malawi, the PIDE, in collaboration with the Malawi government, imprisoned and killed many of them, including a leading political mobiliser, Rui Alberto Mutumul:

3 A. Cortesão, *African Realities and Delusions*, Lisbon, 1962, p. 21.

4 *Mozambique Revolution*, 51, April–June 1972.

5 Conversation with Daniel Mbanze (Vice Minister of the Interior in the early post-Independence period), Dar-es-Salaam, Nov. 1974.

6 *Mozambique Revolution*, 19, June 1965.

7 *Notícias de Beira*, 22 May 1975.

8 E. Mondlane, 'The Crystallisation of a Struggle for Freedom', in Pan Af., *Eduardo Mondlane*, London, 1972, p. 154.

9 UN Economic and Social Council, *Assistance to Mozambique*, *E/5812*, *30/3/1976*, p. 20.

10 *Boletim de Informação*, 10, Aug. 1964.

11 Interview with Adelino Siculava, Political Commissar of Manica Province, Chimoio, 24 April 1975.

12 UN Special Committee on the situation with regard to the implementation of the Declaration of the Granting of Independence to the Colonial Countries and Peoples, *Document A/AC 109/SR419, 17/6/1966*, p. 5.

13 This was verified in many interviews carried out in the former liberated zones.

14 *Mozambique Revolution*, 21, 1965.

15 This is according to the official census statistics. These are to be treated with caution, as they are generally unreliable and certainly do not include people in the liberated zones.

16 Interview with Asani Ali, responsible for Mobilisation and Organisation for the locality at the Frelimo Central Base, Eastern Niassa, 19 July 1976.

17 N. Rocha, *Guerra em Moçambique*, Lisbon, 1969, p. 147. The author was a Portuguese reporter who travelled with the colonial army in Niassa Province.

18 Interview with Jorge Carpinteiro, Commander of an FPLM Company, Marrupa, Niassa Province, 16 July 1976.

19 *Mozambique Revolution*, 27, Oct.–Dec. 1966.

20 E. Mondlane, 'The War in Mozambique', *Venture*, xx, 7, July–Aug. 1968.

21 M. Monsted and P. Walji, *A Demographic Analysis of East Africa*, Uppsala, 1978, p. 146.

22 E. Mondlane, 'The War in Mozambique'.

23 *Tempo*, 200, 21 July 1974.

24 Interviews with Father Miguel Buendia and the Sisters at Murraca Mission (Marima Olmas, Joaquina Neves, Concepcion Vecino and Mother Cesária Gonzales), Murraca, Manica and Sofala Province, March 1975. They estimated that many hundreds of students went from their mission to join Frelimo as a result of Gwenjere's teaching.

25 Frelimo, *Breve recapitulação sobre a Situação dos Estudantes Moçambicanos no Exterior e Sua Inserção na Luta de Libertação Nacional*, Dar-es-Salaam, Dec. 1967.

26 This reply was translated and reprinted in the *Journal of African Historical Studies*, iii, 1, 1970.

27 *Mozambique Revolution*, 51, April–June 1972.

28 *Mozambique Revolution*, 34, April–June 1968.

11 The crisis

By 1967, after overcoming some early setbacks, Frelimo had established a firm foothold in the north of the country. The military threat to the colonial power here and in Guinea Bissau and Angola had already produced significant effects on Portugal itself. Between 1960 and 1968 the Portuguese army more than tripled in size from 60 000 to 200 000 men. This placed a considerable strain on manpower reserves to the extent that national service was increased to a four-year term. The financial burden also grew. Only 25 per cent of the national budget was spent on defence in 1960, whereas eight years later this had risen to 42.4 per cent. In Mozambique, the nationalist struggle was reaching a turning point and the movement was not without its own problems. Tensions and conflicts were mounting, as it slowly became clear that there were irreconcilable differences among the leaders over a wide range of issues. A point was being reached where drastic new decisions would have to be taken if any further progress was to be made. We have seen how the collapse of the southern and central fronts and in particular the new 'open door' policy towards foreign investors had terminated any hope of an early capitulation by the Portuguese. It was against this background that the Central Committee of Frelimo held its second meeting in 1966.

Divided aims

After a lengthy analysis of the war, it was agreed that the movement would have to wage a protracted struggle.[1] For some inside the leadership, this decision had far-reaching implications. A protracted struggle and a people's war were synonymous in their eyes. The people themselves would have to participate fully in the political process as active agents of their own destiny rather than a passive mass carrying out orders emanating from on high. The overthrow of Kwame Nkrumah in Ghana that same year was a poignant reminder of the dangers of attempting a 'revolution' solely from above. Frelimo did not miss the point, and commented at the time:

> fundamentally it is necessary to encourage the people to partake in the political life of the country. Further it is necessary to reject a concept in which the revolution (socialism) is built by an active nucleus of leaders who think, create and give everything and are followed by a passive mass who limit themselves to receiving and executing. This concept is the result of a weak political conscience and expresses a lack of

confidence in the fighting and revolutionary capacity of the people. This is the lesson that recent events in Africa teaches.[2]

This failure to involve the population in politics was not confined simply to Ghana but was an almost universal malaise in Africa.

The Central Committee noted the existence of a conflict between the Department of Defence and the Department of Interior Organisation concerning their respective areas of responsibility. The artificial division between military and civilian members was attacked in the strongest possible manner on the basis that if all the people were to be mobilised to participate in the war, then the guerrillas would have to play an active role in politicisation. The Central Committee meeting formally ended the difference between military and political cadres, as it was argued that an ideology without weapons to defend it would easily be neutralised by any armed group; whereas weapons in the hands of the people who were not conscious of their political responsibilites could launch the country into chaos and anarchy. All were to be integrated in the practice of the principal struggle, which was defined as being the political struggle. At the same time, all were to participate in the politics of the main task, armed combat.

In practice, however, some of the political leaders within the liberated zones refused to implement these decisions. The chairmen of Cabo Delgado, who were members of the Department of Interior Organisation, were opposed to delegating what they saw as 'their' political functions either to the fighters or to the peasants in participatory democratic structures. They wanted the FPLM simply to remain a fighting force, and they themselves refused to participate in military combat and often remained for long periods in the safety of Tanzania. The commanders deeply resented these attitudes. In the day-to-day life of the war, they increasingly appreciated the central importance of their own political role. When Samora Machel became Secretary of the Department of Defence in 1966, after the assassination of its former head, Filipe Samuel Magaia, by Portuguese agents, he was in a good position to reinforce the earlier work of politicisation carried out amongst the guerrillas in the training camps. Through the guerrillas, the peasants were becoming more politically conscious. The chairmen bitterly opposed this process, intensifying the hostility between the Defence Department and the Department of Interior Organisation. In August 1967, cadres in the FPLM met together to review the course of the war, and this provided an opportunity to discuss their political grievances among themselves. The campaign against the line proposed by the chairmen began to be co-ordinated at this time.

In the four years from 1967 to 1970, Frelimo's period of internal crisis produced two opposing positions on almost every issue of importance to the movement. With the development of the war and the formation of liberated zones certain choices had to be made. Attitudes to a number of different issues showed clearly that there existed two opposed conceptions of the nationalist struggle. The major issue was the emergence inside Mozambique of an expanding area of territory free from colonial control. This was the original meaning of a 'liberated area', one where the colonial presence had been removed. However, it is one thing to destroy the old and yet another to find a replacement. Whatever was created by Frelimo in the areas under its control would present an image (however distorted) of the future independent Mozambique. President Mondlane had envisaged a society 'directed towards economic progress, where all Mozambicans will have the same rights, where power will belong to the people'.[3] Nevertheless, in order to attain this goal not one but two enemies would have to be fought. Within the front there existed people with a very different idea of what a future Mozambique should be. Only after the waging of a bitter internal struggle could Mondlane's vision of 'people's power' begin to be realised.

Conflicts centred on the organisation of production and distribution in the liberated zones, the new structures to be created in these areas, the military strategy and tactics to be pursued, the emancipation of women, education and the very definition of the enemy. It was at first by no means clear that the conflicts and differences had actually split the leadership: it was only after the Second Congress, held in 1968, that the existence of the two lines was openly acknowledged by the Front.[4] On the one side were the proponents of a traditional African nationalist 'independence', and on the other those who believed that this would be meaningless unless accompanied by a social revolution. Having to fight a protracted struggle and build up a new society in the liberated zones highlighted these alternatives in an urgent and practical way. Those who wanted independence alone, as a means to establish themselves as a new ruling class within a neocolonial context, opposed those who wanted to create political structures based on 'people's power' and an economy founded on co-operation between mutual owners rather than on the existing system of private enterprise.[5] For the revolutionaries in Frelimo, the basis of the exploitation of the Mozambican workers was that he was paid less than the value he produced for his employer. They were not thinking in terms of white equalling exploiter, and black exploited, though this was the widespread African nationalist view. Rather, colonialism was seen as a system imposed on Mozambique to create a labour force which would work to produce surplus value for the capitalist enterprises whose interest the colonial state represented. A part of the Mozambican labourer's day was spent in producing the cost of his wage: the amount of money necessary to buy food, clothing, shelter, and so on, to enable him to survive and carry on working. The rest of his working day was surplus labour time or work for which the employer did not pay him. This group had adopted the labour theory of value, the central concept in Marx's thinking, which helped them to arrive at a systemic rather than a racial definition of whom they were fighting and what they were fighting for.

It had become patently obvious to the revolutionaries in Frelimo's leadership that the mechanics of this system were operable by blacks and whites alike – within or outside the colonial system. When the armed struggle removed the colonial administration from the liberated areas it did not at the same time replace the private-enterprise system. The chairmen of Cabo Delgado opposed the collectivisation of production and the formation of co-operatives, or more subtly gave the name of 'co-operatives' to the *machambas* where the peasants produced surplus value for the chairman. In 1966, landowners in the liberated zones of Cabo Delgado began employing people to work on their fields. At the end of a month's work on the cashew plantation, a worker would receive a shirt. For carrying a sack of cashew nuts for eight days, to the Rovuma river, a man would be given a piece of cloth. Returning from the Rovuma he would carry cloth to be sold inside the liberated zone, and for this he received a little salt. The chairmen controlled the trading stores, sold the goods at an inflated price and frequently lined their own pockets. People in Cabo Delgado were well aware of what the real price of goods should be. The Makonde spanned the frontier between Mozambique and Tanzania, and before the war there was a regular flow back and forth between the two countries. Many had visited Tanzania, and were aware, for example, that they should not have to work for one month to be able to afford a cheap shirt. On occasions the peasants received less for their produce, such as cashew nuts and honey, than they did from the shopkeepers who operated under the colonial administration. Usually the trading stores would not pay in cash, but in goods such as hoes or cloth, and only give half of the true value of produce the peasants brought to exchange. Not unnaturally

> The questions began then to be posed – we are fighting against whom? To establish what? The soldiers were giving their lives, the people were making sacrifices, they were carrying heavy loads, for what? Precisely what was the object of the struggle?[6]

People soon began to ask why they should make sacrifices if members of the liberation movement and their own people continued to exploit them. This exploitation was no abstract concept, as the peasants knew how much they should be receiving for their produce from the chairman. In a very real sense, then, many of the commanders in the Department of Defence, and more slowly the peasants themselves, began to argue not only that colonialism was a system to ensure the exploitation of man, but also that ending colonialism *per se* was no guarantee of abolishing exploitation. The revolutionaries within Frelimo argued that there was no point in the people spilling their blood and undergoing the most arduous living conditions if they would be no better off at the end of it all.

Intrinsically linked with this issue was the debate over the definition of the enemy. The revolutionaries argued that the enemy was a system and not a race, as exploitation has no colour, but others declared that the fight was against the whites, and so glossed over their own economic activities in the liberated zones. Racism also proved a useful weapon for attacking the revolutionary line advocated by Mondlane and dos Santos, among others. Both were slandered for having white wives, and the non-blacks within the movement were accused of being agents of imperialism. The level of militancy and patriotism was seen to be 'a function of skin pigmentation'.[7] Lazaro Kavandame, the head of the Department of Interior Organisation in Cabo Delgado (in his capacity as Secretary of the Province), and the chairmen also used tribalism to try and mobilise support, saying that the leaders all came from the south, and the Makonde tribe of Cabo Delgado was not represented in the leadership of the movement. Using his position as head of the Province, Kavandame had built up his power base by appointing chairmen only from within his own tribe.

In order to replace the Portuguese administration the chairmen propounded a mixture of traditional authority and the recreation of the old colonial structures, but with themselves as the administrators. Soon after the First Congress this group formed a Council of Elders which they tried to impose as a superior organ of the Central Committee, with the aim of safeguarding the power of the chiefs and elders. In the early stages, the support of the chiefs was essential. But with the growth of a new society in the liberated zones they increasingly hindered the process of change. Chiefs and elders, who in traditional society exercised absolute authority over women and youths, impeded the full participation of these social groups in the revolution. They rejected women's right to participate in the armed struggle and defended the brideprice system, child marriage and polygamy. Emancipation of women would affect the power of the elders to control, buy and sell women who were both producers and re-producers in traditional society. A Women's Detachment operated within the Department of Defence, and usually one or more of its members would be present at meetings organised by the chairmen. This was resented by the Department of Interior Organisation for the Province, and as the chairmen increasingly tried to mobilise the people against the guerrillas they were afraid that the Women's Detachment would report their activities.

Sergio Vieira, a Frelimo leader, has explained how the revolutionaries attempted to combat the authority of the chiefs:

> How is it that any person becomes a chief? There was a customary feudal law, a customary political law, as venerable perhaps as the British Constitution. It was necessary to abolish this system of entitlement to power, to modify the conception of customary law as the foundation of power, to affirm the principle that sovereignty belonged to the masses as opposed to the ancestors, or the spirits or a lineage.[8]

The revolutionaries within the movement argued that all should participate in the liberation struggle and share more equally in decision making, be they women, youths or elders. Young men in the FPLM and young girls in the Women's Detachment and militias had *won* the right to have their voices heard, and were no longer prepared to accept the traditional system of blind obedience to the elders. By the end of 1967 the movement's publication was able to report: 'Now an awareness had developed for the establishment of new institutions which put more stress on political devotion than on traditional legitimacy of power.'[9]

The chairmen were frightened of a protracted *people's* war as a means to win independence, because its success depended on the growth of people's power. For this reason they proposed an alternative strategy of urban warfare. The Department of Defence refused, arguing logically that this would be tantamount to suicide, as the guerrillas could never win a conventional military confrontation given the overwhelming technical superiority of the colonial army. The chairmen then accused the FPLM of cowardice, and tried to mobilise the people against the guerrillas, exhorting them to refuse to provide food for the bases and transport war materials. Furthermore, rumours were spread that the guerrillas were responsible for the enemy attacks and were not putting any heart into the fighting. Kavandame was prominent here, because the liberated zones were much further advanced in his own province of Cabo Delgado. He and his chairmen had secretly carved up the future government of an independent Mozambique and therefore were anxious for a rapid victory. As hostility grew towards the FPLM and the principles they were enunciating under the leadership of Samora Machel and President Mondlane, the chairmen began to transform the militias into their own private army. All attempts at reconciliation between the two sides broke down.

Meanwhile, in Dar-es-Salaam, from the beginning of 1968, the situation in the Mozambique Institute rapidly deteriorated until the school had to be closed in March after major disturbances engendered by Gwenjere. Although he was the principal protagonist, there were also members of the Central Committee encouraging elitism within the student body. Approximately four-fifths of the 140 students ran away. Some went to their parents living in Tanzania and others to Nairobi, where they provided recruits for the tiny Mozambican splinter groups. On the face of it, this was a serious setback, given the acute shortage of educated cadres. However, the policies necessary to retain these students' support with their elitist aspirations would have seriously compromised the increasingly revolutionary direction the movement was taking.

On 9 May, the Tanzanian police had to be called in when a group of Makonde exiles attacked the Frelimo office for the second time in a week, killing a member of the Central Committee. Later, thirteen people appeared in a court claiming that they wanted to close down the party headquarters after their requests to meet the President had been ignored. However, at the time of the attack Mondlane was visiting the liberated areas and he gave a press conference immediately on his return. These events inevitably led to external pressure being placed on Frelimo to put its house in order. Hence, with pressure building up both inside and outside the movement, it was decided to call a Congress.

The revolutionaries wanted the time to organise and make the necessary preparations for the Congress. They saw this as an opportunity to define new structures for the liberated areas and generally enable the movement to deepen its political line and resolve some of the contradictions. Realising that the longer the Congress was delayed the more likely was their defeat, the chairmen called for an early meeting, thus hoping to disrupt the opposition's preparations. They succeeded in getting the date of the Congress moved forward to July, but failed in their attempts to convene it in Tanzania, where they had powerful allies. The Congress took place in Niassa, in the midst of the crisis. However, the political delegation from Cabo Delgado, comprising Kavandame and the chairmen, refused to attend.

The second congress

One hundred and fifty delegates from the nine provinces attended the Congress. With the reopening in March 1968 of the military front in Tete, there were three provinces now at war. Given that Frelimo had large numbers of people living in the liberated zones of these provinces, they were allocated a greater number of representatives: nine politico-military and eight political delegates. Raimundo Pachinuapa, the provincial commander of the FPLM, led the nine-man politico-military delegation from Cabo Delgado. Basil Davidson was present at the Congress, and described the commander thus:

> Raimundo, I think, is typical of these young Mozambicans who see the insurrectionary war they are fighting as the means of building new political structures of an elective and democratic sort, and for whom the existing structures, promoted largely by the needs of Portuguese colonial rule, appear quite inadequate to the tasks of the post-colonial reconstruction.[10]

These younger men, who had fought in the FPLM, co-ordinated their strategy for confronting the chairmen under Machel. Their representation on the Central Committee increased considerably as a result of the Congress.

Major changes were initiated in the movement's structures. The Central Committee was expanded from twenty to forty members. The inclusion of militants who worked in the front lines made the leadership much more representative. It also strengthened the revolutionary group's influence within the leadership. Later in 1968, Frelimo was able to report that 'The presence of these new members has made a valuable contribution to the work of the Central Committee and has reduced the distance that was developing between the cadres and masses'.[11] Formerly the Central Committee had both legislative and executive powers, but the Congress created a separate Executive Committee composed of the President, Vice-President and heads of the departments. This had the effect of improving communication between the exterior and the interior – or, what came to the same thing, between the Frelimo leadership and its mass support. It was a significant change, as communication had not always been as good as it should be. The result was that it 'eliminated any sense of inaccessibility, which was a contradictory factor in a revolutionary and popular movement like Frelimo'.[12]

The resolutions on the military struggle approved the thesis of protracted people's war. Popular participation and mobilisation were deemed crucial, and the war was to be totally integrated with political and ideological struggle. Prolonged war was considered the only strategy by which the balance of forces could be inverted in Frelimo's favour. On the question of which structures were to replace the colonial ones inside the liberated zones, the Congress resolution was unequivocal: 'The administration of the liberated zones aims at establishing the people's power.'[13] On the race issue, the revolutionaries gained an important victory. Opposition was by no means confined to the chairmen, although they were the ones to show their hands openly at this stage, with their boycott of the meeting. Some actually at the Congress argued that prisoners of war should be killed, but the revolutionaries urged a reconfirmation of their policy of clemency, and this was finally agreed upon. This was important, they said, in order to make a clear distinction between the behaviour of the liberation forces and that of the colonial army. Furthermore, it would have a positive effect on the war effort: 'We would be breaking the fighting morale of the enemy's army and encouraging soldiers' desertion.'[14] As events were to prove, the principled manner in which Frelimo and its fellow movements (the PAIGC, African Party for the Independence of Guinea and Cape Verde, and the MPLA) fought the war, played an important and as yet virtually unchronicled part in the politicisation of the colonial army and the eventual overthrow of the Caetano dictatorship in April 1974.

In August 1966 an alliance was made between the CONCP (Conference of Nationalist Organisations in the Portuguese Colonies) and the broad-based anti-Salazar Portuguese opposition group, the Patriotic Front of National Liberation (FPLN). The CONCP movements collaborated with the FPLN in distributing anti-war publications to Portuguese soldiers in the colonies. They also welcomed Portuguese deserters. Radio broadcasts, appealing for support from civilians and soldiers in Portugal, were regularly made over the FPLN 'Voice of Liberty' in Algiers. Although collaboration with the Portuguese opposition movement had long been Frelimo's policy, reconfirmation at the Second Congress was important, as there was considerable hostility in some quarters to this part of the programme. Moreover, the decision implicitly reaffirmed that the movement was not fighting whites, but a system that employed Portuguese peasants and workers in a conscripted army to defend the interests of its wealthy rulers.

Educational work within the liberated zones was to be accelerated with adult literacy classes, expansion of primary schools, the encouragement of women's participation and the establishment of centres for political training. In addition, production centres were to be set up in all the schools, which emphasised the importance in Frelimo's thinking of self-reliance. Of major significance was the introduction of a system whereby students could interrupt their studies to help in teaching and giving literacy classes. In other words, those receiving education had a duty to teach others and ensure that the maximum benefits would be gained from limited resources. A clear directive was also issued aimed at combating elitist ideas within the student body. The eighth resolution on education read: 'It shall be the duty of all Mozambican students to take part, whenever it may be deemed necessary, in the various tasks of the struggle for national liberation.'

National reconstruction and, in particular, production and commerce were given a high priority. The liberated zones were seen as the material basis for the growth of the struggle. Lessons had been learned from the earlier experience in Niassa Province. Frelimo advocated the resettlement of the population, which was often widely dispersed, and encouraged the return of refugees. Agricultural production was to be developed, its technical level raised and the defence of the fields consolidated. Co-operatives were to be organised in all sectors, and the importance of self-help was stressed. The Arusha Declaration made by Tanzania in 1967 had an important external impact on Frelimo in this regard. Work in the health department was to be improved and the necessary measures also taken to improve the material conditions of the people in the war zones.

The re-election of Eduardo Mondlane as President was a confirmation of his policies of opposition to tribalism, regionalism, racism and sexism and unswerving dedication to national unity and armed struggle. At every crucial stage in the development of Frelimo he had defended the adoption of a revolutionary line. The success of the Second Congress was, in no small way, a tribute to his leadership. Although the Second Congress took place in the midst of a crisis which it was unable finally to resolve, it would be wrong, nevertheless, to minimise the importance of the event and the successes that it did achieve. Holding the meeting inside the liberated zones, having announced the fact beforehand, demonstrated the growing power of Frelimo and the weakening of colonial control. Furthermore, it reflected the strong base of the movement inside the country, and the world could no longer regard Frelimo as just another party in exile. The Congress passed resolutions which would enable a further advance of the national liberation struggle and also set the stage for resolving the contradictions existing inside Frelimo itself. Those who opposed the increasingly revolutionary line that Frelimo was taking had not felt strong enough to show their hand openly, and they would find it increasingly difficult to propound policies in contradiction to those laid out by the Congress without exposing themselves.

The final unfolding of the crisis

For Kavandame, the re-election of Mondlane provoked the final schism. A last-minute attempt at reconciliation was made in August, under the auspices of Nyerere, with the two sides meeting at the southern Tanzanian port of Mtwara.[15] Kavandame was hoping that his ethnic links with Makonde holding important TANU posts in the south of the country would ensure the important external backing of Tanzania. The Tanzanians, however, pressed for compromise, and Kavandame announced his intention of forming a separatist movement in Cabo Delgado thereby hoping to claim half the aid and later negotiate a separate peace with the Portuguese. Perhaps Tanzania's support for Biafra in the Nigerian civil war (then taking place) encouraged the belief that this support would be forthcoming. In the event, after Mondlane rejected the proposal it was then clear that Nyerere had no intention of backing such a movement. The chairmen returned to Cabo Delgado and used their control over the militias to close the border. All entry was barred to the FPLM, and Samuel Paulo Kankomba, a senior commander, was assassinated when he tried to break through. He was one of many political military commanders representing a 'vanguard' within the Front, continually pressing for the adoption of more revolutionary policies.

The chairmen's separatist plan failed, essentially, because the people in the liberated zones completely withdrew their support. It was the closure of the frontier which proved to be the decisive factor. With no guerrillas to protect them, the colonial army intensified their attacks on a now defenceless population. The chairmen were held to be directly responsible for this and thereby forfeited the peasants' allegiance. On 3 January 1969 the Executive Committee of Frelimo met to suspend Kavandame, but it was the peasants' own rejection of the chairmen and their policies that was more important. As if to vindicate their decision, three months to the day after Kavandame's suspension the Portuguese authorities announced that he had defected. If final proof were needed by the peasants, this action provided it. The old political leaders were simply not fitted for carrying out the kind of political work necessary to fight a successful, protracted armed struggle. They did not have the answers to the new kinds of problems which emerged. With their removal, the way was opened up for a more intensive war effort.

For a time, however, it seemed that a mortal blow might have been struck, when, even before the Kavandame affair had time to settle, on 3 February 1969, Eduardo Mondlane was killed by a parcel bomb that arrived at his Dar-es-Salaam office. The assassination was the combined work of PIDE and the internal opposition, which had not been confined solely to the chairmen. Mondlane was the great arbiter of unity, and his loss was keenly felt. However, the movement had never been built around a single personality and was thus able to continue growing after his death. This in itself was a great compliment to Mondlane's work. Nevertheless, his assassination put the revolutionaries' position in new danger. Both Gwenjere and Kavandame had received surreptitious support from the Vice-President, Uria Simango, who immediately called a meeting of the Executive Committee to declare himself the new President.

A meeting of the Central Committee was called in April 1969, and the revolutionaries were sufficiently strongly represented numerically to thwart Simango's presidential ambitions. He was openly accused of having links with those recently dismissed from Frelimo, and a triumvirate presidency of Samora Machel, Marcelino dos Santos and Simango was formed. Simango had backing from those opposed to the new direction that the movement's policies were taking, but he lacked support within the liberated zones, which he rarely visited. He did, however, have certain influential allies abroad. Increasingly isolated within the movement, Simango published a document called 'Gloomy situation in Frelimo', in November 1969. Hoping to take advantage of his external support, he organised the distribution of the document among the embassies of member states of the Organisation of African Unity, and others. It contained the (by now) familiar accusation of ethnic dominance by the southerners and opposition to the employment of foreign teachers at the Mozambique Institute. Once again a thinly disguised package of tribalist and racist ideas was employed by the dissidents. Simango wrote: 'I agree that ideology is very important, but it should never be considered as a uniting or dividing factor of the national liberation forces of

Mozambique at this stage, if all agree and accept the fundamental principles, (a) liberate Mozambique from Portuguese colonial domination, and (b) through armed struggle.'[16] He rejected ideological and class struggle, claiming that they were inappropriate.

But even before the publication of Simango's document, Frelimo's magazine, *Mozambique Revolution*, presented the issues of the crisis clearly. The contradictions present inside Mozambique between the forces of imperialism and the forces of revolution were, it declared, also present within the Front itself, and the emergence into the open of these contradictions was a sign of success. The editorial concluded:

> We have come to the point where certain alliances could no longer objectively be stood, certain contradictions no longer be hidden, certain ideas remain unclarified. . . . All this means that our national struggle is growing and our consciousness is growing objectively, towards a revolutionary struggle and a revolutionary consciousness.[17]

In May 1970 a new era in the history of Frelimo began. At a meeting of the Central Committee, Simango was expelled and the line he defended repudiated. There were several desertions, and one of these deserters, Miguel Murrupa, went to work with the Psychological Warfare Department of the Portuguese army. As was the case with Kavandame, when it came to the 'crunch', the interests of the opposition were found to be more closely aligned with Portuguese colonialism than with the developing liberation struggle. Simango left to join one of the tiny splinter movements which spent most of its time and energy disseminating anti-Frelimo propaganda. During the brief three-day revolt of white settlers in Lourenço Marques, after the Lusaka agreement between Frelimo and the Portuguese government in September 1974, Simango gave them his support and made broadcasts from the occupied radio station. However, the over-all result of the May meeting was positive and the movement gained greater ideological unity. The meeting reaffirmed the centrality of the movement's revolutionary objectives and methods of work. Samora Machel was elected President, and Marcelino dos Santos Vice-President. With the internal crisis resolved and the movement's ideology and leadership strengthened, the way was open for rapid advances in the war of liberation.

Notes

1 Frelimo, *Relatório do Comité Central ao 3° Congresso*, 1977, pp. 12–13.

2 *Mozambique Revolution*, 24, March–May 1966.

3 *Mozambique Revolution*, 23, Dec. 1965 to Feb. 1966.

4 The first document examining the divisions on these issues was a Central Committee document entitled *Os Graves Acontecimentos de 1968 e as Divergências Ideológicas*, 21 April 1969.

5 'People's power' has been defined by one author thus: 'The basic principle is

that every community should organise itself to analyse its own problems and possibilities, find appropriate solutions and policies and act to bring these solutions and policies into force.' (See B. Davidson, 'The Revolution of People's Power; Notes on Mozambique 1979', *Race and Class*, xxi, 2, 1979, 127.)

6 Sergio Vieira, 'O Direito nas Zonas Libertades', a paper given to the Faculty of Law, Maputo, Mozambique, 4 July 1977.

7 Frelimo, *Relatório do Comité Central*, p. 17.

8 Vieira, 'O Direito nas Zonas Libertades'.

9 *Mozambique Revolution*, 34, 1967–68.

10 Letter to the *Guardian*, 7 April 1969.

11 *Mozambique Revolution*, 36, Oct.–Dec. 1968.

12 *Ibid*.

13 Frelimo, *Documentos do Segundo Congresso*, 1968.

14 *Ibid*.

15 I am grateful to Basil Davidson for clarifying some of the details of this event.

16 U. T. Simango, *Gloomy Situation in Frelimo*, Dar-es-Salaam, 1969.

17 See *Mozambique Revolution*, 40, Sept. 1969.

12 The political military struggle

Frelimo's master plan for winning the war was formulated in 1967. In essence the analysis that the movement made was the following. The success of the struggle in Niassa and Cabo Delgado owed much to the existence of Tanzania as a secure rear base; but these two provinces were the most isolated and economically were the least significant in the whole country. Although the cost of the war in the north was a drain on Portugal's budget, the real interests of the enemy were not being directly affected. Only by taking the struggle further than the confines of the north could vital economic arteries be cut. The central region of Mozambique – in particular Manica and Sofala Province and Zambezia Province – was economically of great importance to the colonial economy. The third province in this region, Tete, was of less importance. Neither Malawi nor Southern Rhodesia, which bordered on the two key provinces, would provide the support for Frelimo that Tanzania had supplied. Thus Mondlane and Machel envisaged Tete Province as being the bridge for expanding the struggle to the south and east with Zambia providing a secure external base for entry into Tete. Liberated zones had to be built in this province because only if the people of Tete were fully mobilised and organised would it then be possible to get supplies to the intended new fronts in the two key provinces. The logistical problems involved in carrying supplies hundreds of kilometres from Zambia would be enormous. Only the total support of the people could provide a solution.

The richest agricultural production in the country was to be found in Zambezia Province and Manica and Sofala Province. The agricultural statistics for 1970 show that Zambezia ranked first in the production of tea and second in the production of rice, mapira, maize, (regional) beans, manioc, cotton and sisal; while Manica and Sofala ranked first in the production of maize, potatoes, sugar cane, sunflowers and tobacco and second in the production of vegetables and sesame.[1] Some of the most important linkage mechanisms for Mozambique's integration into the regional sub-system were also to be found in the central provinces of the country. Railways from the port of Beira stretched to Southern Rhodesia and Malawi, acting as important sources of invisible earnings from the transit trade. White settler tourists flocked to Beira and the Gorongosa game park in Manica and Sofala Province, bringing in additional foreign exchange. Tete Province was the site of the grandiose Cabora Bassa dam project, transmitting hydro-electric power to South Africa. The Cabora Bassa dam was no ordinary development project; it was seen by the colonial government as an essential strategic undertaking. The supply of electricity to South Africa was intended to cement further the economic and political alliance between Lisbon and Pretoria. International capital was heavily involved in the Zamco consortium building the dam, and this was seen as the means whereby Portugal could increase its military and diplomatic support from the Western countries, which would naturally be inclined to protect their own investments. A huge lake was to be formed behind the dam which the colonial government believed would be an impenetrable physical barrier to Frelimo's southern thrust. At the same time, the international finance channelled through the project could be used to pay for an acceleration of the programme for building *aldeamentos* (strategic villages). There was much talk also of settling one million white immigrants in the newly irrigated areas to provide a human wall against the nationalist forces.

According to Frelimo's analysis, however, the 'vertebral column' of the enemy was to be found in Manica and Sofala and Zambezia provinces.[2] Not only would the introduction of the war there cause the greatest disruption economically, it would also focus world attention on Mozambique when international communication links were disrupted. Furthermore, it was believed that the higher density of population would permit a more rapid expansion of Frelimo's ranks. On 8 March 1968 Frelimo reopened the war front in Tete. At a press conference to announce the event, Mondlane revealed the presence of a battalion of South African troops to defend the dam site, and went on to explain that the proximity of Tete to Rhodesia would enable Frelimo to lend moral and physical support to the Zimbabwe nationalist forces.[3] This internationalist perspective was a characteristic of the movement from the very beginning of its existence, and was strengthened by the harsh reality of active co-operation by certain governments with Portugal's colonial war effort.

Military co-operation between South Africa, Southern Rhodesia and the Portuguese government (the so-called 'Unholy Alliance') mirrored the extensive economic integration of the region. Although no military co-operation existed officially, there was an extremely close security relationship, plainly visible in the high-level visits of top political, military and security police personnel. In 1967, for example, the Supreme Commander of South Africa's Joint Armed Forces, General Frazer, visited Portugal to confer with heads of the Portuguese armed forces and he also witnessed demonstrations of counter-guerrilla warfare.[4] That same year the Portuguese Minister of Foreign Affairs visited South Africa, and issued a statement that '[we] share the same principles'.[5] Three soldiers of the Rhodesian Light Infantry were killed by a Frelimo mine in 1971 while on patrol deep inside Portuguese territory in the Zambezi valley; so co-operation was by no means merely restricted to consultations.[6] Neither was it simply an agreement between South Africa, Southern Rhodesia and Portugal, although there was strong evidence that these three countries met regularly once a month to exchange information and co-ordinate their plans for counter-insurgency.[7] In December 1971, there were reports of a secret meeting in Lisbon, attended by the South African Army chief, concerning a tripartite military understanding between South Africa, Portugal and Malawi over action to be taken against Frelimo.[8] There were strains within the alliance, however, with the Rhodesian government becoming increasingly doubtful whether the Portuguese could effectively contain Frelimo rebel activity in Mozambique.[9]

Armed struggle spread quickly and reached the banks of the Zambezi river. The colonial government became trapped in a contradiction. When Frelimo announced its intention to 'Bust Cabora Bassa' and with Portugal seeing the dam as the key to its counter-insurgency programme in Tete, thousands of troops were tied up in its defence as the government assumed that this meant a direct attack. The strategy of the nationalists was in fact completely the opposite. A direct attack on the dam would prove fatal, but guerrilla warfare tactics could be employed to ambush convoys carrying materials for use in the construction of the dam, thus effectively hampering the work. This gave Frelimo the space to develop its liberated zones in the surrounding regions. The watchwords 'Bust Cabora Bassa' became a rallying cry for support movements throughout the West to mobilise public opinion against investments going from their own countries into the project. Pressures were also put upon governments to prohibit such investment.

The big push south of the Zambezi river occurred at the same time as the Gordian Knot offensive in Cabo Delgado, launched by General Kaulza de Arriaga, the new Portuguese commander-in-chief of Mozambique. This operation was an attempt to invade and reconquer the liberated zones of the province. A vast array of war machinery plus tens of thousands of troops were employed from May until August 1970, when the whole operation finally ground to a halt. Arriaga used aerial and artillery bombing, deployed battalions of infantry and ploughed makeshift roads into the bush in an attempt to find and destroy the Frelimo bases.

A guerrilla commander who was in Cabo Delgado at the time explained the Frelimo response to Arriaga's plan: 'When we knew the strategy, the guerrillas and the people studied together how to combat him.'[10] Guerrillas in the Tanzanian training camps returned to the country, and all participated in the counter-offensive. The colonial army was attacked by peasants with makeshift weapons fighting alongside guerrillas armed with kalashnikovs. Constant bombardments initially disrupted daytime production, but the peasants soon began cultivating their fields at night. When the attacks reached a certain area, the people dispersed into small groups, abandoning their houses which had been constructed under the shelter of the trees, and fled nearer to the guerrilla bases where they could be better defended. Frelimo then moved the people from the affected area to another zone. A group of guerrillas would bombard the enemy from the front with mortars, while another group circled behind the invaders to mine the roads cleared by caterpillar tractors. Peasants and the militia worked alongside the FPLM cutting trees and digging ditches to block the roads. Getting in to the liberated zones was relatively easy, but getting out again was to prove more difficult.

The failure of Operation Gordian Knot was a turning point in the war. Never again would the colonial army be able or willing to launch a major offensive of this size. The basic reason for the defeat was that

Frelimo had emerged from the crisis period with the revolutionaries firmly in command. Having failed to destroy the movement politically from within, the colonial government had attempted to defeat it militarily with this campaign. This second failure was a heavy blow to Portugal's war effort.

By 1972, the movement controlled most of Tete Province, the bridgehead had been built, and the new front in Manica and Sofala Province was ready to be opened. Confirmation of the success in Tete came indirectly from the Portuguese High Command, which in October 1971 admitted for the first time the nationalist achievements in the province.[11]

Frelimo's new structure

In order to understand fully how the war was being fought and the reasons for its success, it is necessary to examine the new organisation of the FPLM. In over-all command was the Political Military Co-ordinating Committee. Its members were the President, Vice-President, Political Commissar, Chiefs of Security, Defence and Organisation, and Secretaries of the Provinces. Below this organ were the Provincial Commands. The diagram below demonstrates how this latter structure operated.[12]

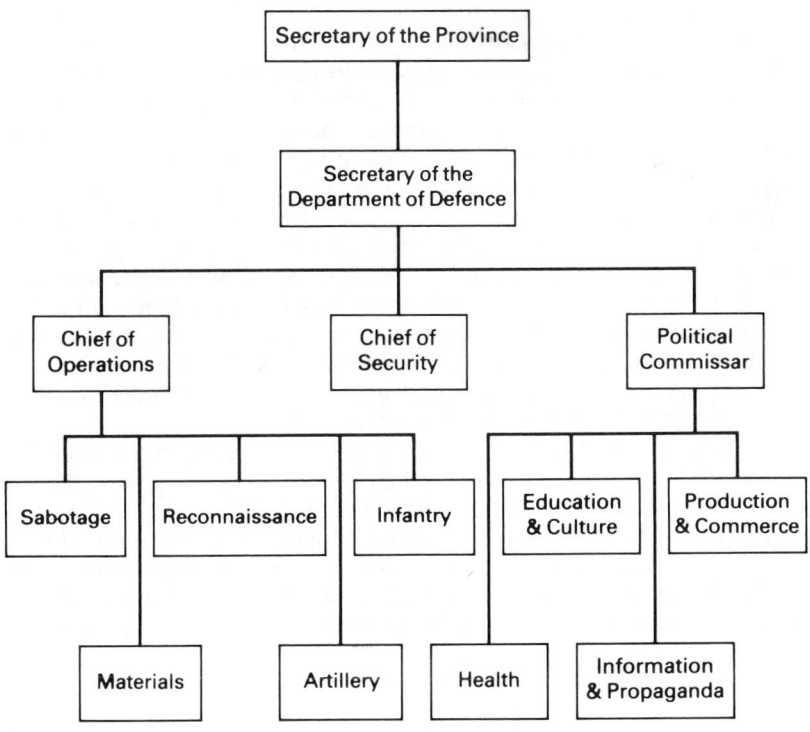

Every three months a meeting of the Provincial Command was held, attended by the Chief of Operations, the Political Commissar and the Chief of Security of the sectoral commands (each province was divided into sectors). The Political Commissariat took over the old functions of the Department of Internal Organisation. Its responsibilities were political mobilisation among both the people and the army and the work of national reconstruction in the liberated zones. Security had three functions: to understand the enemy's strategy and movements, to defend Frelimo's political line and, finally, to infiltrate clandestine militants into the new zones. The Chief of Operations had direct responsibility for the military struggle: he planned and organised the strategy and tactics and co-ordinated all actions against the enemy forces. The Chief of Security was also frequently second-in-command of operations.

The structure at the level of the sector was the same as that of the Province. There was a guerrilla battalion in each sector, and this was divided into companies numbering approximately 150 men. Each company had a base, whose exact location would change periodically but which remained within the given area it was intended to control. The companies were divided into three platoons of about thirty-six men apiece. These were further divided into three sections of a dozen or so men each. Finally, at the lowest level, there was the group (three men). This military structure gave great flexibility to the guerrilla army, enabling various combinations and divisions to execute any given plan. All the chiefs in each sector would try to meet each month to discuss the general situation in their own area.

Creating a Political Military Co-ordinating Committee was a crucially important recognition that the struggle was not purely military but essentially political. However, the political struggle needed an armed component to succeed. Each was mutually dependent on the other. There could no longer be the creation of separate political cadres and military cadres. Although a person could move from being a Political Commissar to become a Chief of Operations, as their training was essentially the same, more important, all cadres had to mobilise the people and be politically conscious of why they were fighting. All had to participate in the armed struggle, as this was the only way to end colonial rule. This perspective was adopted and put into operation at every level. All cadres had to undergo political–military training at the Nachingwea camp in Tanzania. Afterwards, some would be sent for specialised training in military techniques in the socialist states.

Organisational unity and closer co-ordination emerged from the clearer ideological position adopted by Frelimo after the crisis. All was now co-ordinated through the structures of the FPLM, while powers of decision making were more decentralised and communications flowed more easily. The integration of formerly separate departments, at the level of the provinces and sectors within the structure of the FPLM, was open acknowledgement of the interrelationship between the different aspects of the struggle.

Grass roots politicising

When Mondlane gave a press conference to announce the resumption of the struggle in Tete, he stressed that it was only the work carried out by the clandestine militants in the three years since the closing of the military front (at the end of 1964) that now enabled operations in the province to be resumed.[13] One political commissar involved in this work described how he carried out his mission.[14] When he arrived in a new village he would explain that he was interested in finding a wife; this enabled him to establish contacts with the chief and the people. Having won the confidence of the former, the chief would then indicate the people who could help. When sufficient people were recruited and mobilised his work was ended and he would move on to the next village.

Before a new war zone was opened a thorough politicisation of the people had to be carried out. Reconnaissance units would be sent from the guerrilla camp to check out the zone in question. They would cover the area completely and search out possible sites for a base. Where possible this would be in the mountains since it was easier to defend and usually had a supply of water. When these reconnaissance units returned, they reported on the terrain, the level of consciousness of the people, the enemy's strategy and the possible strategy that Frelimo might employ. They also provided tactical reports on the number of enemy troops, how they were positioned and the weapons they carried. Both reconnaissance and politicisation work were carried out by members of the FPLM in civilian dress. When the time was judged to be right, the first armed actions would begin. The over-all aim was to cut communications, isolate Portuguese bases, and cause an ever-greater concentration of enemy troops, thus bringing more and more people and territory under Frelimo's control. Attacks were planned and discussed in detail by the commanders and guerrillas together. Infantry and sabotage groups would begin by blowing up bridges and mining roads. Whenever possible these attacks would be co-ordinated. Thus an operation against an enemy barracks would be accompanied by an ambush on the road to the next enemy base. In this way, the arrival of a column of reinforcements would be impeded. The effect of these co-ordinated actions was to make the enemy fearful of leaving its base in case this was attacked when not at full strength. Constant attacks not only restricted the colonial army to its bases but also created a climate of insecurity. In this way, Frelimo kept the enemy busy trying to defend itself and reluctant to venture out into the bush. This gave time for the liberated zones to be consolidated, and, as we have seen, this was of particular importance in Tete, which had to serve as the internal base for the expansion of the struggle.

The work of politicisation was by no means restricted to those areas pending armed guerrilla activity, but took place all over the country. Clandestine Frelimo cells existed among workers and students in the cities and among migrant workers in the neighbouring countries. In the Munhava suburb of Beira, for example, a group of twenty to forty people met secretly, with the help of the Burgos Fathers missionaries, to study Frelimo's programme.[15] In general, much of the clandestine work in the areas away from the war zones involved recruiting people and getting them out of the country. One particular route took the recruit from Lourenço Marques to Beira by road, then by train from Beira to near the Malawi border at Vila Fronteira. The recruit and the member of the cell designated to look after him or her would then get off the train and make their way through the bush across the border.[16] Usually, there would be four people in a cell, and only one person in that cell would know the other contact person from a cell in another town. The recruit would be passed on from one cell to another until his escape was secured. Many workers from the towns went to join Frelimo in this way. In 1970, President Samora Machel recorded that 'Combatants have come from the ranks of the peasants, industrial workers, and those working on the mines and plantations'.[17] The highly successful commander of the FPLM in Tete Province, José Moiane, was formerly a migrant worker in the mines of South Africa, whose father had been killed in an accident on the mines.[18] Migrant workers in South Africa frequently went to join Frelimo by way of Botswana,[19] where the movement had an office.

The failure of Portugal's counter-insurgency programmes

As the Portuguese Government intensified the campaign to meet the growing challenge posed by the nationalist movements in the colonies, certain new tactics were adopted. Both Tanzania and Zambia were bombed in an attempt to discourage them from continuing their support for Frelimo. With the re-opening of the war front in Tete Province there were open skirmishes between Zambian and Portuguese troops at the border. In addition to an intensification of the military struggle, there was also a move by the Portuguese Government towards a greater psychological and social offensive. In 1970, a glossy monthly magazine called *Permanência* was started by Caetano to improve the image of the colonies. The Portuguese commander-in-chief in Mozambique, Arriaga, wrote a book, *The Portuguese Answer*, in which he stressed that counter-subversion was primarily a hearts-and-minds campaign and only secondarily was concerned with social progress for the population.[20] The capture or destruction of the enemy he listed as having the lowest priority. Ian Sproat, M.P., in an introduction to Arriaga's book, openly conceded that 'The tremendous drive by the Portuguese authorities towards improving the lot of Africans has been a direct result of the struggle in each of the territories'.[21]

The successes of Frelimo brought forth important concessions and changes of policy by the colonial power. A good example of this, which also demonstrates a new development in the parallel but unequal growth of resistance, relates to a strike by Lourenço Marques port workers in June 1972. In that year the stevedores were given a wage increase from 35 to 65 escudos per day, but the dock workers did not receive a similar increase.[22] Three thousand of them marched through the capital to the governor's residence to put their claim for parity. Incredibly, given the heavy repression used in earlier years to crush strikes, not only was there no use of force but the strikers' request was granted. Undoubtedly, the fear of causing greater unrest in the capital (with Frelimo's actions spreading rapidly from the north) was the reason for this new 'soft' approach by the colonial authority. In other words, workers from the capital city in the south were able to benefit from the gains made by Frelimo in the national liberation struggle in the centre and north of the country.

At the centre of Portugal's strategy against Frelimo was the policy of building *aldeamentos*. These were intended to keep the population isolated from the guerrillas and were designed at the same time to provide a better social and economic infrastructure. Potentially there were many advantages to be gained by peasant families living together in larger units; but the success of the scheme depended both on the population being willing to enter the villages and on Portugal providing the necessary amenities. *Aldeamentos* engendered at gunpoint could only be counter-productive, as they alienated the population even further from the government. Time and effort were not taken to explain the advantages of grouping people together, and, in the main, the programme was carried out without the consent of the peasants. Hasty removals to new sites provoked resistance, especially as the traditional land of their ancestors had to be abandoned. Such promises as the government gave about the amenities to be made available were frequently found to be empty.

The traditional system of agriculture was based on dispersed settlement, so that each family originally had its fields near its own house. When more than a thousand people were concentrated together, people were frequently obliged to walk a couple of hours to reach their fields. In addition to the loss of working time, the *machambas* could not be protected from wild animals at night because of the curfew law. For military reasons, the *aldeamentos* were stationed along the roads, without due regard to the suitability of the soil for cultivation.

Even if the colonial government had wished to make the protected villages a more attractive proposition, it was, quite simply, never given the time. The pace of the war was too great for the lumbering, incumbent administration to be able to keep up. Only in 1965, the second year of the war, did the Governor of Cabo Delgado propose the creation of *aldeamentos*, but by this time the embryos of semi-liberated zones were already being formed. Efforts were concentrated on clearing the land immediately to the south of the Tanzanian border, as the government anticipated a conventional invasion force. However, Frelimo's cadres were already operating all over the northern provinces. By the beginning of 1972, the colonial government claimed to have 440 000 people in *aldeamentos*. The overwhelming majority of these, however, were in Cabo Delgado and Niassa, but the focus of the war had by now moved to Tete, where the *aldeamento* programme was still in its infancy. The programme was not a complete failure, however. In particular, there was a large measure of success amongst the Macua people in the south of Cabo Delgado Province. Along with the strategic villages, there was a carefully nurtured campaign to promote ethnic hostility among the Macuas towards the Makonde, whom Frelimo was said to represent. This delayed Frelimo's southward thrust from Cabo Delgado, but the movement outflanked the colonial strategy by rapidly spreading the war in Tete.

By the time the government began constructing *aldeamentos* in Tete, it had gained a greater degree of sophistication. In many cases the *aldeamento* was built around a troop base, so that the military was surrounded by a civilian barrier. This enabled greater control to be exercised over the population. At the same time, in the case of a Frelimo attack, civilian casualties would be higher and this could be used as propaganda against the movement. Frelimo devised a counter-strategy based on mobilising the population of the *aldeamentos*; then, before an attack, the people would be told to flee.[23] The aim of the attacks on *aldeamentos* was to liberate the peasants from what Frelimo termed the enemy's 'concentration camps'.

In order to defend each protected village the *fumo* (the local chief) would usually choose ten or twelve men to be trained as members of a militia. In the province of Tete, most received a three-month course. Each member of the militia had a trade which was pursued during the day, but at night he assumed his para-military role. It was the duty of the militia to check that all the villagers had returned from the fields, and, along with the paid informers, they were supposed to report any suspicious behaviour. A member of the PSP (Polícia de Segurança Pública) was assigned to control the militia in each *aldeamento*, and worked alongside the *fumo*. The militia were paid by the administration and received a relatively high salary. The over-all co-ordination of these forces was left to the colonial army, which sometimes used the units for offensive operations.[24]

One veteran commander in Frelimo explained how the movement coped with the problem of *aldeamentos* in Tete Province: 'Frelimo for the most part was able to politicise the people, including those in the *aldeamentos*. If the people in the *aldeamentos* accepted the politicisation of Frelimo then the *aldeamentos* were not attacked.'[25] At first sight this may seem a paradox, but the commander went on to explain:

> Often secretaries of *círculos* * would be inside the *aldeamentos* mobilising the people. They would give information about the enemy, give food to the guerrillas and leave the *aldeamentos* at night to help with transporting supplies from Zambia, sometimes being away for up to a week.

But it was not always so easy. Nearer to the provincial capital of Tete, colonial propaganda and control were more intense, and this sometimes created big problems for the movement. Commander Lucas Lepewa described the Frelimo response to this situation thus:

> As we were fighting a political struggle, our arms were used to make possible our work of politicisation. So it was those *aldeamentos* where the people had not yet adopted the Frelimo line that were attacked. The people were then taken to Frelimo bases where politicisation could be carried out more effectively.

* The unit at the lowest level of Frelimo's political structure.

As the war intensified, the *aldeamento* programme was speeded up, and by the end of 1973, official claims were being made that one and a quarter million people had been resettled.[26] With the advance of the war the government's security network was strengthened and the vigilance exercised over the people in the *aldeamentos* increased. The Women's Detachment of Frelimo had a vital role to play in combating these measures; formed in 1967, it quickly grew to become a central component of the FPLM. The task of making the first contacts with the population in a new area was usually given to the women guerrillas. Not infrequently, one of the women would have members of her family in the area where enemy troops were stationed, and she would first make contact with her relatives. Her tasks were two-fold: to collect intelligence information, and to begin the work of politicisation. By the early 1970s the vigilance of the colonial authorities was such that any strange male approaching an *aldeamento* would be reported and most likely killed by the militia or army. The women were not immune from this danger, but they had a better chance of escaping detection. Twenty-four-year-old Elisa Geteo, who was a chief of a Women's Detachment, described how they operated:

> Groups of two or three were sent to enter an area and find out the situation of the people and their difficulties. They would return from this mission and report to the political commissar of the base (to whom they were directly responsible). They would then be sent back to contact the people and arrange to meet again at a certain time and place. This time the political commissar would go with them.[27]

A continuous process was involved. The women guerrillas would first find out the grievances of the people, and these grievances were then discussed with the commissar at the base. All the information brought back would be analysed. Then the women returned to the *aldeamento* or village to continue and develop their work of politicisation. One group would have responsibility for a village, *aldeamento* or a particular zone. After a while they would change location. This was not through fear of being caught by the Portuguese but to enable the women to become familiar with different parts of the country. As Elisa went on to explain: 'You could not understand Mozambique if you knew only one place, you had to be aware of the problems of every area.' This work required courage, determination and a cool head. The risks were high, and sometimes cadres of the Women's Detachment were caught by the enemy. Elisa gave a typical example of this happening:

> Sometimes when we were having a meeting at a water hole, other people who were not so well politicised came to fetch water and they might return and inform the Portuguese. The Portuguese would then come and attack – sometimes women would be killed or rounded up and taken for interrogation. One arrival at the enemy base, the Portuguese would ask each one of the group that had been rounded up if we were Frelimo or simply the people. If we replied 'Frelimo', we were immediately killed. If we replied that we were the people, we

were sent to an *aldeamento*. From there we could escape and return to our base.

A new front is opened

With Tete Province secured as the internal base area, a small company of guerrillas was despatched to take the war into Manica and Sofala Province. On 25 July 1972, Fernando Matavele's company launched the first attacks. The work of political mobilisation had been well carried out, and support for the guerrillas was rapidly forthcoming. Clandestine militants had already been operating in the province for a long period of time. A greater concentration of settlers had produced a more intense level of exploitation, and the people proved only too willing to take up arms. Thrusts were made in three directions, to the east, north-east and south. By the end of 1973, Frelimo was operating in the area of the Gorongosa game park, not far from the port of Beira, Mozambique's second largest city. The thrust in the north-east made possible attacks on the rail link with Malawi, but it was the southern advance which was to sever the jugular vein of the colonial economy.

At four minutes after midnight on 1 January 1974, the Chief of Operations for the Vila Pery sector, Commandant Johan Jeova, put into action his carefully co-ordinated series of combined assaults.[28] Both the rail and road links connecting Rhodesia with the Indian Ocean were attacked in ten different places. By February 1974 the railway line had been the scene of no fewer than nineteen separate incidents,[29] causing railway staff to strike in protest at the army's inability to protect them.[30] However, Frelimo's activities were not confined solely to the disruption of communication lines. Inhaminga in the north of the province became the centre for some of the fiercest fighting of the war, with civil administration buildings and barracks coming under heavy fire. Taken unawares by the strength of the movement's presence and by the support it was receiving from the population, the *aldeamento* programme was speeded up, and vast areas of the countryside were made free-fire zones. In the six months to February 1974, 146 000 villagers had been moved into strategic hamlets in Manica and Sofala. According to Colonel Sousa Talles, the governor of the region, even this could not halt Frelimo's progress; the guerrillas were attacking six or seven *aldeamentos* per night, trying to free the inhabitants.[31]

The military offensive was not confined solely to this province. In Cabo Delgado, the district capital of Mueda was attacked by large-scale units, and twenty-one aircraft were destroyed as they lay on the airstrip.[32] On a later occasion, Portugal's top combat officer, Lieutenant-Colonel Alvares Pereira, was shot down in his Dakota reconnaissance plane as he took off from the airport.[33] With the arrival of Soviet-supplied Sam 7 missiles, Frelimo was able to shoot down many more planes in the period March–April 1974.[34]

The disintegration of the colonial army

In response to Frelimo's increasing success, the incidence of civilian massacres by units of the colonial army increased dramatically. Numerous written accounts of these now exist,[35] and secret documents from the Portuguese army (published after the April coup of 1974) have confirmed the authenticity of these events.[36] At the time, much controversy surrounded the Wiriyamu massacre in Tete Province; its very existence was denied by the authorities.[37] My own on-the-spot investigation, which included an interview with one of the few survivors, confirmed the massacre of hundreds of villagers.[38]

Standing in marked contrast to the increasingly well-integrated and efficient Frelimo organisation stood the Portuguese colonial army. Relying in large measure on conscripts serving a four-year term, the signs of degeneration in the early 1970s were remarked upon by many. A. J. Venter, a South African specialist in guerrilla warfare, wrote: 'Judging from personal experience, standards maintained by some of these conscript units are questionable. These troops are sometimes reluctant to attack, inept in the handling of weapons under fire and are often content to sit tight and stay out of trouble until their terms of duty are over.'[39] Kerry Swift, another South African who toured extensively with the Portuguese military, reported many signs of breakdown in morale, including heavy drinking on duty in the convoys, lack of discipline (slovenly dress, misuse of weapons and the murder of Frelimo prisoners), and the widespread use of prostitution.[40] There were conflicts between the secret police and the military, and within the army conflicts existed between conscripts and professionals.

The over-all weakness of the Portuguese military effort had a number of internal causes. No comprehensive plan was worked out; military policy was haphazard and unco-ordinated; the strategy was essentially defensive; local military policy was often inexplicably altered with the arrival of a new commanding officer; there was inter-service rivalry and rivalry between staff and combat officers; senior officers served also on the boards of large companies; professionalism was subordinated to political orthodoxy in the promotion of officers; and, finally, there were conflicts between junior and senior officers. Gallagher has concluded that 'Military favouritism, bad leadership, and profiteering by generals, led the disadvantaged half of the army to seek retribution in 1974'.[41] There was a growing war-weariness as casualties mounted: South African sources gave a figure of 1 300 Portuguese soldiers killed in Mozambique up to 1971.[42] In the following year, official Portuguese sources gave a monthly average of eighteen soldiers killed and twenty-nine seriously wounded, although the real figures must have been greatly in excess of these.[43] Many avoided serving in the army. Between 1961 and 1974, 110 000 conscripts failed to report for military service.[44]

It was more, however, than just war-weariness, the inner tensions and conflicts of the colonial military machine, and the economic costs of the war that produced the officers' revolt and popular uprising which ended almost half a century of dictatorship. The political line of the liberation movements was a vital determining factor. We have already shown how the issue of captured prisoners of war played an important part in the two-line struggle within Frelimo at the time of the Second Congress in 1968. That same year, a number of Portuguese soldiers went over to Frelimo, and the movement regularly published tracts aimed at encouraging such desertions.[45] A Portuguese daily newspaper printed a story (in 1969) concerning the release by Frelimo of two captured soldiers.[46] Inside Portugal, anti-war resistance mounted steadily. During the first half of 1971, for example, there were reports of anti-war speeches at the funerals of dead soldiers, a student demonstration against the war occurred in February, in April a new clandestine journal *No to Colonial Wars* appeared, and the direct sabotage of military equipment took place.[47] In 1973, a new paper, *A Voz do Desertor (The Deserter's Voice)*, was issued while the United Portuguese Opposition published a declaration calling for the end of the war that same year.[48] Some of this opposition was spontaneous, although some was clearly organised. The Portuguese Communist Party (PCP) decided to infiltrate cadres into the colonial army in order to encourage the troops not to fight.[49] There were five identifiable urban guerrilla groups operating inside Portugal by 1973. The ARA (Armed Revolutionary Action) was the armed wing of the PCP, and in addition there were the Revolutionary Brigade, the League for Unity for Revolutionary Action, Revolutionary Communist Action and the Anti-Colonialist Committee. Inside Mozambique, clandestine copies of Frelimo's publications were circulated, having been surreptitiously removed from the *Centro Psicológica* where the authorities had collected them together.[50] Much of the politicisation of the troops undoubtedly came from reading 'revolutionary guerrilla manuals . . . in the African bush'.[51]

When the coup in Portugal took place on 25 April 1974, Frelimo increased its war effort. The wars in the three African colonies had undoubtedly been a major cause of disaffection among the officers; but this did not mean that the Armed Forces Movement was yet prepared to hand over power to Frelimo. The struggle, therefore, was intensified on the firm assumption that success in negotiations depended upon gains made on the battlefield. On 5 June 1974, Frelimo entered into negotiations with the colonial power, but the Portuguese delegation had come only to obtain a cease-fire and had no mandate to discuss the transfer of power to Frelimo. For this reason the negotiations were broken off.[52]

In the middle of the year, a new front was opened in Zambezia Province, and the guerrillas continued their southern offensive. With the increasing pressure of the war, the futile attempts to find a neocolonial solution for Mozambique being proposed by General Spinola – the new head of the government in Portugal – steadily crumbled. By June, the Portuguese military command in Nampula had told Rhodesia not to expect any further co-operation.[53] This was a clear indication that the war was nearing an end. In July 2 000 soldiers from Boane and the Lourenço Marques Engineering Barracks declared their support for Frelimo and refused to be sent to the operational zones; marines stationed at Chire in Zambezia Province reacted in the same way. At Namatil, in Cabo Delgado, a whole garrison of troops was surrounded on 1 August and given the chance to surrender. José Carlos Monteiro, the officer in command who agreed to the surrender, later made a statement which is very revealing of the attitude of many Portuguese officers at that time:

> The decision I made was the only one possible, because a hundred and forty three lives were at stake. Only in this way was I obeying the will of the majority of Portuguese people. Besides, the whole world knows that for ten years we have been sustaining a war which has never benefited us. It might have satisfied the wishes of a capitalist minority, but for the Portuguese people it brought only bloodshed and lost lives. The time has come to decolonise not just Africa but also the minds of many Portuguese who have grown used to a Fascist, oppressive regime.[54]

The clumsy, inefficient bureaucratic administration of the Portuguese state made its mark on the colonial army. Mario Luis Martins Nobre was a sergeant in the Namatil garrison, and explained some of the shortcomings in the colonial military machine:

> The way in which both soldiers and officers were treated in combat left much to be desired. You see, we had a timetable for war. If we went beyond the set time and had any successes we might be considered heroes, but on the other hand, those wounded after four o'clock were not fetched. In some cases people died due to lack of assistance.[55]

A strong backlash occurred among the settlers as a result of the curtain of deceit drawn over the real nature of the war. Colonial propaganda maintained that Frelimo consisted of a small bunch of terrorists making sporadic attacks across the border, and that their activities were confined to the north. With widespread guerrilla operations covering the whole of Manica and Sofala Province, the settler population could no longer be kept in ignorance. In Beira, angry mobs of settlers demonstrated against the army for three days, calling for the resignation of Portugal's leaders, and the Provincial Governor was forced to resign.[56] Demoralisation within the colonial army could not but increase in the face of this pressure. Unofficial cease-fires were being declared by officers in various parts of the country. By the second week in August 1974, photographs and articles were appearing in the Mozambican press showing guerrillas and Portuguese soldiers meeting on the streets of Tete.[57] Mario Soares gave an interview to *Der Spiegel* on 19 August in which he warned that 'there could emerge grave problems if there was a delay in the decolonisation process'.[58] A tacit cease-fire was widely reported, and in September this was made official, with the signing of an agreement to form a Transitional Government – made up of Frelimo and the Portuguese administration – as an intermediate step to the complete handover of power to Frelimo in June 1975. Secret negotiations had continued throughout July and August between the two parties, with Aquino de Bragança, a long-standing militant on the CONCP Secretariat, playing an important intermediary role. These discussions set the stage for the signing of the Lusaka Accord on 7 September 1974 under which Portugal agreed to the unconditional handover of power to Frelimo.

Inside Mozambique, a whole collection of political parties and groups mushroomed after the coup. Only three were to have any significance: GUMO, FICO and the Democrats Movement.[59] GUMO (*Grupo Unido de Moçambique*), the United Group of Mozambique, actually came into existence before the coup, and had the tacit support of the Caetano government. Its leader, Maximo Dias, held a meeting with the Portuguese premier in September 1973. The party's programme called for the granting of a 'progressive autonomy' inside Mozambique. Joanna Simeão, GUMO's best-known spokesperson, explained in a press interview that her party wanted to see blacks and those of mixed blood nominated to responsible positions – not, she hastened to add, 'the anonymous mass' but the 'intellectual class'.[60] Not surprisingly, when GUMO fell apart its members joined up with Simango, Gwenjere and others previously in COREMO to form the National Coalition Party.

FICO was originally an extreme right-wing group for whites only. 'Fico' is a Portuguese word meaning 'I stay'. Increasingly, this party was forced by the speed of events to incorporate token blacks and propound a federalist policy. Its members later formed the core of the Free Mozambique Movement, *Moçambique Livre*, which led some of the settlers in a last-ditch rebellion in September 1974. The Democrats were not strictly a party, but were the traditional anti-fascist, white, opposition group which came to support the Frelimo cause. Control of the media was vitally important during the turbulent post-April period when censorship was lifted for the first time in forty-eight years. Democrats, working in the media, published whatever information they could about Frelimo, especially in *Tempo* and *Notícias de Beira*. They collected data on DGS agents and helped the thousands of newly released political prisoners. In collaboration with many of these prisoners and Frelimo militants who had been working clandestinely, they organised rallies in support of a Frelimo government. Undeniably, the mass of support throughout the country was with Frelimo. In the cities, the vast majority of workers put their weight behind Frelimo and frequently broke up the meetings of the other parties. Although many workers fled to join Frelimo during the war, and others formed clandestine cells, it was in this period that the working class as a whole was to play an important role in ensuring Frelimo's victory.

When the news of the signing of the Lusaka Accord came through, there was a brief three-day revolt in the capital with echoes in the provincial capitals of Beira, Tete, Quelimane and Nampula. It was led by those white settlers unwilling to accept the end of the old era. The radio station in the capital was occupied, and two daily newspapers were seized. Initially, this group made broadcasts calling on the colonial army's elite troops, the commandos, to join them. (Although there was no response at that time, there was a serious incident of fighting in the capital between the commandos and Frelimo troops towards the end of October 1974.) Gwenjere and Simango also made broadcasts, and appeals were made for the customs officials to open the borders, in the hope that South African troops would come in to support them, but this was at a time when the Vorster government was practising its short-lived '*détente*' exercise. A move of this kind would have caused that particular diplomatic house of cards to come tumbling down even sooner than it eventually did.

Furthermore, there were no serious rivals to Frelimo that could serve as a cover for intervention, as was the case with UNITA and the FNLA in Angola. The South African government probably felt that its powerful economic hold over Mozambique and its military superiority would provide it with sufficient leverage even with Frelimo in power. Finally, the South Africans would have required some support from the United States to launch an attack, and the United States was still smarting under the effects of its defeat in Vietnam and the Watergate imbroglio. The government in Portugal also refused its support. In the capital, tens of thousands of African workers massed, ready to march on the radio station, but the surrender occurred before their intervention became necessary.

Why did Frelimo succeed?

An editorial in *Mozambique Revolution* in 1973 examined the reasons for Frelimo's success. It suggested that for some the answer lay in the technical sphere – a better organisational device or more sophisticated weapons. Clearly these were of some importance, but the article spoke of: 'the error of considering that stronger weapons and better techniques are basic to our continued success'.[61] Portugal, as a member of the North Atlantic Treaty Organisation, was receiving all the weaponry it needed from its Western military allies, yet it was losing the war. A belief in this factor, it was argued, would run the risk of cutting off Frelimo from its real source of strength, the people:

> Instead, we have operated on the premise that it is the people who first and foremost must be mobilised, cared for, protected, and that in the words of a recent communiqué from Frelimo's Health Service 'the cadres [must] cultivate love for the masses'. Because ours is a people's struggle.

The work of mobilisation was the work of the cadres – not only political commissars, but the chiefs of operations, teachers, health workers and members of the committees of peoples' power, formed in the zones freed from colonial control. How well the work of mobilisation was carried out depended on the ideological level of the cadres. After the movement's crisis, the leadership was able to lay down a more advanced political line; cadres were encouraged to internalise this line and apply it in practice in their everyday lives. Frelimo considered that 'Stepping up the ideological offensive is the major pre-condition for victory. A correct political line is what transforms weakness into strength.'[62] However, a revolutionary ideology not realised in daily practice remained mere rhetoric. Peasants judged the ideology of the movement by the way in which the cadres treated the people, the solutions they provided for the problems facing them and the personal comportment of the carriers of Frelimo's message. The political advance of the movement was marked by an ever-clearer definition of the enemy – what the movement was fighting against and what it was fighting for.

One particular example may serve to show how important this ideological advance was for the political military struggle. Special units of the colonial army called GEs (Special Groups), GEPs (Special Paratrooper Groups) and Flêchas (a special group linked to the secret police) began to operate in the 1970s. These were to employ 'guerrilla' tactics as part of the general counter-insurgency strategy. Highly trained and particularly brutal in their methods, they were frequently deployed dressed in Frelimo uniforms. Only black Mozambicans were used. They would go into an area, pretending to be Frelimo fighters, commit atrocities and in this way try to spread seeds of discord among the people and Frelimo. The Selous Scouts in Zimbabwe used similar tactics. Intensive mobilisation was necessary to combat these manoeuvres, but, as Samora Machel explained,

The enemy may use the same uniform and equipment as us, may speak in the same terms, use the same language, be from the same ethnic group and have the same colour, but one thing they can never do is to behave as we do and live by our line of serving the people.[63]

He continued by saying that to ensure that the ideological offensive had real life, it was essential that it be lived in practice. The movement's success must point to the fact that in general it was lived in practice.

Frelimo's final victory was not a solo triumph. It was the result of the combination of national liberation struggles taking place in all of the Portuguese colonies, backed up by international support from various countries and political groups sympathetic to those struggles. Yet if one was to search for the core reason for the revolution's accomplishments, it is to be found in the development of the movement's ideology, and it is to this that we now turn our attention.

Notes

1 *Estatísticas Agrícolas de Moçambique*, 1970.

2 Interview with Adelino Siculava, Political Commissar of Manica Province, Chimoio, 24 April 1975.

3 ZANU submitted a plan of action to Frelimo in 1971 which was accepted and put into operation in 1972. The Mozambican peasants in Frelimo's liberated areas gave a considerable amount of logistical support to the Zimbabwe nationalists. See *Zimbabwe News*, x, 2, May–June 1978.

4 *Primeiro de Janeiro*, 24 May 1976.

5 *Primeiro de Janeiro*, 27 July 1967.

6 *Daily Telegraph*, 29 April 1971.

7 *The Times*, 12 March 1968.

8 *Agênce France Presse*, 9 Dec. 1971.

9 *The Sunday Times*, 29 Oct. 1972.

10 Interview with Commander Leonardo Njawala, Vila Pery, Manica and Sofala Province, April 1975.

11 *The Nationalist*, 23 Oct. 1971.

12 This was described in an interview with the Provincial Command of Tete Province, Tete, May 1975.

13 See *Africa Report*, May 1968, p. 34.

14 Interview with Alfredo Wassira, M'temangão, Manica and Sofala Province, 5 May 1975.

15 Interview with António Padicement, a member of the clandestine group of Frelimo supporters, Beira, April 1975.

16 Interview with João Baptista, a former Frelimo clandestine worker, Murraca, Manica and Sofala Province, March 1975.

17 Frelimo, *A vitória constrói–se, A vitória organiza–se,* Textos e documentos da Frelimo, 2, 1977, p. 53.

18 Conversation with José Moiane, Tete, May 1975.

19 Interview with Commander Alfredo Pires de Abrão, Vila Gouveia, Manica and Sofala Province, May 1975.

20 K. de Arriaga, *The Portuguese Answer*, London, 1973.

21 *Ibid.*, p. 11.

22 Interview with Albino Sitói, one of the leaders of the strike, Maputo, 2 March 1978.

23 Interview with Commander Bernardo Beca, Tete, 13 May 1975.

24 Interview with the Chief of PSP in Furancungu, Tete, 24 May 1975.

25 Interview with Lucas Lepewa, Sectoral Chief of Operations, Furancungu, Tete Province, 26 May 1975.

26 H. Portman, 'Os Mitos da Frelimo', *Permanência*, Ano IV, No. 38, Julho 1973, Agência-Geral do Ultramar.

27 Interview with Elisa Geteo, Cazula, Tete Province, 23 May 1975. Note that the clarification in parentheses is mine.

28 Interview with Johan Jeova, Provincial Chief of Operations, Vila Pery, Manica and Sofala Province, 29 April 1975. For a press report of these attacks see the *Guardian*, 3 Jan. 1974.

29 *Daily Telegraph*, 11 Feb. 1974.

30 *The Star Weekly* (South Africa), 23 Feb. 1974.

31 *Daily Telegraph*, 11 Feb. 1974.

32 *Daily News*, Dar-es-Salaam, 2 March 1974. See also *The Times*, 31 Jan. 1974.

33 *Daily Telegraph*, 13 Feb. 1974.

34 *A Voz da Revolução*, 21, Jan.–April 1974.

35 The best-known is A. Hastings, *Wiriyamu*, London, 1974. See also *Terror in Tete*, Special Report No. 2, London, International Defence and Aid Fund, 1973.

36 J. Amaro, *Documentos Secretos, Massacres Na Guerra Colonial. Tete, um exemplo*, Lisbon, 1976.

37 See Ministry of Foreign Affairs, *'Wiriyamu' or a Mare's Nest*, Lisbon, 1973.

38 Interview with João Xavier, Wiriyamu, Tete Province, 31 May 1975.

39 A. J. Venter *The Zambesi Salient*, Howard Timmins, 1974, p. 46.

40 See K. Swift, *Mozambique and the Future*, Cape Town, 1974.

41 T. P. Gallagher, 'The Theory and Practice of Portuguese Authoritarianism in Salazar, the Right and the Portuguese Military, 1926–1968', Ph.D. thesis, University of Manchester, 1978, p. 292.

42 A. J. Venter, *Portugal's Guerrilla War: the Campaign for Africa*, Cape Town, 1973, p. 72.

43 South African Institute of Race Relations, *A Survey of Race Relations in S. Africa 1973*, Johannesburg, 1974, p. 94.

44 D. Porch, *the Portuguese Armed Forces and the Revolution*, London, 1977, p. 32.

45 See *Frelimo Information* (Algiers), 1968 and *Frelimo Information*, July 1969, for details.

46 *Diário de Lisboa*, 6 Oct. 1969.

47 See *Portugal and Colonial Bulletin*, xi, 3, July 1971.

48 *Frankfurter Rundschau*, 26 May 1973.

49 Interview with João P. Quelhas, Maputo, 9 May 1976. He was a member of the PCP who fought in the colonial army between 1970 and 1974.

50 *Ibid.*

51 R. Harvey, *Portugal, Birth of a Democracy*, London, 1978, p. 12.

52 *Mozambique Revolution*, 60, July–Sept. 1974.

53 *Financial Times*, 4 June 1974.

54 *Mozambique Revolution*, 60, July–Sept. 1974.

55 *Ibid.*

56 *The Times*, 7 March 1974.

57 *Tempo*, 203, 11 Aug. 1974.

58 M. Soares, *Democratização e Descolonização*, Lisbon, 1975, p. 75.

59 The others included: CNAM, the African National Congress of Mozambique; FRECOMO, the Mozambique Common Front, which wished for a privileged position for the Makua–Lomwe group; the Commercial Agricultural and Industrial Association of Niassa, formed in May 1974, which also claimed to represent the Makua–Lomwe; UNIPOMO, a Makonde group formed by Lazaro Kavandame; MONA, a single race group, this time based in the capital; COREMO, which returned from exile; and the CDM, associated with the powerful pro-Caetano industrialist Jorge Jardim.

60 See *Tempo*, 192, 19 May 1974; and *Tempo*, 193, 2 June 1974.

61 *Mozambique Revolution*, 56, June–Sept. 1973.

62 *Mozambique Revolution*, Special Issue, 25 Sept. 1973.

63 *Ibid.*

13 The theory and practice of Mozambique's revolution

Frelimo was founded as a front uniting various classes, but was largely composed of workers and peasants who were the overwhelming majority of the population. The other classes represented in the front were numerically small, but highly significant nevertheless: namely, the traditional 'feudal' chiefs and embryonic bourgeoisie, more properly called the petty bourgeoisie. All that united these classes was their common opposition to Portuguese colonialism. Beyond this platform their interests diverged, and as the nationalist struggle progressed the different class interests within the front entered into ever-greater conflict. The traditional chiefs and embryonic bourgeoisie wished to replace colonialism in order to take control of the state and then use this political power to establish themselves as a new ruling class. In essence, they envisaged retaining the same economic system (capitalism) and the same state structures to defend the interests of the dominant class within an essentially neocolonialist system.

Workers and peasants, on the other hand, could benefit only if the system based on the exploitation of their labour power was abolished. As a result of *chibalo* and migrant labour, most male Mozambicans had the experience of selling their labour power, freely or otherwise, in return for a pittance. Peasants, particularly the women, laboured through the seasons of the agricultural cycle to sell a portion of their harvest at grossly deflated prices. An unequal exchange took place between the buyers and sellers of agricultural commodities; this was guaranteed by the colonial state itself.[1] Only a new state, built to serve and represent *their* class interests instead of the interests of those who exploited their labour power, could bring about a real change. A formal independence of flag and anthem would make little meaningful difference to the lives of the majority of the people.[2]

All ideologies have a class base: that is to say, they represent the interests of a particular class. The development of Frelimo's ideology must be seen in terms of the class struggle taking place within the movement itself. Frelimo moved beyond nationalism to adopt a revolutionary programme, and it is this which sets Frelimo apart from most other nationalist movements in Africa, although putting it alongside of its sister movements, the MPLA in Angola and the PAIGC in Cape Verde and Guinea Bissau. Independence for the majority of the continent did not bring an end to the exploitation of peasants and workers. Rather, it served to camouflage the real nature of that exploitation and enabled foreign companies to continue extracting their profits. At the same time it facilitated the creation of a new native class of exploiters. Imperialism operates through colonialism and neocolonialism alike. It cannot continue in the post-independence phase without an alliance with a new indigenous ruling class to defend the interests of the capitalist system within a country. The fight against imperialism during the national liberation struggle had also to be conducted against imperialism's potential allies within the nationalist movement itself.

The development of Frelimo's ideology

Ideological struggles reflecting the different class positions represented by leaders of Frelimo had taken place from the very beginning. With the start of the armed struggle and the formation of semi-liberated zones, the ideological struggle intensified as new kinds of decisions had to be taken. The revolutionary line, representing the interests of the majority of the population, made steady advances. At the Central Committee meeting of 1966, racism, tribalism and regionalism were declared enemies to be fought in the same way as colonialism.[3] These, however, were precisely the ideological weapons used by the neocolonialist line inside the leadership when it tried to take control of the movement. Having these principles enshrined in Frelimo's policy did not prevent them from continuing to employ racist tactics, but it did strengthen the revolutionaries in their struggle. Setbacks did occur, however. In the midst of the crisis, in 1968, the neocolonialist elements were able to manoeuvre with some members of the Tanzanian government (but not President Nyerere) to have white Frelimo militants expelled from the country. Only later, after the removal of Simango, were they able to return to resume their duties.

The 1966 Central Committee meeting also called for an end to the distinction between military and political cadres. This gave the revolutionary vanguard forces, strongly represented in the army, the possibility of playing a more decisive role in the work of political mobilisation. Commanders of the FPLM were only too aware of the need for a popular war involving the active participation of the people, in carrying weapons, giving information, fighting alongside the army in the militias and so on. Peasants would only give their unconditional support if the leaders were really seen to be defending their interests. Kavandame was opposed to the popularisation of the war and wanted a purely military fighting force, autonomous from the people, with politics kept as the preserve of the political leaders – in particular, of himself and his followers. They were more concerned with ruling than with raising the consciousness of the people to enable them to take political control over their own lives. With this aim in mind, Kavandame did not hesitate to use tribalism and regionalism to further his own ends.

With the creation of the Women's Detachment the mass base of support for the movement was enlarged, and this was seen as bringing a new and decisive force to the revolutionary struggle.[4] All the advances in the movement's ideology produced gains on the battlefield. However, with the expansion of zones of combat and the consolidation of liberated areas, it became clear, both in discussions within the Central Committee and in the practical application of policies, that Frelimo was far from being a homogeneous entity. As we have already examined the events of this period in some detail, it now remains to underline that the defeat of Gwenjere, Kavandame and Simango was primarily a defeat of their ideology. Frelimo made the decisive break with neocolonialism, and revolutionary positions were consolidated as a result. This, then, created the possibility for the political military offensive to begin in earnest.

At the Central Committee meeting held in May 1970 significant ideological advances were made. The direct enemy was defined as being colonialism and imperialism; but in addition, the Central Committee noted the existence of an internal and indirect enemy within the Front itself. The enemy was not defined by colour, nationality, race or religion, rather as 'Whoever at a certain moment practises the exploitation of man by man, whatever the methods and forms that exploitation takes'.[5]

In a speech made the following year, Samora Machel neatly summarised the essence of Frelimo's ideology that had emerged from the bitter internal struggle: 'Our war is a war of national liberation against Portuguese colonialism, against imperialism and against the exploitation of man by man.'[6]

At the meeting of the Central Committee in 1970, a deep and penetrating assessment of the weaknesses and strengths of the movement was made. A certain disequilibrium was noted between the development of the struggle and the general level of political consciousness. As a result, a major reorganisation of all the structures of Frelimo took place the following year. Schools and the health services, as well as the army, became centres for diffusing the new ideology. Political work was intensified at all levels. The liberated zones were to be consolidated and turned into bases for the formation of cadres; as the movement saw it, they were to be staging posts, points of departure for the advance of the struggle. The new ideology – in other words, a different way of seeing the world and acting upon it – was to be put into practice in the liberated zones. This meant that discipline in the schools was to be organised by the students; patients in the hospitals were to take part in the problems of health care; and elected committees of peasants rather than the traditional chief were to direct the life of the village.

Towards the end of 1971 the tasks for the coming year were set.[7] Priority was given to work among the cadres. The reasons are not hard to discover; only a well-prepared group of militants could do the necessary work of mobilisation over the vast area which Frelimo now controlled. The people living in the liberated zones had to be taught to assume their new responsibilities. Cadres had to lead the combat against old ideas, such as those concerning the inferiority of women and youth. The ideology of so-called 'African socialism' in many states within the continent, defying as it does traditional communalism, neglected the repressive aspects of these pre-capitalist societies. A real revolution – working towards socialism – could never be a return to an earlier mode of production and traditional way of life. It had to move towards a more advanced form of social organisation. Cadres were decisive in making this transformation possible, and the movement concentrated on raising their political and educational knowledge. Frelimo's ideology could be spread only through the work of the cadres. Uniting the cadres with the people was considered to be essential if the new ideas were really to take root.

Criticism and self-criticism were encouraged as the means by which old ideas could be replaced by new ones. Self-criticism was the open acknowledgement that mistakes are made but that lessons can be drawn from them. It was a way of encouraging each militant to fight a personal, internal battle in the struggle to assume the new ideology. Methods of leadership were to be continually democratised, and a warning was given about the dangers of resolving political problems with administrative solutions. These tasks laid out at the end of 1971 were to be recurrent themes guiding the struggle, even in the post-independence period. Samora Machel explained the qualitative change taking place in Frelimo thus:

> The seventh year began with the transformation of our armed struggle into a revolution, it began with an intense battle to create a new mentality. The seventh year was the point of departure for the conscious evolution of the nature of our organisation, its evolution towards becoming a vanguard party of the working masses of our country, a vanguard party with a vanguard ideology.[8]

'Armed struggle' is not synonymous with 'revolution'. In Kenya, during the Mau Mau rebellion, armed bands had operated in the Aberdare forest region, but liberated zones with a functioning alternative society did not exist and the ensuing Kenyatta regime became a virtual parody of neocolonialism.[9] Revolution involves making a break with old ideas and structures, creating entirely new economic and social relationships in their stead. Only a political vanguard guided by a revolutionary ideology which represented the interests of the working people of Mozambique could lead and direct this process of change. The leadership of Frelimo came to Marxism from their search for a way forward that would make a decisive break with the past. It was no foreign import but something that emerged from the real struggles taking place both inside the movement and in the country. Marxism was adopted as the theory which represented the interests of the working people of Mozambique. Frelimo applied the theory creatively to its own situation; to do otherwise would have been a recipe for disaster. Frelimo explained its position on this issue in 1970:

> The Mozambican revolution is essentially Mozambican. It is not copied from any other revolution, but is dictated by the interests of our people and by the solidarity with other peoples who are fighting against colonialism and imperialism. But a people's revolution has characteristics in common with other people's revolutions, no matter in what time or in which place; the experiences of other revolutions help us to find solutions for certain of our problems, to foresee certain phases of our revolutionary process, to find the most suitable formulas to characterise our situation at each moment.[10]

Frelimo eschewed the labels traditionally employed, and during the national liberation struggle never categorised the movement as having a Marxist–Leninist ideology: to do so would have meant little to the peasants inside the country. What was significant for the peasants, and therefore the reason why they supported Frelimo, was the real content of the movement's programme and the way in which it was implemented in practice. It is here that we find some of the main features of Marxism: the struggle to end class exploitation, to overcome the division between intellectual and manual labour, and to integrate theory and practice. On the latter theme, Machel has written: 'for ideas to live and develop they need praxis, as a plant needs water . . . we have to live our ideology at the level of the structures and in our daily work'.[11]

At a meeting of the Defence Department held in July 1972, an attempt was made to develop a synthesis of the ideological and class struggles that had taken place within the movement during the crisis.[12] The class content of ideology was carefully analysed, and from the ensuing debate there emerged the necessity of a clearer definition of ideology and of its application in the political practice of the FPLM and Frelimo as a whole. In December of the same year, these discussions were renewed and further developed at a meeting of the Central Committee, the fifth such meeting since the Second Congress. The decisions taken at that time, Frelimo believed, set the movement on its final road to victory. Armed struggle was to be made an integral part of the life of the Mozambican people, it proclaimed, and the war to be truly popularised. Each Mozambican was to be encouraged to live the political line, thus giving the movement's ideology a real and material form in day-to-day social practice. This involved making sure that all the people knew the movement's principles, the tasks to be fulfilled and the objectives of the struggle. Methods of work were clearly defined, and it was openly stated that these had to be democratised so as not to make them the monopoly of a single group. Finally, there was the call for a generalised offensive on all fronts.

The primacy of the ideological struggle was further reaffirmed at the 1973 Central Committee meeting, which was convened chiefly in order to study how to apply the decisions of the previous year. As Samora Machel was later to remark:

Our struggle was a struggle at the level of ideas, it had to stop being a simple liberation struggle because national unity was no longer sufficient. . . . Only with revolutionary ideological unity could we conduct the liberation struggle in a fruitful way, in a way which would lead to victory.[13]

In his speech at the Independence celebrations, the President explained that this ideological unity had to be founded on a clear vision of what Frelimo wanted for the future and the society that it proposed to construct.[14] He stressed that the principles had to be lived and developed in practice. The ideology manifested itself in the new society growing in the liberated areas, and there was a clear demarcation between these, and those areas still under colonial control. In this speech Samora Machel attributed the defeat of Portuguese colonialism to a just line and correct political practice – that is, that the ideology of the movement was lived on a daily basis by the cadres. This meant that great emphasis was placed on the comportment of Frelimo militants – on the sound assumption that people would make their judgement of the movement not only by what was said but essentially by what was done.

A vanguard party, on the lines established by Lenin, was the way chosen by Frelimo to lead the process of transforming society in general and the individuals forming that society in particular. The year 1973 saw the formation of the first party committees inside the FPLM, and in January 1974 the party school began operating, in order to provide a sounder theoretical base for the cadres. The work of the school involved teaching the classics of Marx and Lenin in addition to the concrete experiences of Frelimo's own history and class struggles. Both the President and the Vice-President gave the work of the school the highest priority, personally giving lectures on the courses. Frelimo's approach has always been one which sees the need to apply Marxist theory creatively to the concrete circumstances confronting each particular country. It has rejected the erroneous notion of Marxism–Leninism providing a single blueprint for action. Such a crystallisation of dogma as occurred under Stalin is roundly condemned.

The emergence of a vanguard revolutionary leadership within the broader nationalist front was a vitally important ingredient for the transformation of Frelimo. We should now, perhaps, try to analyse more theoretically the processes involved.

Why a revolutionary leadership emerged

Frelimo's victory in the Mozambican struggle owed much to the decisive break made with the mainstream of traditional African nationalism and to the choice of a revolutionary path. The Italian writer Antonio Gramsci can help us conceptualise how this revolutionary leadership came into being. Gramsci's writings were frequently produced under the worst possible conditions of prison and censorship in the early decades of the century, inevitably without either the experience or the focus of our own study. However, certain Gramscian concepts employed and reinterpreted for our own purposes appear to cast new theoretical insight on the problem of how the intellectuals who formed the revolutionary leadership emerged within the Mozambican nationalist movement. The focus of Gramsci's analysis is precisely on the role of the intellectual, in particular the question of whether intellectuals are an autonomous and independent social group or whether every social class has its own specialised category of intellectuals.[15] The problem is complex, because the real historical process has created a variety of ways in which categories of intellectuals are produced. Every class coming into existence creates organically within itself a strata of intellectuals which give it homogeneity and an awareness of its function in the economic, social and political fields. These *organic* intellectuals Gramsci differentiates from the *traditional* intellectuals – priests, professionals, academics and others, who appear to be outside of the class structure but who ultimately derive from past social class relationships. The organic intellectuals are not distinguished by their profession, which may be anything within their class, but rather by the function they perform in directing the consciousness of their class. It was erroneous to distinguish intellectuals by the intrinsic nature of intellectual activity, Gramsci argued, rather than by the ensemble of the system of relations in which those activities took place.[16]

There are important implications in Gramsci's analysis of the intellectuals for the question of political organisation. We may draw a parallel between his remarks on the Russian intellectuals and (for our own purposes) the African intellectuals of the Portuguese colonies. In his analysis of Russian intellectuals he shows how an elite group of the most active, energetic, enterprising and disciplined members of the society emigrated abroad and there assimilated the experiences of the most advanced countries of the West. They did this without breaking their sentimental and historical links with their own people. Then, 'Having [thus] performed its intellectual apprenticeship it returns to its own country and compels the people to an enforced awakening, skipping historical stages in the process'.[17] Some of Mozambique's intellectuals, like those of Russia, were to undergo this same process. A small number of blacks and people of mixed race were assimilated as intellectuals in the arts, literature and science. A small fraction of this group, who studied first in Lisbon at the turn of the 1950s and later in the major metropolitan centres, were to become the founders and leaders of the nationalist movements. In Angola these included Agostinho Neto (a poet and medical doctor) and Mario de Andrade (a literary critic and author); in Mozambique, Eduardo Mondlane (a university academic) and Marcelino dos Santos (engineer, sociologist and poet); in Portuguese Guinea, most notably Amilcar Cabral (an agronomist by training). A small proportion of those traditional intellectuals who had studied abroad formed a Marxist embryo which grew within the womb of the broader nationalist front. The Marxist 'traditional' intellectuals combined with the growing numbers of organic intellectuals from the worker and peasant classes. The latter (the organic intellectuals) were formed as intellectuals of their class both in the training camps and in the day-to-day experience of the political and military struggle. Access to Marxist literature and the presence of those gifted and committed cadres who were able to assimilate and creatively apply the theory to their own concrete situation were invaluable necessities. Together, the organic and traditional intellectuals grew, in every conceivable aspect, in the process of the struggle itself. It was the complex inter-reaction between the struggle and Marxist theory which formed them into a *de facto* revolutionary vanguard within the broader front.

Lenin wrote of the need to obliterate the distinction between workers and intellectuals within a political organisation, with all the members becoming professional revolutionaries.[18] Frelimo was a nationalist front and not a vanguard party, but a 'vanguard' of professional revolutionaries (not simply militant nationalists) crystallised within it. The task of the political organisation that Gramsci saw was to channel the activity of the organic intellectuals who provided the key link between their class and a section of the traditional intellectuals. In the African context a distinction must be made between the traditional intellectuals of pre-capitalist social formations, the chiefs and the spirit mediums, and those produced under colonial capitalism. The former had to be won over in the early stages of the armed struggle in the Portuguese colonies as they commanded the allegiance and support of the peasants. Gramsci has written:

> One can understand nothing of the collective life of the peasantry and of the germs and ferments of development which exist within it, if one does not take into consideration and examine concretely and in depth this effective subordination to the intellectuals. Every organic development of the peasant masses, up to a certain point, is linked to and depends on movements among the intellectuals.[19]

By harnessing the legitimacy of the traditional intellectuals of the pre-capitalist social formations, the nationalist movement was able to win the support of the peasants. Only later were the organic intellectuals of the under-classes, in combination with a revolutionary fraction of the traditional intellectuals formed under colonial capitalism, able to establish the 'moral isolation' of both colonialism and the chiefs and spirit mediums. This is the process which we saw unfolding in the later part of the book. The mere presence alone of the vanguard was not sufficient to ensure the revolutionaries' success. A series of inner battles had to be fought against what Bragança has termed 'the class block of the *bourgeois-feudal* alliance' (he is here using Gramscian terminology).[20] This block, we would argue, was composed of traditional intellectuals of the pre-capitalist social formations (the chairmen) and bourgeois intellectuals (Simango, Murrupa and others) who, together, were opposed to a systemic transformation which would eliminate the possibilities for their class aspirations to be realised. The successful inner struggle, won by the Marxist traditional and organic intellectuals, produced a series of policies representing the interests of the working class and the peasantry. With the resolution of the crisis, the movement's programme and policies more closely articulated the grievances of the under-classes, and in the liberated areas a viable and positive *living* alternative was provided. Foretelling Machel's emphasis on the need for principles to be lived in practice, Gramsci wrote, 'The mode of being of the new intellectual can no longer consist in eloquence, which is an exterior and momentary mover of feelings and passions, but in active participation in practical life, as constructor, organiser, "permanent persuader" and not just simple orator.'[21] Finally, the success of the revolutionary vanguard's inner struggle owed much to the perspicacity with which the battles were fought within the Front. The vanguard ensured that, both internally and externally, people were aware of the issues and supported its positions at the decisive moments. The quality of the leadership, therefore, in choosing when the battles could be fought and won, was highly important. But the element of good fortune must never be overlooked, and having President Nyerere as the head of the external host country was surely an example of such good fortune.

In the final section of this chapter we examine the liberated areas. It was here that the new ideology took on a palpable form. The new structures existing in the liberated areas were a concrete manifestation of the ideology, providing proof to the people that Frelimo's alternative was not only desirable but was also possible.

The liberated areas

Inside the expanding liberated areas economic, health, educational and political structures were growing up alongside an emerging new culture. We can only touch on a few of the many and varied aspects of all of these, beginning with the economic. Given constant Portuguese army incursions into Frelimo's areas, maintaining agricultural production was not always easy. Initially, when new areas were liberated, the movement aimed only to keep up a constant rhythm of production in spite of enemy bombardments.[22] Then, in a second phase, production in general was developed and internal trade organised; finally, a network of shops was set up to organise imports and exports.

Advances in the political–military struggle increased the number of peasants cultivating in Frelimo's areas and the amount of land available to be worked. This in its turn had a reciprocal effect on the progress of the war. One Frelimo publication described the wider impact of the liberated zones in this way: 'Its message and its promise permeates the consciousness of those who still live beyond the forward lines.'[23] In addition to quantitative changes in the productive forces (labour and the means of production), there were also qualitative transformations. New seeds and crop techniques were introduced. Centres of agricultural experimentation were established at major military bases where a combination of modern agricultural science and traditional experience was brought to bear on such persistent problems as plant disease and the optimum nutrition for plants.[24] The Frelimo army had an important role to play here. People from all regions and ethnic groups were in the guerrilla army, facilitating the spread of successful techniques used in the traditional agriculture of their home areas, and sometimes these techniques would be combined and improved upon.[25] The enormous prestige enjoyed by the guerrillas enabled traditional barriers of prejudice towards innovations of any kind to be gradually overcome. Animal husbandry was introduced in those parts of Cabo Delgado where the tse-tse fly was not present, and tree cultivation was carried out in all the liberated areas. Irrigation was encouraged, and peasants were urged to utilise the many small streams and rivers wherever possible. This involved the use of gravity-fed ditches and the watering can. A Chinese delegation visiting Muidumbe district of Cabo Delgado found that every household had built a storage bin of straw and wood for maize and cashew.[26] Not all the innovations, however, were a success, the introduction of oxen and donkeys being a case in point. Fish-drying, salt-production and the small-scale manufacture of agricultural and domestic implements took place inside the liberated areas, but still many things had to be brought in from Tanzania. However, as one Frelimo leader commented during the war:

> As far as certain goods are concerned this is only temporary, because the development of handicrafts is making it possible to solve certain problems internally. Indeed, in some zones fewer and fewer axes, hoes and knives were being sold because the old blacksmiths freed from the constraints of forced cotton cultivation or forced labour, have resumed their iron-working with fragments of shot-down aircraft and destroyed vehicles.[27]

Increases in exports from the liberated zones demonstrated the progress being made in the economy. A part of the surplus produce went to support the new war zones where production had yet to begin, and the remainder was exported to pay for the import of essential goods which were unable to be produced internally, such as cloth, matches and soap. Cabo Delgado produced by far the greatest volume of exports, mainly cashew nuts, sesame seeds and groundnuts. The total weight exported grew from 997 982 kilogrammes in 1969, to 1 229 304 kilogrammes in 1971.[28] All exports and imports, it should be remembered, had to be carried on the heads of the peasants, sometimes over distances of hundreds of kilometres. By 1973–1974, over all the provinces, cashews were still the leading export, but sesame seed and beeswax were rapidly gaining in importance. Groundnut exports fell because Frelimo took the decision that these should be used for home consumption. This stands in stark contrast with patterns of protein export prevailing in so many neocolonial countries throughout the third world. Other important exports towards the end of the war included castor-oil seed and wood carvings. From 1973 Frelimo started exporting produce to Zambia from the liberated areas of Tete Province.[29] Having removed Kavandame and the private traders (who were paying low prices), the peasants proved far more willing to trade their surplus. Prices were increased three-fold for cashews and one-and-a-half times for honey over those paid previously.[30]

No less important than the development of the productive forces in the liberated areas, and indeed crucial to these very developments, were transformations in the social relations of production. Four identifiable forms of production relationships existed inside Frelimo's areas, and of these individual production by peasant families remained the dominant one to the end of the war. Secondly, there were the so-called pre-collective *machambas*. Here the peasants had their own individual plots, but these were adjacent, enabling the peasants to organise themselves collectively to defend their crops from predators. Thirdly, there were collective *machambas* which were worked in addition to the private plots, and each person's labour time was recorded and the harvest was distributed according to the number of days worked. Finally, there was total collective production organised within Frelimo's own structures. All the schools and health posts produced their food collectively, as did the FPLM. Self-reliance was a cornerstone of Frelimo's policy. The new and varying forms of social production released a great quantity of creative energy and initiative among the peasants, which helped overcome the problems of severe material shortages during the war. However, for the peasants, full co-operative production emerged only in the liberated areas of Cabo Delgado, and even there not extensively.

One important feature of Frelimo's ideology meriting special attention is the political role that production was seen to play. Absolutely everyone was expected to produce, not only the peasants. Marcelino dos Santos, one of the guiding spirits of the Mozambican revolution, made a poignant commentary on this principle, and his words go a long way towards explaining the reasons for Frelimo's success during the war:

> If we seem to place undue importance to the area of production it is because we believe that this activity, productive labour, has the best educational value for our militants in the revolution. . . . The fact that everyone, without exception, works in the fields – the president, vice-president, military cadres and other Frelimo leaders at all levels – has helped to create good communications and good relations among the revolutionary Mozambican people, regardless of their particular areas of training and responsibility.[31]

In the health field great strides were also being made. A foreign delegation visiting the liberated zones of Cabo Delgado at the beginning of the 1970s reported that in addition to the main health centre in the Province, Frelimo had eleven district and field hospitals and fifty-six mobile first-aid stations.[32] Niassa Province had two regional hospitals, fourteen district medical posts and eighteen first-aid posts.[33] By 1972, over all the liberated areas, Frelimo had 420 health workers operating in forty district hospitals and a much larger number of first-aid centres.[34] Nevertheless, conditions were extremely difficult for those cadres involved in health care; in 1973, for example, the Cabo Delgado main hospital was burnt to the ground in a raid by the colonial army. The training programme for health workers had been interrupted for three years as a result of the movement's internal crisis, and was only re-started in 1971.[35] Like every other sphere of activity, health policy was profoundly affected by the movement's developing revolutionary political line. The emphasis was placed on preventive health care, involving mass mobilisation; health education was to be integrated with political education. All the nurses received political–military training and were expected to mobilise the people and fight, as well as being concerned with health care. In addition, health care was not restricted to health workers. As one health worker put it:

> all our Frelimo cadres are health educators. It's done through what we call our 'circles'. These are the units of the agricultural collectives. . . . We meet to discuss what to grow and how to dispose of our produce. So we also discuss health questions at that time. . . . We talk about three things mostly, sanitation, nutrition, and [people] coming to the clinic when they're ill.[36]

The massive expansion of health facilities in the liberated areas (however inadequate compared with the absolute need for such services), was an entirely new phenomenon unknown under colonial rule. Colonial health services were concentrated in the cities and were geared towards the needs of the settler population. Medicine was private, and the cost far exceeded the budgets of most African households. The provision of free medical treatment in the Frelimo zones provided important proof to the peasants of the movement's political claims to represent their interests.

In the field of education important changes were made, many of which we have previously examined. A new Frelimo secondary school, set up forty miles north of Dar-es-Salaam, without the comforts and distractions of city life, initially accommodated fifty-two students.[37] The numbers of children receiving schooling within the liberated areas expanded considerably. By 1972, in total there were estimated to be 160 primary schools attended by 20 000 children.[38] Iain Christie visited the liberated areas of Cabo Delgado in 1973, and reported that 9 000 students were attending the first three years of primary schooling in the Province, whilst a further 135 were studying in their fourth class of primary school.[39] Students had an integrated programme of study and manual work, and political education naturally played an important part in the syllabus.

A visit to a pilot education centre south of the Zambezi river in the liberated areas of Tete Province revealed some of the difficulties under which the schools had to work. The pilot centre, initially attended by some 200 children, was attacked by Rhodesian army forces in September and October 1972.[40] A major offensive was launched again in October 1973, this time lasting for three months;[41] lessons had to stop completely on this occasion. A further attack occurred in May 1974; but every time the work of the school was rapidly resumed after the assaults, though the school would be based in a different location. During the rainy season from November to March, there was no shortage of drinking water, but as the dry season progressed the situation grew appreciably worse. Not infrequently, at the height of the dry season, the Rhodesian army would place a guard on the few remaining water points in the area. This periodic military harassment, combined with shortages of educational materials, food and water, made the maintenance of the work of the school extremely difficult.[42] Only the high level of political consciousness among the teachers, pupils and the surrounding villagers made this possible. Some idea of the suffering involved may be gauged from statistics supplied by the secretary of the local *circulo*. In the 1973–1974 period, 208 people died of hunger and 100 were killed.[43] Hunger was the great killer, and this was a result of the efficiency of the Rhodesian troops, who effectively were in command of counter-insurgency operations south of the Zambezi river in Tete Province.[44] People in the liberated areas of this sector lived only by hunting and by collecting the fruit of the baobab tree. The gathering was organised collectively, but agricultural production *per se* never proved to be possible.[45] In spite of all these difficulties, Frelimo's educational structures grew up rapidly in the expanding liberated zones. John Chivanuvanu (who was head of education in the fourth sector of Tete at the time) and Crispen Matches set up this particular pilot centre on 4 June 1972; within three months they had established a further twenty-eight schools in the sector, employing thirty-eight teachers.[46]

Frelimo's new *poder popular* political structures also spread dramatically. When people first fled to join the movement, one of the Frelimo cadres would help to organise them into a *círculo*. This was the base level unit of the political structure. When there were three or more *círculos* in a given area, then a locality committee would be set up. After the political commissar had spent a certain time holding meetings to politicise the people, a mass meeting would choose who their representatives were going to be and where the headquarters of the locality committee was to be based.[47] Mass meetings would be held approximately twice a month. More frequently, the secretaries of the *círculos* would meet with the political commissar of their locality, and the district political commissar in his turn would hold meetings with the commissars from the localities. There were no hard and fast rules for the number of meetings to be held; this clearly would depend on the local conditions and the problems needing to be solved. Kumeta Mchenga, Political Commissar of Sapenba Locality in Tete, for example, toured his *círculos* three times a month on average.[48] The members of the committees were appointed to more senior levels according to their political consciousness and general abilities. Several times a year the District Political Commissar would hold seminars to raise the political consciousness of people in positions of responsibility.[49]

The highest democratic political structure within the Province was the *Conselho Provincial* (Provincial Council), which theoretically was supposed to meet once every year. In reality, the problems of the war made it impossible to hold the statutory annual meeting. In Tete Province, for example, it met only in 1970 and 1972.[50] Representatives from all the different levels met at the *Conselho Provincial*, including the secretary and perhaps five or six villagers from every *círculo*. This meeting, of more than 1000 people, would last for two days, with the Provincial Secretary or the Secretary of the Defence Department presiding. At the meeting, all of the problems of the war and the liberated zones would be discussed. Frelimo's political structures aimed to maximise direct participation by the people in decision-making and problem-solving. The various levels in the hierarchy were to provide channels of two-way communication between the base and the top of the movement. Undoubtedly, the functioning of a genuine grassroots democracy helped to transform the tacit support for Frelimo into active involvement in the national liberation struggle.

Many of the developments in the liberated areas, however, took on a far less tangible form than those already described, but they none the less signified real advances. Eliza Sumahili summarised the changes that she personally had undergone as a woman in the following way:

> I gained a wide experience of speaking to men and the public in general – of communicating – and I stopped feeling afraid, which is what I felt whilst living at home. Traditionally in my village, a girl could never speak with either a man or a boy. . . . Now we discuss on an equal footing.[51]

Women also took part in dances formerly reserved for men, and the old sex and age barriers dividing the communities gradually began to be eroded. Song, dances and poems reflecting the course of the national liberation struggle became widespread, and were constantly changing their themes to meet the needs of each new phase or situation in the war.[52] A profound cultural transformation, therefore, was taking place in the lives of the people.

The experience gained in the liberated areas was continually referred to as a model for the development of post-independence Mozambique, and it undoubtedly proved to be a valuable experimental ground for Frelimo's policies. However, the magnitude of the problems facing the movement after the takeover of power were to be of a different order, and many of the circumstances were new. In the final part of the book we turn to examine the post-independence situation.

Notes

1 Where landlordism is not an issue, it may very well be that peasant farmers are more likely to see the state as being the agent of exploitation.

2 Frelimo's theoretical analysis of the state and revolution is to be found in *Estabelecer o Poder Popular para Servir as Massas*, Maputo, 1979.

3 *Mozambique Revolution*, 27, Oct.–Dec. 1966.

4 'Discurso de Estado do Camarada Presidente da Frelimo, Samora Moisés Machel na tomada de posse da República Popular de Moçambique', in *Datas e Documentos da História da Frelimo*, J. Reis and A. P. Muiuane (eds), Maputo, 1975, p. 498.

5 *Mozambique Revolution*, 43, April–June 1970.

6 'As vitórias de Frelimo historiadas pelo Camarada Samora Moisés Machel no Tofo (Inhambane)', in *Datas e Documentos*, p. 454.

7 'Mensagem do Presidente da Frelimo nos Combatentes das FPLM e ao Povo Moçambicano, por ocasião do 7 aniversário da luta armada de Libertação nacional', in Frelimo, *A vitória constrói – se, A vitória organiza – se*, Textos e documentos da Frelimo, 2, Maputo, 1977, pp. 73–86.

8 *Ibid.*, pp. 83–84.

9 On the changing political dimension of guerrilla war in Africa see B. Davidson, *The People's Cause: a History of Guerrillas in Africa*, London, 1981.

10 'Lenin and the Revolution', *Mozambique Revolution*, 42, Jan.–March 1970.

11 *A vitória constrói – se*, p. 84.

12 *Report of the Central Committee to the Third Congress*, Maputo, 1977.

13 'Discurso do Camarada Presidente Samora Machel na abertura do Comité Central em Inhambane', in *Datas e Documentos*, p. 434.

14 'Discurso de Estado do Camarada Presidente da Frelimo, Samora Moisés Machel na tomada de posse da República Popular de Moçambique', in *Datas e Documentos.*, p. 500.

15 A. Gramsci, *Selections from the Prison Notebooks*, London, 1973, especially pp. 3–23.

16 *Ibid.*, p. 8.

17 *Ibid.*, p. 20.

18 V. I. Lenin, *What is to be Done?* London, 1970, p. 156.

19 Gramsci, *Prison Notebooks*, pp. 14–15.

20 A. de Bragança, 'La longue marche de Samora', *Afrique-Asie*, 18 April 1977.

21 A. Gramsci, *Prison Notebooks*, p. 10.

22 Armando Guebuza (Frelimo), *Report on the Liberation Struggle in Mozambique*, a paper given at the International Conference of Support to the Peoples of the Portuguese Colonies, mimeo, Rome, 1970.

23 *Mozambique Revolution*, 50, Jan.–March 1972.

24 Darlib Support Group, interview with Joaquim Carvalho, Secretary of the Department of Production and Commerce, mimeo, Dar-es-Salaam, 30 May 1974.

25 Mozambique Institute, *Frelimo Social Development*, Dar-es-Salaam, August 1971.

26 *Daily News*, Dar-es-Salaam, 4 May 1972.

27 'Statement by Jorge Rebelo of Frelimo at the 915th Meeting of the Special Committee of 24', mimeo, 13 Feb. 1973.

28 *Mozambique Revolution*, 51, April–June, 1972.

29 See the interview with Joaquim Chissano in *Ceres, F.A.O. Review*, Aug. 1973.

30 Interview with Inaçiao Nunes, who was put in charge of trade in Cabo Delgado in 1970, Dar-es-Salaam, Jan. 1975.

31 Boubaker Adjali, 'Interview with Marcelino dos Santos', Liberation Support Movement, Richmond (Canada), 1971, p. 14.

32 *Daily News*, Dar-es-Salaam, 4 May 1972.

33 G. Watts, 'What to Do When the Doctors Leave', *World Medicine*, xii, 8, 26 Jan. 1977, 18.

34 Darlib Support Group (Working Group on Health), 'Frelimo's Health Services on the Eve of Independence: The Challenge of National Reconstruction', mimeo, Dar-es-Salaam, Sept. 1974.

35 S. Machel, *Mozambique. Sowing the Seeds of Revolution*, Committee for Freedom in Mozambique, Angola and Guinea, London, 1974, p. 46.

36 M. Segall, 'Health and National Liberation in the People's Republic of Mozambique', *International Journal of Health Services*, vii, 2, 1977, 320.

37 *The Standard*, Dar-es-Salaam, 7 April 1971.

38 *Daily News*, Dar-es-Salaam, 4 May 1972.

39 *Afrique-Asie*, 10–23 Dec. 1973.

40 Interview with Crispen Marcus Matches, Head of the school, Pilot Centre Jeque, Tete Province, 14 May 1975.

41 Interview with Gonçalves Chaora, a teacher, Pilot Centre Jeque, Tete Province, 15 May 1975.

42 Interview with Augusto Denge, chief of education in the 4th sector of Tete, Pilot Centre Jeque, Tete Province, 15 May 1975.

43 Interview with the Secretary of Jeque Círculo, May 1975.

44 Interview with Augusto Denge, *op. cit.*

45 *Ibid.*

46 Interview with Crispen Matches, *op. cit.*

47 Interview with Kominet Itani, Political Commissar of Mavudzi Locality, Tete Province, 23 May 1975.

48 Interview with Kumeta Mchenga, Political Commissar of Sapenba Locality, Tete Province, 23 May 1975.

49 Interview with Joaquim Norte, Political Commissar, Sabundo, Tete Province, 21 May 1975.

50 Interview with Lucas Lepewa, Sectoral Chief of Operations, Furancungu, Tete Province, 26 May 1975. Similarly, meetings of Congress were statutorily to be held every four years; but in practice six years separated the first from the Second Congress and nine years separated the Second from the Third Congress.

51 M. Manceaux, *As Mulheres de Moçambique*, Lisbon, 1976, p. 77.

52 See, for example, Frelimo, *Poesía de Combate*, Maputo, 1977, and Associação Portugal–Moçambique, *As Armas Estão Acesas Nas Nossas Mâos*, Porto, 1976.

PART FOUR

Preparing the transition to socialism

14 Political development

Frelimo had succeeded in its primary aim of winning independence, and that was where many African political parties were content to let the matter rest – collecting for themselves the benefits accruing from control of the post-colonial state machine. Along the way and in the course of the armed national liberation struggle Frelimo had set itself a further goal, to be crystallised at the movement's Third Congress held in 1977 – the building of a socialist society. This was a far more ambitious project, implying a permanent struggle and entirely new policies to wrench the country out of the quagmire of underdevelopment. On the whole, those states maintaining rather than destroying the inherited system had failed to achieve this, and Frelimo was determined to try a new approach.

The obstacles were formidable, not least because of a continuing economic dependency on apartheid South Africa. There was chaos in industry and agriculture precipitated by the mass exodus of colonial settlers, who took with them all the skills that they had formerly monopolised. The population was illiterate, diseased and frequently malnourished. In short, this state of affairs was the sorry legacy of Portuguese colonial rule. We will examine how the movement tackled these problems, the mistakes it made and its attempts, successful or otherwise, to meet the new situation. The struggles and the processes we have previously been describing were to continue with added intensity in the post-independence period. As yet any final evaluation of the post-independence phase would be precipitate, but we can present such evidence as does exist, and show how certain major themes, previously examined, continued to evolve.

Mozambique became independent on 25 June 1975 after a nine-month period of Transitional Government under a Frelimo-appointed Prime Minister, Joaquim Chissano. Under him were six Frelimo ministers, and three were nominated by the Portuguese. Many new problems confronted the movement, not least what to do with the newly occupied urban areas.[1] Each of the three major cities posed a different kind of problem. In Nampula this was militarism, with all its attendant vices. The city had been the colonial army's headquarters, and anti-Frelimo propaganda had been strongly inculcated amongst the urban population. Beira faced the problem of racism, as a result of the strong Rhodesian influence and the history of British company rule. Lourenço

Marques was the bastion of foreign and national capital, the stronghold of both the companies and the settlers.

Frelimo also had to cope with ruling all the country's nine provinces, including rural areas previously untouched by the movement's presence. The situation was not made any easier by the compromises engendered on sharing power with the Portuguese.[2] Among a few cadres material corruption occurred, as some decided that the time had come to enjoy the 'fruits' of independence after years of sacrifice. Retribution swiftly followed, and their dismissal was a sign that the leadership was determined to continue the ethos of self-denial created during the war. This, indeed, was vital, because essentially the new government had to rely on its political impact to tackle the grave problems of dependency and poverty facing the country. Maintaining the political dynamic had been crucial for winning the war against the Portuguese army. It would prove no less crucial for winning the war against underdevelopment. President Machel highlighted this theme in his Independence Day address: 'In establishing our development strategy', he said, 'we must attach special value to what is our chief strength, the mobilisation and organisation of the people.'[3]

If the successes of the national liberation struggle had to be explained in as few words as possible, these would have to be that Frelimo knew how to mobilise and organise the population. Beginning under the Transitional Government, for the first time in generations there was freedom of expression and assembly in the zones not liberated during the war, with thousands of meetings being held in every part of Mozambique. Welding together a single nation was an important preoccupation of the leadership, given the diversities existing in this huge country. Apart from language and cultural differences, the vast disparities in levels of political consciousness between the liberated and the non-liberated zones made the development of national unity an urgent priority. This was a major theme of all the meetings.

But Frelimo's message went beyond this, as it declared its intention of radically transforming the way in which production was organised. Essentially this was to be achieved by creating communal villages in the rural areas and structures of workers' control in industry, both of which depended on a high level of politicisation among the workforce. Mobilisation entailed giving political education to peasants and workers, encouraging them to take an active part in the political process. Organisational work provided the practical extension of this. The energy and initiatives of peasants and workers had to be harnessed if they were to become an effective force for change. Mobilisation and organisation were also important to provide some insurance that the revolutionary process would not grind to a halt, or become diverted from its original goals. The greatest danger was that the state might well be able to transform the revolution before the revolution could transform the state. Bureaucratisation of the state and party were real dangers which many countries had so far failed to overcome. With this in mind, perhaps, when Marcelino dos Santos was asked how a movement ensures that it achieves a real socialist revolution, he replied:

The main defence must be to popularise the revolutionary aims and to create such a situation that if for one reason or another at some future time some people start trying to change these aims, they will meet with some resistance from the masses.[4]

Dynamising groups

With the investiture of the Transitional Government, Frelimo produced a political innovation in Africa when it set up the *grupos dinamizadores* (dynamising groups) to carry out the work of mobilisation and organisation throughout the country.[5] The g.d.s., as they became known, were formed in every place of work or study as well as in the residential areas. They served a number of functions, but principally they were to incorporate the mass of the population into the political process by holding regular meetings and acting as a local catalyst for change. This was not always an easy process given such handicaps as a severe lack of transport in most areas. Up in the northernmost district of Niassa Province, for example, the secretary of the g.d. had to walk 170 kilometres to visit the farthest outlying cell.[6] In Maua, just to the south, there was not a single vehicle in the whole district.[7]

The antecedents of the g.d.s were the people's committees of the liberated areas, and the g.d.s were to become the earliest structural forms of *poder popular,* people's power, stretching throughout the nation. From the beginning they held a sweeping brief. Given the crisis in the colonial state apparatus and the overwhelming ground-swell of support which Frelimo initially enjoyed, people began to go to the g.d.s to resolve their problems rather than to the administration. They were never intended to be permanent structures, and their functions were later to be assumed by party committees, people's assemblies, production councils and various other organs established by Frelimo. The g.d.s were organised from the base up to the province, although it took some time for the structure to become operative at all levels. However, by the end of 1976 there existed a fairly comprehensive national coverage. A typical g.d. would have a secretary, assistant secretary and a *responsible* * with an assistant, for the following areas: mobilisation and organisation, information and propaganda, education and culture, women, social affairs, production and commerce and finance. The secretary acted as the convener and representative for the group as a whole.

Although the tasks of the individual *responsibles* is fairly self-explanatory, a word could usefully be said about two of them. Through the auspices of the education and culture section of the g.d.s, a massive literacy campaign was initiated, with those possessing little education teaching those with none at all. Particular emphasis was given to the cultural dimension of mobilising work. New songs and dances

---

* The term *responsible* (*responsável* in the original Portuguese) will be maintained throughout. There is no adequate translation of the term, which bears the connotation of leadership as a responsibility rather than as privilege, service rather than the power of officership.

addressed to the particular problems of the moment were continually being devised. Through the medium of culture the movement hoped to implant new values and briefs. By transforming culture, in the widest meaning of the term, it was hoped that the very fabric of society could itself be changed. The encouragement of cultural exchanges between different regions provides one such example, thus helping to overcome tribalism and weld together a single national culture. The importance of this was reflected in one of the watchwords of the g.d.s: 'unity'. This message was also spread by the information and propaganda section through its *Jornal de Povo*, people's newspaper. This was a selection of important news items, photographs and political writings displayed in a prominent public place so that all the constituents of a g.d. could read it. Given that many areas would not receive a magazine, newspaper or any written material at all, the *Jornal de Povo* was assured of an important role.[8]

Besides 'unity', the other watchwords of the g.d.s were 'work' and 'vigilance'. The encouragement of production was vital not only in order to overcome widespread economic sabotage but also to try to transform people's consciousness from the attitudes of work avoidance and 'laziness' characteristic of popular resistance under colonialism. Without 'work' the problems of underdevelopment could never be tackled. 'Vigilance' referred to the continuing threat posed by foreign invasions and the internal opposition,[9] and we shall examine both of these in due course.

When Frelimo came to power, many members of the petty bourgeoisie and opportunists of every description came forward, hoping to gain a position within the political structure either for personal reward or some more sinister motive. These included former members of the secret police and the counter-insurgency special forces. Because it was aware of the dangers that this posed, Frelimo was reluctant to permit a massive inflow of new recruits directly, and one of the tasks of the g.d.s was to provide a platform on which the inevitable class struggles of this phase of the revolution could be played out.

A good example of this process in operation is provided by the provincial g.d. of Manica Province in the first half of 1975.[10] The whole committee was under the influence of Senhor Fragoso, one of the richest businessmen in Vila Pery, the provincial capital. Fragoso was the manager of the local beer factory. He was highly articulate and had a (verbal) command of Frelimo's writings and Marxism. As his personal adjutants, Fragoso had an ex-Franciscan priest and a former hippy. Although there were a few honest men on the committee, virtually all were petty bourgeoisie office workers, mostly employed by the Administration. Through financial inducements, the loan of his Mercedes car, and the liberal dispersal of whisky, Fragoso managed to undermine not only the provincial g.d. but also the provincial political commissar, who should have been the one to prevent corruption within the g.d. The provincial commissar was a Frelimo militant from the very beginning, a man who had fought and suffered the hardships of the war. With independence, he had decided that the time had come to reap some of the rewards – an understandable attitude perhaps, but the Frelimo line was perfectly clear that comfort and revolution were incompatible.

For the May Day celebrations in 1975, the workers at the huge SOALPO textile factory in the town wished to organise a march. But the provincial g.d. refused permission and instead arranged a free football match. The *Jornal de Povo* displayed notices at the stadium proclaiming that 'The revolution means free football'! In June, Jose Moiane flew in to Vila Pery, to become the new governor of Manica. A senior Frelimo veteran who had directed the struggle in Tete Province in the closing years of the war, he soon rectified the situation. Fragoso flew off to Portugal and the political commissar was removed, in addition to five members of the provincial g.d.[11]

In order to understand the processes operating at that time, we have to place the formation of the g.d.s in their historical context. Frelimo was largely unaware at the time of the coup who were their actual supporters. The more articulate and educated members of the petty bourgeoisie were quick to present themselves as longstanding sympathisers. Within the colonial hierarchy they occupied the junior grades, but still enjoyed a social superiority in relation to the overwhelming proportion of black Mozambicans, who were workers or peasants. The latter let them take over control of many g.d.s, in part as a result of deference to their superior wealth, education and social standing. Secondly, the habit of silence engendered by repressive colonial rule was not an easy one to break, even for Frelimo's clandestine workers. Many opportunists occupied positions in the g.d.s as a result. Nevertheless, Frelimo gave continuing support to the class struggles being fought out within them. In a speech to a meeting of g.d. members from factories in the Maputo, Matola and Machava areas, the National Political Commissar stressed that the composition of the g.d.s must be constantly reviewed to see if they really represented the working class and incorporated the vanguard of the workers, removing those members potentially allied with capitalism.[12] These struggles were of immense benefit for people's political education, instilling an important sense of self-confidence in their ability to determine their own future. The g.d.s were a genuine political innovation, and demonstrated a determination to involve the people in the political and developmental processes in a manner rarely seen in an independent African country. They harnessed the ground-swell of enthusiastic support for the movement, which had, after all, ousted the most tenacious of the colonial powers.

Class and party

Rigid censorship and the difficulties of clandestine work under colonialism meant that many people had only a superficial idea of Frelimo's programme. They supported the movement because it brought independence, but beyond this their level of political understanding was limited. Even early members of Frelimo who had been imprisoned and were released after April 1974 knew little of the ideological developments since the crisis period. There was an urgent need for extensive political work over the whole country, but there was an equally desperate shortage of cadres to fulfil this task. Excluding children and those wives of members not operating actively within Frelimo, the movement had about 15 000 militants at the time of the coup.[13] Of these, only a few hundred would be top-quality cadres with an extensive political formation and several years' experience.

Given the acute shortage of cadres at independence, people were frequently placed in senior positions for which their previous experience had hardly prepared them. Many proved remarkably resilient and capable in the face of huge responsibilities, growing into their positions. Not surprisingly, though, a few proved unequal to the task. A movement is judged by its cadres. For the rural population of a remote region Frelimo *was* the particular political cadre in the area. For this reason, the movement always took scrupulous care both in training and in ensuring that those who slipped from the high standards set were speedily removed. In any particular district, one or more of the five leading officials would be a trusted Frelimo cadre. This might be the District Administrator, the Political Commissar, the Chief of Police, the FPLM commander (if there were a significant number of troops in the area), or the Secretary of the district g.d.

New party schools were opened to meet the increased demand for cadres, in Maputo, Cabo Delgado and Nampula provinces. In an address to one of the schools, soon after independence, Samora Machel outlined their central aim as being 'to prepare [cadres] with the instruments of social and political analysis that will permit them to detect the multiple forms which the class struggle assumes in our country at each moment'.[14] The cadres had to 'popularise the revolutionary aims' as Marcelino dos Santos had said, giving political leadership to the people. However, the role of the movement was not only to prepare the cadres, but also to ensure that the political leadership they gave was both coherent and unified and suited to the new phase of the revolution that Frelimo was entering. The question arose of whether the very nature of Frelimo would have to change in order to meet the new challenges.

Given Frelimo's stated determination to carry on the revolution, following the successful struggle against Portuguese colonialism, it had to be decided how the new enemy would be both defined and fought. Such a decision would have to be discussed at the highest level possible, and, as a result, the Third Congress of Frelimo was called for February 1977. A series of theses were presented for nationwide discussion as preparation, in a document entitled *Frelimo and the Mozambican Labouring Classes in the Building of People's Democracy*.[15] The second thesis presented the clearest short class analysis the movement had made of the immediate post-independence struggles, and it began by stressing that the winning of state power had intensified (rather than resolved) the class struggle. The new fight was against 'internal reactionaries and imperialism, the permanent enemy'. The exploiting classes were the colonial bourgeoisie who had virtually abandoned the country and the small and medium-sized internal bourgeoisie. With a weak economic base, the latter were desperately trying to substitute themselves for the colonial bourgeoisie. These two groups were in alliance with those who had formed the special indigenous combat units of the colonial army and those in the criminal unemployed strata. 'Taken together they are weak, but their penetration in the state apparatus and economy, and above all their position as internal representatives of imperialism makes them highly dangerous', the document warned. Opposed to them were the 'overwhelming majority of our people, who belong to the worker-peasant alliance'. They were 'in radical and frontal opposition to the handful of old and new exploiters'.

In order to fight these new battles, in what was characterised as the next stage in the revolutionary process – the Popular Democratic phase – a major change in Frelimo was called for. The most significant act of the Third Congress was beginning the long and difficult process of transforming Frelimo from being a front to a vanguard party. The reasons for such a change were outlined in the Central Committee's report to the Congress. The abolition of all forms of exploitation depended upon the labouring classes (the workers and peasants) imposing their own power on society; but, it was declared, 'The workers will only be victorious in this struggle if they are united, organised and conscious of their objectives'.[16] These objectives were then stated clearly as being the transition to a socialist society where class exploitation would become a thing of the past, and that a vanguard party representing the interests of the labouring classes was required to lead that transition.

Such a decision followed on quite naturally from the direction that Frelimo had been pursuing after the crisis period and Marxism-Leninism was embraced as the revolutionary theory to guide the party's work, distinguishing the Mozambican experience from the various brands of African socialism practised in the rest of the continent. Nevertheless, a warning was given that this was not a static doctrine; rather, it had to be 'applied and developed creatively'. Other aspects of the new vanguard party were its committed internationalism and its democratic centralist principles of internal organisation. Stress was given to the fact that 'Our experience of centralism has always valued its democratic aspect highly', and this was reinforced by reference to the continued mass meetings to discuss all manner of problems that Frelimo had employed during the war and after. Samora Machel explained it thus, on another occasion: 'Our decisions must always be democratic in both content and form. "Content" means that they must reflect the real interests of the masses. "Form" means that the broad masses must take part in arriving at the decision, feeling that it is theirs and not something imposed from above.'[17]

The criterion for membership of the party changed; only those living from their own labour and with 'outstanding political and moral qualities' could now be chosen. Following the Congress, the party had to be set up throughout the country and the choice of the right people was clearly vital. Those who put their names forward were not only vetted by the party itself, to see if they had been former members of the secret police, and so on; this was the least rigorous of the tests. They had also to appear in front of a massed meeting of their workmates, convened by a special brigade of the party, when a full and frank discussion of the political, working and moral life of the intended party candidate would be held. All in the meeting were encouraged to tell of their personal knowledge of the candidate, who was approved or rejected by the mass meeting as a whole. Full admission to the party followed the successful completion of a year's candidature with the person's conduct being carefully monitored throughout.

There were two difficulties in obtaining cadres for the vanguard party. The first was that the party leading the transition to socialism was doing so in a country having only a small permanent working class with a relatively weak history of working-class organisation and consciousness. The point of production for many workers was outside the national boundaries, and inside Salazar's repression had prevented trade unions developing. Although extensive labour migrancy may have helped cement the worker–peasant alliance, as most peasants supplemented their livelihood with wage labour, this also meant that the permanent working class was small. The level of consciousness was not highly developed even in the most established sectors such as the ports.[18] Because Marxist theory is clear that the proletariat is the only class which can lead a transition to socialism, Frelimo had both to recruit more of its members from the working class, while at the same time pursuing development policies to build up that class nationally. Secondly, in lieu of a powerful and class-conscious working class, the national liberation struggle, pursuing a policy of protracted people's war, had produced cadres by the very process of the struggle itself, as we have previously argued. When these conditions no longer existed, it was difficult to create them artificially.

Another serious weakness also became apparent. There was no clearly established formula for the articulation of the various organisational levels in the provincial party hierarchies, and this produced a certain degree of confusion and disorganisation.[19] Furthermore, in the first three years after the Congress not one senior Frelimo leader was given sole responsibility for directing the work of the party. The reason for this was that Frelimo had to take control of the state before it had made the transformation into a vanguard party. All the top cadres had been absorbed into the state, and although they supposedly had tasks in both the party and the state, it was the pressing demands of the latter which took up most of their time. With the leadership totally absorbed in affairs of state, the setting up of a party whose independence from the state was vital to exert the necessary political control over it proved a difficult assignment. With the gradual disappearance of the g.d.s there was a visible waning of political mobilisation in many areas, which contributed to problems in the economic and social development programmes. As one party official explained, 'Our leading cadre could simply find no time to attend to party matters: ninety per cent of their time was spent on government, and the party . . . was getting weaker. With a weak party, national discipline breaks down. This is one of the main sources of all this inefficiency.'[20] In the final chapter we will be examining not only the manifold problems in the economy but also the 'offensive' launched by the party to correct some of these earlier mistakes. Now, however, we must say a word about the mass organisations linked to the party which acted as a further channel for mobilisation, before concluding with a brief section on the state.

The Organisation of Mozambican Women (OMM) was set up in 1972, and its general orientation was defined by the over-all political struggle being waged by Frelimo. The struggle against sexual discrimination has continued to remain subordinate to this broader goal. At the Second Conference of the OMM, held in November 1976, a certain rejuvenation of the movement was called for and its tasks were redefined.[21] These essentially involved integrating women into both the political process and socially productive labour, combating reactionary institutions (such as child marriage and polygamy) and ideas of inferiority and subordination, especially prevalent in the rural areas. Compared to other African states Mozambique has achieved at least some degree of participation by women in the political process, but there is still a long way to go. In relation to the economy, the content of women's work has remained, with some exceptions, much as it always has been.[22] Unless the sexual division of labour is seriously attacked, the emancipation of women will long remain on the agenda. There is a considerable amount of legislation supporting women's equality, but the problem is to transform this into daily practice. The Mozambican Youth Organisation (OJM) is another mass organisation having an important role to play in the work of political mobilisation and organisation, and both the OJM and OMM provide channels for would-be party members.

Finally, we must turn to examine the role of the state.

The state

Frelimo inherited a lethargic, cumbersome, bureaucratic, racist and corrupt Portuguese colonial state machine, festooned with red tape and special tax stamps – to be affixed in appropriate denominations in specific places on a million forms and filled in for virtually every activity the citizen wished to undertake. It was nothing short of a nightmare. The state existed to serve the interests of the metropolitan bourgeoisie and the settlers and therefore to control the African population through its economic, ideological and repressive apparatuses; the complicated procedures virtually excluded most Africans from such limited rights as they might legally have enjoyed. Frelimo's experience with the democratically elected people's committees of the liberated areas provided the beginnings of an alternative state, but the problems associated with taking over, transforming and controlling this grotesque monster were of an altogether different order.

Given the exodus of most of the settlers and the illiteracy of most Mozambicans, there was the immediate problem of how the administration of the state could be kept going. Political and technical cadres were few in number, and much reliance was placed on those members of the petty bourgeoisie (mainly *mixtos* and *assimilados*) already in the bureaucracy, who were rapidly appointed to middle and senior positions. People barely literate and with no office skills filled the positions beneath them. There were sufficient problems keeping the machine running without necessarily mastering it sufficiently to know how to transform it. As a consequence, much of the time-wasting form filling remained. The shortage of personnel was compounded as new socialist measures, such as nationalisations, expanded the state's ambit, particularly in the social and economic sectors.

Frelimo's president summarised the essential problem in the following way: 'We cannot found a people's State with its laws and administrative machinery on the basis of a State whose laws and administrative machinery were wholly designed to serve the exploiters . . . . To "Africanize" colonial and capitalist power would be to negate the meaning of our struggle.'[23] Within the state apparatuses themselves, a new class base for recruitment was introduced, new laws were passed, new work methods introduced, as well as compulsory political study and the forming of party cells. In these ways serious attempts were made to transform the state itself. Important measures were also taken to erect mechanisms of democratic control over the state; in particular, elections were held for a whole range of popular assemblies in 1977, stretching from the level of the locality to that of the nation (see Appendix 1). These were to provide the legislative organs and also to exercise control at all levels of the state hierarchy. Maintenance of the party's separation from the state and control over it were clearly vital considerations. Production councils and people's militias also had a role to play here, along with the popular tribunals which began to emerge at the end of the 1970s. The extent to which all the various organs of *poder popular* were firmly implanted and functioning democratically would determine whether the revolution could truly transform the inherited state and ensure popular control over it. These were essential to safeguard the revolution's objectives.

Frelimo had at least drawn up its own constitution, unlike the other African states where this was done by the colonial power, and Article Two stated clearly that in the People's Republic of Mozambique power belongs to the workers and peasants. Having reasserted Marx's theory that 'The state is the organised form through which a class exercises power in society, and the state apparatus is the instrument through which this power is put into practice',[24] Oscar Monteiro (in a speech in 1976), went on to explain that all too often the reverse was the case: 'We can now see that instead of impressing upon the state apparatus throughout Mozambique the popular and revolutionary character that it had assumed in the liberated areas, we were swamped by the administrative machinery left by colonialism. *Instead of giving directions, we were controlled and directed.*'[25]

Nowhere was this more apparent than in relation to the economy, and in the final chapter we examine this and related problems of national reconstruction in the light of continuing foreign aggression and a radical new offensive to tackle the problems.

Notes

1 The problem of the cities was explained by Daniel Mbanza (later Vice-Minister of the Interior) in a conversation in Dar-es-Salaam, 11 Dec. 1974.

2 For a summary of these, see Frelimo, *Documentos da 8a Sessão do Comite Central*, Maputo, 1976, pp. 31–33.

3 A brief extract of this speech, available in English, is to be found in *Principles of Revolutionary Justice*, Mozambique, Angola and Guinea Information Centre, London, 1979, p. 7.

4 M. dos Santos, 'Frelimo Faces the Future. An Interview with Joe Slovo', in *African Communist*, 55, Fourth Quarter, 1973, p. 49.

5 A key task given by Samora Machel to the Transitional Government was to create the conditions necessary for extending popular power to the whole country. See *Tempo*, 5 Jan. 1975.

6 Interview with Manuel Saidi, Secretary of Mecula g.d., Niassa Province, 21 July 1976.

7 Interview with the District Administrator of Maua, Niassa Province, July 1976.

8 The district of Malema in Nampula Province, for example, is on the main railway line to Malawi; yet in 1976 only the district administrator received the weekly periodical, *Tempo*, and no-one received regular newspapers. This emerged while the author was doing research in the area in July 1976.

9 One of the earliest manifestations of internal opposition was a brief rising by a group of disgruntled soldiers in December 1975, which was swiftly put down by the g.d.s and loyal troops.

10 This example is taken from a large number of interviews conducted in Vila Pery in the first half of 1975.

11 *Tempo*, 20 July 1975.

12 *Tempo*, 4 Jan. 1976.

13 Conversation with Daniel Mbanza, Dar-es-Salaam, Nov. 1974.

14 *Tempo*, 4 Jan. 1976.

15 Frelimo, *A Frelimo e as Classes Trabalhadoras Moçambicanas na Edificação da Democracia Popular*, Colecção 'Palavras de Ordem', No. 4, 1976.

16 *Central Committee Report to Frelimo Third Congress*, MAGIC, London, 1978.

17 S. Machel, *Establishing People's Power to Serve the Masses*; an English translation is published by the Toronto Committee for the Liberation of Southern Africa, Toronto, 1976, p. 21.

18 See the earlier discussion on this issue, but also *Tempo*, 26 Oct. 1976, for the text of an important speech by Machel on the limits of working-class consciousness in Mozambique.

19 An important self-criticism was made on this point at the 5th Central Committee meeting held in 1979, see *Voz da Revolução*, 67, July 1979, 11–12.

20 Quoted in *Africa*, 105, May 1980.

21 *Documentos Da 2a Conferência Da Organização Da Mulher Moçambicana,* Imprensa Nacional de Moçambique, 1977.

22 See United Nations, *Mozambique: Women, The Law and Agrarian Reform,* 1980, for a useful and detailed analysis. See Appendix 1 for the number of women elected to the People's Assemblies.

23 Machel, *Establishing People's Power,* p. 17.

24 See *Principles of Revolutionary Justice,* p. 29.

25 *Ibid.,* p. 30.

15 War and reconstruction

In the Popular Democratic phase of the revolution, the Third Congress declared, the new task was to create the material and ideological bases for making a transition to socialism. The two were closely interrelated, as political mobilisation was employed to the end of economic and social reconstruction whilst the development of industry and state farms necessarily implied building up the working class. Explicitly the strategy was based on the assumption that Mozambique was unable to make an immediate transition to socialism, but that the conditions had first to be created. In the last chapter we examined the political and ideological developments taking place with this end in mind, but now our focus must turn to the social and economic policies.

Severe economic problems were compounded by continuing external aggression to make this the most difficult of tasks. The generalised offensive launched as an integral part of the plan to make the 1980s 'a decade of victory over underdevelopment'[1] was an attempt to overcome some of the shortcomings of the first few years, particularly in the economic sphere. With Gross Domestic Product growing at 3.6 per cent it was not far outstripping the projected population growth rate of 2.8 per cent. In spite of the enormous and as yet unresolved difficulties in industry and agriculture, huge advances were being made in the health, education and social-welfare sectors. These in their turn would help pave the way for revitalising the economy.

The economy

The seeming paradox of all revolutions is that their success has been continually jeopardised by the negative constraints of their economic and social situation. Yet it is precisely these economic and social conditions which have so greatly contributed to engendering the revolution in the first place. As the analysis in Part One of the book indicated, the political economy of Mozambique was dominated by its role on the periphery of a regional sub-system with South Africa as its centre. Severance of the links with Portugal was soon accomplished,[2] but this still left intact a regional and global dependency. The development of a thriving and well-integrated economy was central to breaking out of this position, and it is to these efforts that we first turn our attention.

Between the April coup of 1974 and the Frelimo Third Congress of February 1977 the economy went through a period of crisis. Most of the settlers left, taking with them all the managerial, organisational and technical skills previously denied the African population by the colonial system. There was a definite cost associated with the elimination of the settler bourgeoisie, petty bourgeoisie and skilled working class. Industrial and agricultural production declined drastically. The removal of the settlers was not a deliberate policy but rather was provoked by nationalisations and the widespread rumours and panic which surged in waves through the white community. More than 10 000 did remain, however, taking out Mozambican citizenship – a situation made possible by the continuing adherence to anti-racist policies. Because Frelimo had drawn certain basic lessons from the period of the armed struggle – in particular, that people were the determining force and that self-reliance was essential, it was not afraid to cope with this situation. The loss of secondary-school students from the Mozambique Institute in 1968 had provided a precedent. This presents only one example of how the experiences gained during the nationalist struggle and the principles then developed were to guide post-independence policy making.

Initially there was no over-all coherent plan for the economy, and it was only with the Congress that clear guidelines were laid down. The government could then move on from the crisis management of the first two years when it had reacted on an *ad hoc* basis to the sabotage and closures of numerous enterprises. Those abandoned, or where sabotage was detected, had an administrative commission put in. Nationalisations in the economy were essentially a reaction to events, and slender resources were stretched to the limit. The g.d.s played a vital role in keeping production going at this time but were unable to prevent output plummeting overall. Although this was the cost of losing the settlers, the gain was the elimination of those classes (the colonial bourgeoisie and petty bourgeoisie) who would have directly opposed the transition to socialism. Independent Zimbabwe has had to cope with these classes remaining, at the same time safeguarding, in the short term at least, its own economic production.

The exodus of the settlers produced massive unemployment with the closure of many enterprises. A United Nations study in 1976 estimated that employment in transport, building and selected industries had fallen 40 per cent since independence.[3] The average number of job-seekers registering monthly in Maputo and the adjacent industrial town of Machava rose three-fold from 1976 to 1978,[4] and the trend could not be immediately halted. The problem of unemployment was exacerbated by the decision of the South African Chamber of Mines to reduce the recruitment of Mozambican miners from 115 000 in 1975 to 36 800 in 1977.[5] With the closure of the Rhodesian border in compliance with United Nations sanctions policy, a further 10 000 people, mainly around Beira, were made redundant. New employment opportunities had to be found. For those who berated the Mozambican government for not unilaterally breaking off all economic relations with South Africa, there was the experience in Niassa Province in the mid-1960s which served as a warning against taking such precipitous action. The failure to organise alternative production then had led to serious setbacks. Frelimo was determined to avoid a repetition and would try to provide alternatives to the population before breaking off all such links.

The existing industrial structure had to be changed, especially given the inheritance of factories producing luxury goods for the settler market. The over-all directive given at the Congress was to make agriculture the base and industry the dynamising factor for development. Without the eventual creation of a heavy industrial base, intermediate goods would always be dependent on imports. The need for a balanced and integrated economy was recognised as being essential to break out of the mire of underdevelopment. The production of agricultural implements was obviously one area of importance. In 1974, Mozambique produced only 7 000 shovels and hardly any ploughs,[6] and plans were soon made to change this appalling situation.

The first target, of achieving pre-independence production levels by 1980, was certainly not met. Mismanagement, excessive bureaucracy, a lack of technical skills and sufficient political mobilisation, along with foreign exchange shortages which prevented parts and raw materials being purchased from abroad, all played a part. Because a long-term problem revolved around the continuing need to import food, much-needed foreign currency was spent on something which could and should have been grown locally. This made the process of paying for industrialisation all the more difficult. Nevertheless, by the early 1980s the government clearly controlled the commanding heights of the economy – in 1978 alone nationalising such important enterprises as the oil refinery, the Moatize coal mine (near Tete) and Sena Sugar estates. The latter provided an extraordinary example of the economic sabotage that had to be faced. Over the five years to 1978, production dropped by almost three-quarters, the company's main factory was at a standstill and cane was left to rot in the fields. Incredibly the company had run up a debt of US$45 million to the Bank of Mozambique, equivalent to virtually 15 per cent of the country's ordinary state budget expenditure.[7] Given all the problems, some early successes were notable. In 1980, sugar once again became the major export crop,[8] and the coal-miners of Moatize exceeded their production target of 400 000 tons.[9]

The basic problem remained, however, that the Mozambican economy did not have a secure internal base for accumulation prior to independence. How, then, was it to provide the necessary level of accumulation to fund its socialist development option in the post-independence phase? Great reliance was inevitably placed on external sources, in particular Scandinavian aid. Western investment in general was not forthcoming and only the German Democratic Republic, Bulgaria and Romania made any significant investments from the countries of the socialist bloc. One reason for the latter shortage was the difficulty of coordinating Mozambique's needs into the long term planning cycles of these countries. Mozambique's foreign currency reserves were necessarily diminished and the burden of debt increased given this tremendous inherited difficulty of internal accumulation.

Frelimo was not only concerned with increasing production. What differentiated its approach from that of most other African states was the determination also to transform relations of production in the workplace. Given the nature of the working class and its background, this would inevitably be a long process, but an important beginning was made with the launching of production councils in October 1976. Their task was to raise workers' consciousness, be involved in decision making, help increase productivity and assume control of discipline in the workplace (rather than leave it in the hands of management). They were explicitly seen as 'a weapon which will lead to the destruction of the old capitalist relations of production and the establishment of new social relations of production'.[10] One unanticipated side effect with the creation of these councils was to add to the confusion of responsibilities already existing between the g.d.s and the factory administration, but over time this was sorted out. Within the context of the drive to increase production and introduce new structures, class struggles continued to occur within various factories, and the case of one such, CIFEL (the state steel works), has been well documented.[11] Both factory administrators and the g.d.s were replaced at various times as a result of the complex struggles that occurred, and by 1978 the results, in this factory at least, were favourable for increasing worker participation. Even so, the level of consciousness achieved by the working class generally was still not deemed to be sufficiently advanced that trade unions could be formed, even into the early 1980s, although this was the eventual stated intention.

If agriculture was to be the base of Mozambique's development strategy, then in the early 1980s that base still looked very shaky. The country was only growing about a third of the food that it consumed by the beginning of the decade,[12] and the ambitious state farm programme was proving to be costly, both in terms of low production and the drain on foreign exchange. The Limpopo agro-industrial complex in the south was intended to be the food basket for the country, but the 1981 harvest was a failure, producing only 25 500 tons of rice where twice that amount had been expected.[13] Heavy rains added to the problems in the following harvest also.[14] Some increases in state farm production did occur, but adverse weather conditions, overcentralised management, and lack of maintenance and spares for machinery continued to bedevil the state farm sector. The weakness of the party in the complex also had a role to play.

This was intended to be but one arm of the government's agrarian strategy and was to be coupled with an emphasis on transforming family agriculture through the creation of communal villages. Together, these were to lead to the progressive 'socialisation of the countryside', where 85 per cent of the population still lived. According to the provisional long-term plan, this was intended to triple productivity in the countryside, bring social benefits to the peasants (by means of the amenities offered in the communal villages) and reinforce the worker–peasant alliance 'with the creation of an agricultural working class and [of] a peasantry organised in cooperatives'.[15] More than a million people were already living in a thousand communal villages by 1979, and this was undoubtedly a great achievement;[16] but only 7 per cent of them were in producer cooperatives.[17] Even where cooperatives had been formed, they did not always benefit the right people. In Gaza province, for example, some cooperatives were dominated by the richer peasants and were not used for the good of the communal village as a whole.[18] The communal village programme was still at a very early stage and its prospects for success would depend greatly on the amount of political and economic resources invested in it.

The crisis in agriculture was directly related to the nature of an economy based on migrant labour. Not only were the mining companies and plantations dependent on the peasant base to subsidise their wage labour, but the peasants relied on their off-farm income to purchase the agricultural implements and other inputs that they required. There was an interdependence, in other words, between the two. The crisis in employment previously outlined could not but affect the peasantry also. This was particularly devastating given that the networks for transporting and commercialising their crops disappeared with the departing Portuguese rural shopkeepers.[19] At independence, peasant marketed output dropped by a staggering 60 per cent.[20] Because the difficulty of getting produce to market was compounded by an absence of goods for sale, the peasants lacked even the incentive to market their crops. Worker-peasants in the south of the country began drifting to the towns as their earnings from the South African mines and cash-crop production began to dry up. This raised the important question of whether a smaller proportion of the investment in agriculture should be placed in the highly mechanised state farm sector.[21] The injection of more resources into the communal village programme and the pursuit of a 'labour-absorbing' strategy could perhaps help to alleviate the peasant crisis and the problems of urban unemployment which increasingly stemmed from it.[22]

A major preoccupation of the government was the feeding of the cities. A warning of the dangers incurred by not guaranteeing the supply of food was provided in Angola. An attempted coup led by Nito Alves in May 1977 against President Neto and the MPLA leadership involved the creation of food shortages in the capital.[23] Previously, the settler farmers had provided most of the food for Mozambique's cities, although a certain amount had always been imported. When they left, the government created state farms on the abandoned land in order to try to make up the inevitable shortfall in food supplies. Perhaps this policy was inevitable. However, the crisis of the worker-peasants in the rural areas was creating a flux to the towns, thereby increasing the food requirements of the cities while diminishing the numbers growing it. A spread of the investment on a broader basis might perhaps have absorbed the labour in the rural areas, have sped up the collectivisation of production in the communal villages and produced a food surplus. There was no easy solution to the problem, however, and the debate on the most appropriate agrarian strategy would undoubtedly long continue.

Substantial wage rises and a significant increase in the standard of living of many of the population increased the food shortages. Speculation and black marketeering began to grow to alarming proportions. Queues were a frequent sight in the city (not surprisingly, perhaps, given Frelimo's determination not to raise the prices of basic commodities and so reduce demand in the traditional way). It was clear that some measure had to be taken, and in March 1981 rationing was introduced for eleven basic products.[24] This succeeded in drastically reducing the queues. As the number of consumer cooperatives grew, they provided a longer-term solution to the problem. These had 325 000 registered members by the beginning of the 1980s, and when dependants were included this accounted for one in seven of the population.[25] These provide a success story in Frelimo's ambitious attempt to transform Mozambican society. The people's shops, on the other hand, were a failure. These were set up to deal with the vacuum in the retail trade created when the settlers left. As the President put it, 'our state cannot waste energy selling needles and razor blades or running tea-rooms and barbers' shops'.[26] The realisation of the limited capacity of the state to handle certain areas of life marked a key step forward.

An attempt to put Mozambique's economy on a firm footing was vital if the battle against dependency and underdevelopment was to be won. However, Mozambique was not the only fly trapped in Pretoria's web. Another important policy avenue was the initiation of mutual cooperation among all those states in the region which were to a greater or lesser degree dependent on South Africa. In 1979 the Southern African Development Co-ordination Conference (SADCC) was formed. Each of the nine member states (Zambia, Swaziland, Zimbabwe, Angola, Tanzania, Botswana, Malawi, Lesotho and Mozambique) was assigned responsibility for a particular area of cooperation. Mozambique was allocated transport and communications, arguably the most important part of the plan. More than 40 per cent of the proposed total budget of $2 billion was to be spent in Mozambique, essentially on transport and communication infrastructure.[27]

Transport links with neighbouring countries were slowly improved. From April 1980, goods began flowing from newly independent Zimbabwe to the port of Beira.[28] From 1983, Tanzania and Mozambique were to be linked by a road bridge,[29] and in December 1980 a new tarred road connection with Zambia became operational.[30] For the plan to succeed, not only would the nine politically disparate states have to continue to agree and work together, but Mozambique would have to get both the ports and railways operating efficiently. South Africa, meanwhile, would not stand by and see one of its trump cards of economic control wrested from its hand. Warning pressure was applied in March 1981, when South African railways put a temporary ban on freight going into Mozambique.[31] This was only part of the South African counter-attack, which was also to employ more overt military tactics.

War continues

The problem facing all revolutions is that they are never allowed to carry out their social experiment in peace. Development plans are not only constrained by the inherited dependency of the economy but also by constant military and economic attack. Since independence, Mozambique has been continually in a state of (undeclared) war. The application of United Nations sanctions against the illegal regime of Ian Smith and the permitting of Zimbabwean camps in Mozambique in spite of the enormous costs it would entail were important expressions of Frelimo's internationalist principles. The result, however, was invasions by the

Rhodesian army and the infiltration of anti-government bands. In one attack at Nyazonia refugee camp in August 1976, 600 men, women and children were killed. By the time the Lancaster House independence agreement was signed, Mozambique had lost 1 338 of its own citizens killed, 1 538 wounded and a further 751 people had disappeared without trace.[32] The financial cost of the war was US$0.5 billion for the imposition of sanctions and a further $47.7 million for damage inflicted militarily.[33] What is perfectly clear is that Mozambique's own economy and socialist experiment were also under attack, and not simply the Zimbabwean camps. Communal villages and state farms were frequently singled out for aerial bombardment, such as the Sussundenga complex in Manica Province in June 1978,[34] and in Gaza Province the centre of agricultural production at Chokwe in March 1979[35] and Aldeia de Barragem in September.[36]

With the end of the independence struggle in Zimbabwe, Mozambique had only a temporary respite. The National Resistance Movement (MRN) was the name given to the principal internal opposition group. It was financed by ex-Portuguese settlers and by Rhodesia, but after the latter's independence the MRN transferred its base to South Africa and intensified its operations, frequently still using Zimbabwean territory to gain access to Mozambique. South African advisers were in the MRN camps, and special training teams were regularly flown in.[37] Although the Mozambican army had some successes, taking the main base camp at Sitatonga in mid-1980,[38] sabotage actions continued, including the blowing up of the Zimbabwe–Mozambique oil pipeline and railway link in October 1981[39] and the capture of a British expatriot biologist in a publicity-seeking exercise.[40]

From May 1980, coordination existed between the governments of Mozambique and Zimbabwe in order to try to eliminate the bands,[41] but with South African military and logistical support guaranteed, they will inevitably be a persistent irritant to the government. Infiltrating through the centre of the country, the MRN then moved both north and south, establishing bases in most of the provinces. Sabotage operations concentrate in the main on transport and communication links, intending to prevent the success of SADCC and maintain Mozambican dependency on South Africa. The MRN also tried to use the traditional chiefs in some areas to mobilise support against the communal village programme.

Direct South African military intervention was heralded by a raid on the homes of African National Congress members, just outside Maputo in January 1981. An escalation of fighting seemed inevitable as the situation worsened within South Africa itself. South Africa's nuclear arsenal, especially its tactical nuclear bomb shells delivered by artillery, could not but loom as the ultimate threat.[42] Mozambique seemed determined to continue with its support of the liberation movement, however, regardless of this. It was not slow to respond to the threats either. An American spy network run by the Central Intelligence Agency was broken up, and six people were expelled in March 1981. This network had been collaborating with the South Africans to collect information both on the Mozambican armed forces and on liberation movements based in the country.[43] A Treaty of Friendship and

Cooperation signed with the Soviet Union was a useful diplomatic counterweight to the support that South Africa received from many Western governments.

One of the most serious side effects of the continuing war was that it forced Frelimo to divert resources needed for development purposes into the army. In spite of this, great strides were being made in the fields of education, health and social affairs generally, as we shall go on to see.

Social affairs

The great emphasis given to mass education during the guerrilla war continued after independence. Schoolchildren were seen as the *continuadores* (the continuers) of the revolution. Given the policy of deliberate neglect for the many, and of assimilation for the elite few, coupled with the incredibly powerful influence of the Catholic church, there was much that Frelimo had to tackle. The first move was to take education under state control and inaugurate a rapid expansion of primary, secondary and adult literacy training. After five years of independence, the results were remarkably impressive. The school population totalled 1.5 million, with 90 051 in secondary schools, 12 707 in technical schools and 1 744 taking pre-university courses, the remainder being in primary schools.[44] Between 1974 and 1978 0.75 million Mozambicans attended literacy courses, and in 1980 a further 300 000 were registered, over 10 per-cent up on the previous year. A new department of adult education was created, and the plan was to establish adult education structures within every economic and social unit, whether state or privately owned.[45] Given a total population of 12 130 000 in the 1980 census, these statistics are confirmation of the government's success in this field.

The principles adopted during the war yet again provided the guidelines for the post-independence education policy: the integration of intellectual and manual labour, political education, collective work, and the strong emphasis always placed on cultural activities. 'Make the school a base for the people to take power'[46] was the title given to the major text on education written in the war, and it continued to be the policy guide.[47] Chris Searle's detailed and illuminating study of the transformations occurring in one Nampula secondary school show how these were implemented in practice.[48]

There was no shortage of problems, however, with the desperate lack of teachers and an inevitable drop in standards given such a massive expansion programme. At a meeting to initiate a new National Teachers' Organisation, late in 1981, some of these problems received an airing.[49] Bureaucratic attitudes in the Ministry of Education were criticised, and inadequate training and support for teachers sent to their first posting, insufficient consideration of the degree of responsibility or length of service in determining teachers' pay were some of the more specific problems mentioned. Perhaps one of the greatest weaknesses was the planning of education in general, and a considerable shake-up here was certainly necessary for the 1980s.[50] Teachers felt that having their own organisation would help to deal with some of these problems.

In the health sector, the inherited situation was worse than in education. Of the 550 doctors in the country in 1973, only 87 remained by May 1975.[51] An expensive private medical system based in the towns, for the use of the settlers, had left an appalling legacy of ill-health and infant mortality in the countryside and shanty towns. Nationalisation was the first measure taken, 'in order to create the conditions for a new health care system, namely the provision of free preventive services, such as vaccinations and examinations and the free distribution of certain basic medicines'.[52] Private medicine was banned, and the creation of an organised rural health service was made one of the earliest priorities.[53] Paramedics were trained to be able to diagnose the most common complaints and prescribe up to about fifty drug products.[54] Primary health care within the community was given the main priority. National vaccination programmes were launched as well as campaigns to dig pit latrines and provide clean water. A change of emphasis towards preventive rather than curative medicine was initiated. A directive in 1975 urged the replacement of individualised, bureaucratised and anti-democratic management by 'a new democratic and collective structure, that permits the organised participation of all workers in the study and solution of problems in the hospital'.[55]

Although it still remains impossible to give meaningful mortality statistics, the evidence on surface provision is extremely impressive.[56] Proportionately, expenditure on health in the state budget rose more than three-fold from 1974 to 1980, when it stood at 10.6 per cent.[57] By then the Central Hospital in the capital absorbed only a tenth of the total budget rather than the half that it had previously. In spite of the low population density and terrible transport problems, more than 90 per cent of the population was covered by the vaccination campaigns running from 1976 to 1979 (11 million people in total); the World Health Organisation confirmed the enormous success of the operation.[58] It was only the high level of political organisation existing in the country that permitted this almost unprecedented coverage. One statistic that is available is that for infant mortality, which declined by a fifth over the first five years of independence.[59] Substantial achievements were clearly in evidence here as well.

In housing, the nationalisation of land laid the foundation for sweeping changes. Not only did this prevent the ownership of multiple property in the 'cement city' (as the European areas were know), but also among the 'caniço' shanty towns (named after the reeds used in their construction). All rents were considerably lowered, and many African families were relocated into good-quality, inner city housing. Pilot schemes were set up to rebuild homes and provide essential services in the 'caniço' areas, again relying on the local political structures to mobilise people in a self-help approach.[60] The communal village programme was the lynch-pin of the policy for improving housing and social welfare generally in the countryside. Yet, as in many other areas, housing was bedevilled by problems of bureaucracy. In the State Housing Corporation (APIE) inefficiency became coupled with corruption as some of the best houses were allocated to the families and friends of officials. The revelation of such activities was to be a central feature of a far-reaching campaign launched in 1980, both to reassess the direction and reinvigorate the revolution in Mozambique.

The offensive

With the signing of the Lancaster House agreement at the end of 1979, signalling the end of settler rule in Zimbabwe, Frelimo felt able to turn its full attention to the internal situation. The President declared that it was no longer possible to blame the external enemy for everything that went wrong in the country. Their arms had now to be turned inwards, to tackle the problems in their midst. What followed can best be described as a political, economic and social blitz, although its official designation was the *ofensiva*. Seizing the breathing space afforded by the end of the Zimbabwe war, the internal economic turmoil and bureaucratic ineptitude became the new subject of attack. In a series of presidential initiatives Samora Machel paid a number of unannounced visits to ports, warehouses, airports, factories, clinics and the Central Hospital. He found warehouses filled with mountains of food and other items in short supply, widespread apathy and incompetence.

Many of the problems were related to bad management and general inefficiency, but at another level they were a result of the party's inability to transform the state. 'We found organised red tape, bureaucracy transformed into a system to paralyse our economy', the President said, in a keynote speech in March 1980.[61] The corruption in the State Housing Corporation was unearthed and the guilty punished. Nepotism and corruption compounded by the inexperience of those running the state shops had resulted in empty shelves and long queues. Goods were sold on the black market at exorbitant prices or were hoarded by the employers and their friends. The people's shops were abolished completely. Part of the solution to the problem posed by the state apparatus was recognising where to limit its involvement. Although the consumer cooperatives were seen as the key to the eventual socialisation of retailing, private shopkeepers were also to be encouraged, to help overcome the distribution problems. Peasants were also offered higher prices for their produce, but the family sector needed more support generally.

A shake-up in a number of government departments took place. The ministers of Public Works and Housing, Internal Trade and Health were removed, and later other ministries were reorganised. Mario Machungo, who was carrying two heavy portfolios for Planning and Agriculture, was left with only the former, and Sergio Vieira, who had successfully reorganised the national bank, took over at Agriculture. Offices of control were introduced within each ministry to improve efficiency. In relation to the economy a central committee meeting at the end of 1981 declared that 'state firms cannot be a refuge for indiscipline, laziness, negligence and lack of punctuality. They should be a model of efficient and profitable management'.[62] The launching of the offensive coincided with the first serious attempts at planning the economy, and the two were seen to go hand in hand. Foreign capital was also invited in, on strictly controlled terms, to help finance development policy.

Efficiency, good planning and organisation were some of the more important considerations in the early stages of the offensive. Weaknesses in management had to be tackled, but an early emphasis on the heightened role of the manager was subsequently followed by a drive to strengthen party structures amongst the workforce. A permanent tension will inevitably exist between moves towards greater participation and democratic control on the one hand and managerial hierarchy and authority on the other. Depending on the particular weaknesses of the time, one or the other may be emphasised. A very strong policy statement followed up by action at the centre is always required for changes to permeate the country as a whole. The effect is similar to that of the ripples on a lake when a stone is thrown; the more distant from the impact, the weaker the ripples. An early emphasis on management authority was necessary for the sake of efficiency at the beginning of the offensive. This in its turn created strains between the political and administrative structures in individual enterprises.[63] There followed new moves to revitalise the party, and in particular to develop its economic role, reflecting a somewhat different policy accent, countering the abuse of managerial power that may have emerged in certain places as a result of the earlier emphasis.

This is the job of the vanguard political leadership in a nutshell: to assess the strengths and weaknesses at a particular time and place and launch initiatives to correct the chosen course, furthering the process of socialist transition. The right decision may not always be taken, but what is important, in the words of Armando Guebuza, is that the leadership must learn from its own mistakes.[64] The offensive was above all an act of merciless self-criticism, as in the first few years of independence there had been a 'tendency to see what's good coming from the inside and what's bad from the outside'.[65] The colonial heritage, war, flood and drought were all being blamed for the country's problems. Undeniably they had no small part to play, but the internal weaknesses presented no less of a problem. These were now being recognised and tackled with the launching of the offensive. It was by resolving just such internal problems in the late 1960s that Frelimo was able to make the massive post-1970 gains, but no less of an internal class struggle would now be required.

In the last resort, Frelimo's successes had always been based on its ability to mobilise and organise the population. Having realised its shortcomings in this regard after five years of independence, a main thrust of the offensive was to reorganise and revitalise the party. Towards this end two of the most senior figures in the leadership were relieved of their governmental responsibilites to devote all of their time to the party. Marcelino dos Santos became Party Secretary for Economic Policy and Jorge Rebelo, Secretary of Ideological Work. This was ample demonstration that Frelimo was determined to strengthen the party as a crucial means for controlling the state apparatus and genuinely encourage mass participation.

In July 1981 the sector responsible for ideological work within

171

Frelimo produced a highly critical statement about the party's work. Over large areas of the country the party had little contact with the people, it said; directives either did not reach the people or were distorted when they did. Jorge Rebelo warned, 'we must radically alter our style and methods of work. We have to get out of the offices and spend most of our time among the people.'[66] The party was accused of being bureaucratic and office-oriented. In general, the weaknesses of party work among the people were considered to be the result of a lack of cadres and good internal organisation, incorrect work methods, poor training and an incorrect conception of party discipline.[67] Several measures were proposed to improve the situation, and it was apparent that strengthening and reinvigorating the party was to be a major task in the 1980s. Upon its success much could depend, as the party, too, could become bureaucratised.

The need to maintain a strong defence force was not only a drain on material resources as it also diverted the work of many political cadres. This was certainly necessary, as the President reported that 'In the Defence and Security Forces in general, we find that numerical and technical growth has not been accompanied by a corresponding political growth.'[68] In the 1981 offensive much stress was laid on imposing a series of tough measures to control abuses by individuals within the security forces. An increase in the party's influence as well as the establishment of punitive measures were considered equally important. By 1982, 400 members of the security police had been expelled over the previous two years for a variety of offences, indicating Frelimo's seriousness of intent,[69] and it provoked a former director to go over to the South Africans.

Conclusion

Six years after independence Mozambique's school population had tripled and the health budget had increased three-fold.[70] In spite of the great strides made in the provision of social welfare, the magnitude of the problem facing the government should not be minimised. Even with the introduction of a new national system of education (in 1982), moving towards the statutory provision of education for all children, by 1990 an estimated 2 million people will still not have completed their compulsory education programme.[71] Enormous problems in the economy remained, and the constant threat of South Africa's military might loomed not only on the borders but within Mozambique itself, with raids and sabotage by the MRN. However, Frelimo has succeeded in spite of the enormous odds in pursuing its own development strategy informed by an indigenous Marxism. This centred on the politics of mass participation forged during the national liberation struggle, based on the principle that people were the determining factor. Essentially it relied on integrating political organisation with economic and social development.

The frankness with which the Frelimo leadership assessed its failures as well as its successes augured well for the continuing revolutionary process in Mozambique. To downplay the difficulties of building socialism on the periphery of a regional sub-system dominated by an aggressive and militaristic power like South Africa would do but scant justice to Frelimo's achievements. Much remained inconclusive in terms of the long-term prospects for their success, but no-one could deny that their experiment was breaking new ground on the African continent.

Notes

1 See S. Machel, *Façamos de 1980–1990 a década da vitória sobre o subdesenvolvimento*, Colecção 'Palavras de Ordem', No. 11, 1979, for the speech launching the ten-year offensive against underdevelopment.

2 Portugal was providing 18% of Mozambique's total imports and receiving a third of its exports in 1974. Even by 1977 its share of both had halved. See Direcção Nacional de Estatística, *Informaçao Estatística*, 1978.

3 United Nations ECOSAC, *Assistance to Mozambique*, A/32/96, 19 Oct. 1976, pp. 9–10.

4 Universidade Eduardo Mondlane, *Relatório provisório sobre o desemprego*, Maputo, 1978, p. 7. (Note that the information for 1978 refers only to the first two months of the year.)

5 *Ibid.*, p. 25. South Africa reduced the numbers recruited because the special gold payments system to Mozambique became too costly.

6 B. Wisner, 'Agriculture in Mozambique', *Science for People*, 34. A new factory was planned to be opened in the 1980s at Beira, producing annually 800 000 hoes, 20 000 ploughs, 7 000 harrows and 4 000 seed sowers. (*AIM Bulletin Dossier. Fourth Session of the Central Committee of Frelimo*, Aug. 1978.)

7 See *Tempo*, 13 Aug. 1978.

8 *African Economic Digest*, 19 Sept. 1980.

9 *AIM Bulletin*, Mozambican News Agency, 56, Feb. 1981.

10 'Workers Control in Mozambique', *Peoples Power*, 10, 1977.

11 See P. Sketchley, 'Problems of the Transformation of Social Relations of Production in Post-independence Mozambique', *Peoples Power*, 15, 1979; and *Casting New Moulds*, Institute for Food Development Policy (San Francisco), 1980.

12 See *An Appeal: Food Aid for the People's Republic of Mozambique*, Maputo, 1980, memo.

13 *Tempo*, 30 Aug. 1981.

14 *Tempo*, 13 Dec. 1981.

15 *Our Plan is the Key to Economic Victory*, the opening address to the eighth session of the People's Assembly by President Machel, in October 1981 (see *Supplement to AIM Bulletin*, 64, 1981).

16 *Supplement to AIM Bulletin*, 36, 1979.

17 O. Marleyn, D. Wield and R. Williams, *The Political and Organisational Offensive in Mozambique. Its relationship to state agricultural policy*, a paper

given at the Transition to Socialism in Africa conference, University of Leeds, May 1982.

18 See the article by L. Harris in *Journal of Peasant Studies*, vii, 3, April 1980.

19 No fewer than 25 000 vehicles disappeared between 1973 and 1977 (according to the VIAK, *National Transport Survey*, 1978).

20 See M. Wuyts, *Peasants and Rural Economy in Mozambique*, Centre of African Studies, Maputo, 1978, p. 30.

21 In 1977, for example, more than 1 000 of the 1 200 tractors imported went to the state farms; see J. Hanlon, 'Does Modernisation Equal Mechanisation?'', *New Scientist*, 24 Aug. 1978.

22 See M. Wuyts, 'The Mechanization of Present-day Mozambican Agriculture', *Development and Change*, xii, 1, 1981, for a discussion of these issues.

23 See P. Fauvet, 'Angola: the Rise and Fall of Nito Alves', *Review of African Political Economy*, 9, 1978, 94.

24 *AIM Bulletin*, 57, March 1981.

25 *AIM Bulletin*, 56, Feb. 1981.

26 *AIM Bulletin Dossier. Fourth Session of the Central Committee of Frelimo*, Aug. 1978.

27 *Financial Times*, 27 Nov. 1980.

28 *AIM Bulletin*, 46, April 1980.

29 *Daily News*, Dar-es-Salaam, 12 Sept. 1980.

30 R. Young, 'Zambia in 1980', in *The Annual Register of World Events in 1980*, H. V. Hodson (ed.), London, 1981.

31 *Guardian*, 11 March 1981.

32 S. Machel, *A Vitória do Povo do Zimbabwe é Fruto da Luta Armada, da Unidade e do Internacionalismo*, Colecção 'Palavras de Ordem', 16, 1980, p. 16.

33 See *Mozambican Appeal. Consequences of Sanctions and Rhodesian Aggressions. A Need to Reconstruct*, Maputo, 1980.

34 *The Herald* (Zimbabwe), 27 June 1978.

35 *Financial Times*, 15 and 16 March 1979.

36 See reports in the *International Herald Tribune*, 2 Sept. 1979, *Financial Times*, 8 Sept. 1979.

37 *The Herald*, 22 July 1980. This was, of course, denied by MRN spokesmen; see *The Herald*, 28 May 1980.

38 *The Herald*, 10 July 1980.

39 *The Observer*, 1 Nov. 1981.

40 *Daily Telegraph*, 28 Dec. 1981.

41 *Daily Telegraph*, 27 May 1980.

42 *World in Action*, Granada Television, 1980.

43 See the *Guardian*, 6 March 1981, *AIM Bulletin*, 57, March 1981, and *Covert Action* (US), 13, July–Aug. 1981.

44 I. Christie and J. Hanlon, 'Mozambique', in *Africa Contemporary Record 1981*, C. Legum (ed.), London.

45 The provisions of the Council of Ministers decree were published in *Notícias*, 9 Feb. 1981.

46 S. Machel, *Fazer da Escola Uma Base Para o Povo Tomar o Poder*, Colecção Estudos e Orientações, 6, 1979.

47 It is quoted at the beginning of an education policy text written in 1980, for example. See S. Machel, *Na Educação Só Investiremos em Terreno Fertil*, Colecção 'Palavras de Ordem', 20, 1981, p. 9.

48 C. Searle, *We're Building The New School! Diary of a Teacher in Mozambique*, London, 1981.

49 See *Tempo*, 25 Oct. 1981.

50 See R. Carr-Hill, *Education Planning for Scientific Socialism in Mozambique*, a paper given at the Development Studies Association conference, 1981, for one critical view of the education sector.

51 Interview with Helder Martíns, Minister of Health (conducted by Polly Gaster), June 1975.

52 Ong Bie Nio, *Medicine and Culture in Mozambique*, a paper given at the Fifth Joint Scientific Meeting of the Society for Social Medicine and 'L'Association Villerme', Manchester, 1979.

53 M. Segall, 'Health and National Liberation in the Peoples Republic of Mozambique', in *International Journal of Health Services*, vii, 2, 1977.

54 *New Scientist*, 7 Sept. 1978.

55 S. Machel, *Transformar o Hospital Central Num Hospital do Povo*, Colecção Estudos e Orientações, 11, 1980.

56 For an extensive and detailed case study in Maputo, see D. M. Jelley, *Primary Health Care in Practice – A Study in Mozambique*, a thesis submitted to the University of Nottingham Medical School, 1982.

57 World Health Organisation and UNICEF, *Country decision making for the achievement of the objective of Primary Health Care*, Geneva, 1980, p. 80.

58 World Health Organisation and UNICEF, *National Decision Making for Primary Health Care*, Geneva, 1981.

59 See *Afrique-Asie*, July 1980.

60 B. Pinsky, 'Mobilising for a New Life: 'Caniço Settlement Rehabilitation in the Bairro of Maxaquene, Mozambique', *Antipode*, xii, 3, 1980.

61 For an English translation of a part of the speech, see *Supplement to AIM Bulletin*, 45, 1980; otherwise S. Machel, *Desalojemos o Inimigo Interno do Nosso Aparelho de Estado*, Colecção 'Palavras de Ordem', 19, 1980.

62 *AIM Bulletin*, 66, Dec. 1981.

63 *Boletim de Célula*, 1, 1981.

64 Conversation with Armando Guebuza, Vice-Minister of Defence, Manchester, 27 June 1981.

65 *Ibid*.

66 *AIM Bulletin*, 61, July 1981.

67 *Notícias*, 3 July 1981.

68 *Supplement to AIM Bulletin*, 65, Nov. 1981.

69 *Tempo*, 23 Feb. 1982.

70 *AIM Bulletin*, 61, July 1981.

71 Graça Machel, 'The National System of Education', *Supplement to AIM Bulletin*, 66, Dec. 1981.

Appendix 1

The results of the first elections to the People's Assemblies (1977)

Level	No. of Assemblies	No. of Deputies	Workers and Peasants (%)	Women (%)
Popular Assembly	1	226	60.10%	12.39%
Province	10	734	48.50%	14.70%
City	10	460	48.56%	20.87%
District	112	3,390	57.99%	23.81%
Locality	894	22,230	–	28.30%

Note: More than 2 000 candidates were rejected by the voters in the locality elections, 206 in the districts, 26 in the provincial capitals and 11 in the provinces (see *AIM Bulletin*, 18, Dec. 1977).

Appendix 2 The leadership of the party and state in Mozambique (1982)

Standing Political Committee of the Central Committee of the Frelimo Party

(Members of the Standing Political Committee are *ex-officio* members of the Council of Ministers)

Samora Moisés Machel, Marcelino dos Santos, Joaquim Alberto Chissano, Alberto Joaquim Chipande, Armando Emilio Guebuza, Jorge Rebelo, Mariano Matsinhe, Sebastião Marcos Mabote, Jacinto Soares Veloso, Mario da Graça Machungo.

The Secretariat of the Central Committee of the Frelimo Party

President: Samora Moisés Machel

Secretary for Economic Policy: Marcelino dos Santos
Secretary for Foreign Relations: Joaquim Chissano
Secretary for Ideological Work: Jorge Rebelo
Secretary for Party Organisation: José Oscar Monteiro

The Standing Commission of the People's Assembly

Samora Moisés Machel (Chairman), Marcelino dos Santos (Secretary), Joaquim Chissano, Lt-Gen. Alberto Chipande, Mariano Matsinhe, Oscar Monteiro, Rui Baltazar, Maj-Gen. Tomé Eduardo, Maj-Gen. Américo Mpfumo, Fernando Matavele, Salomão Munguambe, Fernando Ganhão, Augusto Macamo, Maj-Gen. Joaquim Munhape, Osvaldo Tazama.

Council of Ministers

President of the Republic: Samora Moisés Machel
Minister of Foreign Affairs: Joaquim Chissano
Minister of National Defence: Lt-Gen. Alberto Joaquim Chipande
Resident Minister of Sofala Province: Armando Emílio Guebuza
Minister of the Interior: Mariano de Araujo Matsinhe
Chief of the General Staff of the Mozambique Armed Forces and Deputy Minister of Defence: Lt-Gen. Sebastião Marcos Mabote
Minister of Security: Jacinto Soares Veloso

Minister of Planning: Mario da Graça Machungo
Minister in the Presidency: José Oscar Monteiro
Minister of Finance: Rui Baltazar dos Santos Alves
Minister of Education and Culture: Graça Machel
Minister of Information: José Luis Cabaço
Minister of Public Works and Housing: Julio Zamith Carrilho
Minister of Foreign Trade: Salomão Munguambe
Minister of Agriculture: Sergio Vieira
Minister of Justice: Teodato Hunguana
Minister of Industry and Energy: António Lima Rodrigues Branco
Minister of Health: Pascoal Manuel Mocumbi
Minister of Ports and Surface Transport: Luís Maria Alcantara Santos
Minister of Posts, Telecommunications and Civil Aviation: Rui Lousa
Minister of Internal Trade: Manuel Jorge Aranda da Silva
Minister-Governor of the Bank of Mozambique: Prakash Ratilal

Deputy Ministers
Security: Salesio Teodora Malyambipano
Health: Fernando Everard do Rosário Vaz
Interior: Carlos Raposo Pereira

Secretaries of State
Accelerated Development Programme in the Incomati and Limpopo
Regions: Rui Gonzalez
Coal and Hydrocarbons: Abdul Magid
Cotton: João Ferreira
Cashew: Gaspar Zimba
Fisheries: Joaquim José Tenreiro de Almeida
Culture: Luis Bernardo Honwana
Foreign Affairs: Valeriano Ferrão
Labour: António José Carvalho Neves

Provincial Governors
Cabo Delgado: Armando Panguene
Niassa: Aurélio Manave
Nampula: Feliciano Salomão Gundana
Tete: João Baptista Cosme
Zambezia: Osvaldo Tazama
Manica: Manuel António
Sofala: Resident Minister Armando Guebuza
Inhambane: Alberto Sithole
Gaza: João Pelembe (suspended April 1982 and the post left vacant)
Maputo: José Moiane
Greater Maputo City: António Hama Thai

A note on sources, translations and currencies

Collecting material and doing the research on a revolution is never easy. Opinions are inevitably polarised, and frequently there is a received wisdom handed down on both sides. I was uniquely fortunate in that much of my field research was carried out during the transition period (1974–1975) when I was given open access to travel all over the country and interview senior and middle-level cadres of Frelimo and many other people besides. There was no official interpreter travelling with me; all translations were made by me when the interviews were in Portuguese and by the most suitable person locally available when African languages were used. The data were gathered before any post-independence official version of events was established, and the interviews form an important and original core of evidence for Part Three of the book. Oral data have been used only to supplement written primary and secondary sources in the rest of the text, but I feel that the testimony of the people interviewed fulfils a vital role in constructing the country's history. The position or occupation of the interviewee given in all footnotes refers to the time at which the interviews were conducted.

In order to make the book readable, I have tried to cut down the exhaustive reference system used in the doctoral thesis, on which the early part of the book is based; for those interested, they may refer to B. Munslow, *Frelimo and the Mozambican Revolution*, Ph.D. thesis, University of Manchester, 1980. Similarly in the bibliography, I refer people only to available English language sources and not to the Portuguese, French, Italian, Spanish and German texts also consulted (a complete list is available in the Select Bibliography of the thesis).

Various archives were consulted: the Arquivo Histórico in Maputo; selected district administrations in Niassa, Cabo Delgado, Nampula and Inhambane provinces; the Mission School of Cambine; the Sindicato Nacional dos Professionais de Estiva do Porto de Maputo; and the official port and railways archive also in Maputo; the John Rylands Library at the University of Manchester, the library of the Instituto de Investigação Científico in Maputo, and the city library in Dar-es-Salaam. The private collections of Polly Gaster and Iain Christie were most useful, as was the Jeanne Penvenne collection deposited with the archive of the Centro de Estudos Africanos (Maputo). The author's own extensive private collection will eventually be deposited with the John Rylands Library. Over fifty different newspapers and journals were referred to, as well as *Facts and Reports* produced by the Angola Comité in Holland. A wide range of Frelimo publications and United Nations reports were utilised and many other sources besides, in a study which has spanned more than a decade.

All currency values, unless otherwise stated, are given at the value of the time to which they refer.

Select bibliography

General works on the history of Portuguese colonialism

D. M. Abshire and M. A. Samuels, *Portuguese Africa: a Handbook*, London, Pall Mall Press, 1969.

P. Anderson, 'Portugal and the End of Ultra-Colonialism', *New Left Review*, 15, 16, 17, 1961.

M. de Andrade and M. Ollivier, *The War in Angola*, Dar-es-Salaam, Tanzanian Publishing House, 1975.

K. de Arriaga, *The Portuguese Answer*, London, Tom Stacey, 1973.

G. Bender and A. Isaacman, 'The Changing Historiography of Angola and Mozambique', in *African Studies Since 1945: a Tribute to Basil Davidson*, Christopher Fyfe, ed., London, Longman, 1976.

G. J. Bender, *Angola under the Portuguese: the Myth and the Reality*, London, Heinemann, 1978.

C. R. Boxer, *The Portuguese Seaborne Empire 1415–1825*, London, Hutchinson, 1969.

N. Bruce, *Portugal: the Last Empire*, Newton Abbot, Devon, David & Charles, 1975.

A. Cabral, *Unity and Struggle*, London, Heinemann, 1980.

M. Caetano, *Colonizing Traditions, Principles and Methods of the Portuguese*, Lisbon, 1951.

R. H. Chilcote, *Portuguese Africa*, Englewood Cliffs, N.J., Prentice-Hall, 1966.

R. H. Chilcote, ed., *Emerging Nationalism in Portuguese Africa: Documents*, Stanford, Cal., Hoover Institution Press, 1972.

B. Cornwall, *The Bush Rebels*, London, Andre Deutsch, 1973.

B. Davidson, *The Liberation of Guiné*, Harmondsworth, Mdx., Penguin, 1969.

——. *In the Eye of the Storm*, London, Longman, 1972.

J. Davies, 'Allies in Empire. Part I', *Africa Today*, xvii, 4, July–Aug. 1970.

M. Dickenson, *When Bullets Begin to Flower*, Nairobi, 1972.

J. Duffy, *Portuguese Africa*, Cambridge, Mass., Harvard University Press, 1959.

——. *A Question of Slavery*, Oxford, Oxford University Press, 1967.

A. Ehnmark and P. Wastberg, *Angola and Mozambique: the Case Against Portugal*, Roy Publications, 1963.

E. de Sousa Ferreira, *Portuguese Colonialism from South Africa to Europe*, Freiburg, Aktion Dritte Welt, 1972.

——. *Portuguese Colonialism in Africa: the end of an era*, New York, Unesco, 1974.

A. de Figueiredo, *Portugal and Its Empire: the Truth*, London, Gollancz, 1961.

P. Fryer and P. Pinheiro, *Oldest Ally: a Portrait of Salazar's Portugal*, London, Dobson, 1961.

P. Guinee, *Portugal and the EEC*, Amsterdam, Angola Comité, 1973.

R. J. Hammond, *Portugal and Africa 1815–1910: a Study in Uneconomic Imperialism*, Stanford, Cal., Stanford University Press, 1966.

M. Harris, *Portugal's African Wards*, New York, 1958.

M. A. El Khawas, 'Foreign Economic Involvement in Angola and Mozambique', *The African Review*, iv, 2, 1974.

J. Marcum, *The Angolan Revolution: the Anatomy of an Explosion (1950–1962)*, Vol. 1, Boston, Mass., M.I.T. Press, 1969; Vol. 2, 1978.

W. Minter, *Portuguese Africa and the West*, Harmondsworth, Mdx., Penguin, 1972.

B. da Ponte, *The Last to Leave: Portuguese Colonialism in Africa*, London, International Defence and Aid Fund, 1974.

O. Salazar, *Doctrine and Action*, London, Faber & Faber, 1939.

Tricontinental, *Portuguese Colonies: Victory or Death*, Havana, Tricontinental, 1971.

Selected works on Mozambique

Forthcoming from Longman is a volume of the collected speeches and writings of Samora Machel, edited and introduced by Barry Munslow. This will bring together for the first time in the English language the major works of Frelimo's President. Also appearing in the near future is an edited collection on post-independence Mozambique by John Saul, London, Monthly Review Press; S. Katzenellenbogan, *South Africa and Southern Mozambique*, Manchester, Manchester University Press; and a book on twentieth century Mozambique by Allen Isaacman.

E. A. Alpers, *Ivory and Slaves in East Central Africa*, London, Heinemann, 1975.

American University, *Area Handbook of Mozambique*, Washington, D.C., U.S. Government Printing Office, 1977.

G. Arrighi and J. S. Saul, *Essays on the Political Economy of Africa*, London, Monthly Review Press, 1973 (the chapter on Frelimo).

W. Burchett, *Southern Africa Stands Up*, New York, Urizen Books, 1978.

Centre of African Studies, *The Mozambican Miner: a Study in the Export of Labour*, Maputo, Instituto de Investigação Científico de Moçambique, 1977 (this appears in book form as *Black Gold*, Brighton, Harvester Press, 1983).

Centre for African Studies (Edinburgh) *Mozambique*, Edinburgh, Edinburgh University Press, 1979.

B. Davidson, 'The Revolution of People's Power: Notes on Mozambique, 1979', *Race and Class*, xxi, 2, 1979.

B. Davidson, J. Slovo and A. R. Wilkinson, *Southern Africa: the New Politics of Revolution*, Harmondsworth, Mdx., Penguin, 1976, (the section by Davidson).

M. dos Santos, 'Frelimo Faces the Future: an Interview with Joe Slovo', *African Communist*, 55, Fourth Quarter 1973.

Frelimo, *Central Committee Report to Frelimo Third Congress*, London, Mozambique, Angola and Guinea Information Centre, 1978.

——. *Principles of Revolutionary Justice. Documents on Law and Justice in the Peoples Republic of Mozambique*, MAGIC, 1979.

A. Hastings, *Wiriyamu*, London, Search Press, 1974.

T. H. Henriksen, *Mozambique: a History*, London, Rex Collings, 1979.

A. F. Isaacman, *Mozambique: the Africanisation of a European Institution. The Zambezi Prazos, 1750–1902*, Madison, Wis., University of Wisconsin Press, 1972.

——. *The Tradition of Resistance in Mozambique: Anti-Colonial Activity in the Zambezi Valley 1850–1921*, London, Heinemann, 1976.

——. *A Luta Continua: Creating a New Society in Mozambique*, Binghampton, NY, Braudel Centre, 1978.

F. M. Lappé and A. Beccar-Varela, *Mozambique and Tanzania: Asking the Big Questions*, San Francisco, Cal., Institute for Food and Development Policy, 1980.

S. Machel, *Mozambique: Sowing the Seeds of Revolution*, London, Committee for Freedom in Mozambique, Angola and Guinea, 1974.

——. *Establish People's Power to Serve the Masses*, Toronto Committee for the Liberation of Southern Africa, 1976.

K. Middlemas, *Cabora Bassa: Engineering and Politics in Southern Africa*, London, Weidenfeld and Nicolson, 1975.

J. H. Mittelman, 'Mozambique: the Political Economy of Underdevelopment', *Journal of Southern African Affairs*, iii, 1, 1978.

E. Mondlane, *The Struggle for Mozambique*, Harmondsworth, Mdx., Penguin African Library, 1970.

Mozambique, Angola and Guinea Information Centre, *Peoples Power*, a quarterly journal issued by MAGIC, 34 Percy Street, London W1P 9EG.

B. Munslow, 'Leadership in the Front for the Liberation of Mozambique', in *South African Research in Progress. Collected Papers 1 and 2*, C. R. Hill and P. Warwick (eds.), York, University of York, 1977, 1978.

B. Neil-Tomlinson, 'The Nyassa Chartered Company, 1891–1929', *Journal of African History*, xviii, 1, 1977.

M. D. Newitt, *Portuguese Settlement on the Zambezi*, London, Longman, 1973.

Panaf, *Eduardo Mondlane*, London, Panaf Books, 1972.

J. Paul, *Mozambique: Memoirs of a Revolution*, Harmondsworth, Mdx., Penguin, 1975.

C. Searle, *We're Building the New School! Diary of a Teacher in Mozambique*, London, Zed Press, 1981.

M. Segall, 'Health and National Liberation in the People's Republic of Mozambique', *International Journal of Health Services*, vii, 2, 1977.

P. Sketchley, *Casting New Moulds*, Institute for Food and Development Policy, San Francisco, Cal., 1980.

A. K. Smith, 'The Peoples of Southern Mozambique: an Historical Survey', *Journal of African History*, xiv, 4, 1973.

——, 'António Salazar and the Reversal of Portuguese Colonial Policy', *Journal of African History*, xv, 4, 1974.

C. F. Spense, *The Portuguese Colony of Mozambique*, Cape Town, 1951.

K. Swift, *Mozambique and the Future*, Cape Town, Don Nelson, 1974.

H. Tracy, *Chopi Musicians*, Oxford, Oxford University Press, 1970.

L. Vail and L. White, *Capitalism and Colonialism in Mozambique*, London, Heinemann, 1981.

G. Watt, 'What to Do When the Doctors Leave', *World Medicine*, xii, 8, January 1977.

G. Watt and A. Melamed, *Changing Health Care in Mozambique: Inside Views*, Zed Press, 1983.

D. L. Wheeler, 'Gungunyane the Negotiator: a Study in African Diplomacy', *Journal of African History*, ix, 4, 1968.

M. Wuyts, *Peasants and Rural Economy in Mozambique*, Centre of African Studies, Maputo, 1978.

——. 'The Mechanisation of Present-day Mozambican Agriculture', *Development and Change*, xii, 1, 1981.

INDEX